T0243987

In an age where theology is to   or
mushy and hesitant, the directn   vin
Ortlund's writing is a balm. Whether or not you agree with him,
this is as generous and wise a presentation of the case for historic
Protestantism as I think you'll find.

ALEC RYRIE, PROFESSOR OF THE HISTORY OF
CHRISTIANITY, DURHAM UNIVERSITY

In posing the question of what it means to be Protestant, Gavin Ortlund
launches the reader into a debate in which there is little consensus and
which defies easy answers. Through a combination of robust arguments, theological and historical insight, and generosity toward other
traditions, Ortlund admirably captures the restless, rebellious nature
of a religious movement constantly striving for renewal. The author
makes a case for Protestantism that will not find universal agreement,
but which inspires response, reflection, and humility. An important
read for all Christians.

BRUCE GORDON, TITUS STREET PROFESSOR OF
ECCLESIASTICAL HISTORY, YALE DIVINITY SCHOOL

Much of contemporary Protestantism, conservative to liberal, has
little connection to the Reformation. But Ortlund reminds us why
the "Protestant" label is worth saving. He has a real gift for distilling
complex issues into something easy to understand. This is a well-
informed but also passionate defense. Before running to Rome or the
East, please read this terrific book first!

MICHAEL HORTON, J. GRESHAM MACHEN PROFESSOR
OF SYSTEMATIC THEOLOGY AND APOLOGETICS,
WESTMINSTER SEMINARY CALIFORNIA

Gavin Ortlund is one of the most effective defenders and articula-
tors of Protestant theology at work in the world today. His YouTube
defenses of Protestant perspectives are viewed by hundreds of thousands. More importantly, they're clear, fair-minded, and reliable.
Protestants maintain a wide array of views on how catholic and traditional Protestants should be. But if you want a mainstream view—one
that offers a good summary of Protestant distinctives from a Reformed

point of view—this book is for you. I pray that God will use it to help all of us understand the gospel more clearly and follow the Lord Jesus more courageously.

DOUG SWEENEY, DEAN AND PROFESSOR OF
DIVINITY, BEESON DIVINITY SCHOOL

Gavin Ortlund presents a compelling case for mere Protestantism by showing how a Protestant faith is a recovery of the apostolic gospel and answers the abiding questions of church, authority, and tradition. It is a robust program to be both evangelical and ecumenical. An authentic church, Ortlund teaches us, should be constantly conforming itself closer to the gospel. This book provides a model for how Protestants should initiate conversations with other Christian traditions.

REV. DR. MICHAEL F. BIRD, DEPUTY PRINCIPAL;
RIDLEY COLLEGE, MELBOURNE, AUSTRALIA

Neither shying away from disagreements between Christian traditions nor triumphing in them, this book offers a wonderful introduction to the riches of the historic Protestant tradition. In conversation with other traditions, Ortlund's approach embodies a convicted civility that is humble and irenic yet rooted. For anyone looking for an introduction to what it means to be Protestant that avoids common caricatures of Protestant, Catholic, and Eastern Orthodox positions, this is a great book!

GAYLE DOORNBOS, ASSOCIATE PROFESSOR OF
THEOLOGY, DORDT UNIVERSITY

With a heart aching for Protestants to understand their own heritage, Gavin Ortlund builds a strong, historically grounded case for the advantages of their tradition. And he makes bold claims for the potential of mere Protestantism, as a renewal movement, to serve as the best cultivator of true catholicity. The result is a vigorous and engaging apologetic for a *semper reformanda* approach to theology and the Christian life.

GWENFAIR WALTERS ADAMS, PROFESSOR OF CHURCH HISTORY
AND SPIRITUAL FORMATION, CHAIR OF THE DIVISION OF
CHRISTIAN THOUGHT, DIRECTOR OF SPIRITUAL FORMATION
STUDIES; GORDON-CONWELL THEOLOGICAL SEMINARY

What It Means to Be Protestant

The Case for an Always-Reforming Church

Gavin Ortlund

ZONDERVAN REFLECTIVE

ZONDERVAN REFLECTIVE

What It Means to Be Protestant
Copyright © 2024 by Gavin Ortlund

Published in Grand Rapids, Michigan, by Zondervan. Zondervan is a registered trademark of
The Zondervan Corporation, L.L.C., a wholly owned subsidiary of HarperCollins Christian
Publishing, Inc.

Requests for information should be addressed to customercare@harpercollins.com.

Zondervan titles may be purchased in bulk for educational, business, fundraising, or sales
promotional use. For information, please email SpecialMarkets@Zondervan.com.

ISBN 978-0-310-15634-5 (audio)

Library of Congress Cataloging-in-Publication Data

Names: Ortlund, Gavin, 1983– author.
Title: What it means to be Protestant : the case for an always-reforming church / Gavin Ortlund.
Description: Grand Rapids, Michigan : Zondervan Reflective, [2024]
Identifiers: LCCN 2023057856 (print) | LCCN 2023057857 (ebook) | ISBN 9780310156321
   (softcover) | ISBN 9780310156338 (ebook)
Subjects: LCSH: Protestantism—History. | Theology, Doctrinal. | BISAC: RELIGION /
   Christianity / Protestant | RELIGION / Christian Theology / History
Classification: LCC BX4805.3 .O78 2024 (print) | LCC BX4805.3 (ebook) | DDC
   280/.4—dc23/eng/20240223
LC record available at https://lccn.loc.gov/2023057856
LC ebook record available at https://lccn.loc.gov/2023057857

Published in association with the literary agency of Wolgemuth & Associates.

Cover design: Brian Bobel Design
Cover image: © Faith Stock / Adobe Stock
Interior design: Denise Froehlich

Printed in the United States of America

24 25 26 27 28 LBC 6 5 4 3 2

*This book is dedicated with love and allegiance
to the one, holy, catholic, and apostolic Church,
the precious bride of Jesus Christ.
May she be always honored and blessed.*

The Church . . . is the society of all the saints, a society which, spread over the whole world, and existing in all ages, yet bound together by the one doctrine, and the one Spirit of Christ, cultivates and observes unity of faith and brotherly concord. With this Church we deny that we have any disagreement. Nay, rather, as we revere her as our mother, so we desire to remain in her bosom.

—JOHN CALVIN, 1539[1]

Contents

Acknowledgments

Some of the material in chapters 5–6 is developed from my comments during a debate with Trent Horn on March 2, 2023, "Is Sola Scriptura True?", at Franciscan University, Steubenville, Ohio, hosted by *Pints with Aquinas*. During my research for this book, Andrew Harrah, Damian Dziedzic, Jason Engwer, Joel Chopp, and Joshua Schooping sent me several helpful resources. The entire team at Zondervan and especially Kyle Rohane have strengthened this project in countless ways. Thank you to my dear wife, Esther, for supporting my writing! Not one book could be written without her support.

How I Accidentally Became a "Protestant Apologist"

I never set out to defend Protestantism. I got sort of pulled into it. In August 2020 I started a YouTube channel called *Truth Unites*. My intent was to release content mainly in apologetics, as well as some general theology. I was completing a book arguing for the existence of God, and I had come to see YouTube as a space where I could engage on such questions with a wider and more diverse audience.

As I began putting out videos, I found myself drawn into the various issues that separate different Christian traditions. On YouTube there is a huge amount of energy in conversations between Roman Catholic, Eastern Orthodox, and Protestant Christians (among other traditions as well). I began to engage a bit in this space. One video led to another. I started connecting with other channels addressing these questions.

Quickly I realized there was a huge need for greater Protestant representation. For one thing, there were simply fewer Protestants involved in these conversations. Beyond that, I noticed that traditional Protestant argumentation was often not articulated in the contemporary conversations, such that historic Protestantism was misunderstood or altogether invisible.

So I immersed myself in classical Protestant texts, hoping to represent my tradition as best I could. Soon I began to do dialogues and debates. Before long I had become, to my surprise, a "Protestant apologist."

This whole experience has been a fascinating journey of discovery from which I have learned and profited immensely and made many wonderful friends. Four observations stand out and form the background to this book.

First, there is currently an *enormous* amount of interest in church history. Many evangelicals, in particular, are currently exploring more sacramental, liturgical, and historically conscious traditions. It's hard to convey how strong this hunger for historical rootedness is right now. People are aching for the ancient, the transcendent, the stable, the deep. I routinely get emails or Facebook messages from Protestants who have suddenly come to terms with the sheer hugeness of Roman Catholicism or Eastern Orthodoxy and are struggling with it. When I address issues like the real presence of Christ in the Eucharist, the essence-Energies distinction, or apostolic succession, I am flooded with comments like, "I was *just* wondering about this!" or "I've been *waiting* for help on this!" And I hear testimony after testimony of those who, seeking a more historically rooted expression of Christianity and finding the anti-Protestant arguments of popular YouTube ministries unanswered, leave Protestantism for another tradition.

Related to this, there is an enormous amount of what I call "ecclesial angst" right now (i.e., anxiety about being in the true church). Over and over I hear from people who feel completely overwhelmed by the complexity of ecumenical disagreements. Some are concerned about their salvation (or that of a loved one).

I am deeply burdened that those in that lonely and confusing place find the rest and security that comes from the gospel.

The second thing I noticed is that, among evangelicals, there appears to be insufficient awareness of, and response to, this phenomenon. This is not to say there are *no* evangelical Protestants engaging in these conversations. But the resources available to struggling Protestants are shockingly sparse. On the Roman Catholic and Eastern Orthodox side (especially Catholic), there is a huge body of literature, social media presence, and apologetics ministries that are unmatched on the Protestant side. Just do an Amazon search for books in the genre of "Roman Catholic apologetics," compare that with a search for "Protestant apologetics," and you'll see what I mean. And although I increasingly hear from people who have friends and family members transitioning out of Protestantism to different Christian traditions, many evangelicals remain completely unaware of this trend.

Thus, when it comes to explaining why we are Protestant, we have our work cut out for us.

This was the opposite of what I expected. I had assumed that, since these conversations have been happening for five hundred years among groups with hundreds of millions of people on each side, there would be little to say that hadn't already been said. Trying to make a fresh contribution would be like pouring water into the ocean. But I have come to the opposite conclusion. There is a gap that needs to be filled. It's like there is a gash in the side of the Protestant boat, and water is pouring in—yet too few people are fixing the hole.

A third observation: Gradually throughout this process, through both study and dialogue, I came to see that many of the perceptions I had gathered about older traditions like Roman Catholicism and Eastern Orthodoxy were caricatures, or at least simplified or warped to some degree. I also gained a more accurate understanding of other Eastern traditions like the Oriental Orthodox Church and the Assyrian Church of the East. I had always found it easy to respect these other traditions and learn from them, disagreements notwithstanding. But I never really felt the *pressure* to explain why Protestantism was the better option. I functioned in contexts that were mostly Protestant, so I easily assumed my own tradition as the respected default option.

On YouTube the sociological dynamics I encountered were the opposite: I began to encounter huge numbers of people who were mystified at how anyone could be Protestant. Slowly I learned to see Protestantism through their eyes. What was once obvious as a recovery of the gospel, I could now understand as they saw it—a historical deviation and oddity.

I also began to see the complexity of the issues better. Let me put it plainly: The issues that divide Christendom are rarely if ever so obvious that everyone will come to the same conclusion about them if only they would study them long enough with a good will. Rather, sincere and intelligent people will and do disagree about them because they are not simple. They are enormously complex—historically, theologically, and in terms of the range of values and concerns represented on each side.

Throughout this process, my Protestantism has been challenged and chastened in various ways. At the same time, I've ultimately become more committed to Protestantism and more convicted about the nobility of the Protestant cause. I'll say more about this as we go. The point for now is that this journey has helped me understand the powerful allure of these non-Protestant traditions and burdened me that they are often not treated with sufficient respect and thoroughness.

Fourth, and finally, I have come to appreciate that the caricatures go both ways. Unfortunately, Protestantism is frequently misunderstood and poorly represented by those who criticize it (and occasionally by those who defend it!). People often characterize the whole of Protestantism through the lens of their anecdotal observations of this or that Protestant church or tradition. There is large-scale ignorance of historic Protestant creeds, confessions, catechisms, and major canonical theologians. In many cases, low-church, evangelical Protestantism (predominantly Baptist and nondenominational) is equated with Protestantism as a whole. And many particular Protestant views are mangled by caricature. (I have especially noticed this with *sola fide* and *sola Scriptura*, but it happens in other areas as well).

Sadly, I believe imprecise conceptions of Protestantism are a huge factor in defections from it. For instance, people often compare a particular experience in a Protestant context to what they read about the church fathers on an apologetics website. They are in effect comparing the worst of Protestantism to the best of the non-Protestant traditions, and as a result, they leave Protestantism for other traditions without an authentic grasp of what Protestantism really is (and often without fully looking into the other traditions). Of course, I am not saying *all* conversions are like this. But it does happen a lot.

Before moving on, let me give an example of how Protestantism is often unfairly represented and contrasted with other traditions. In early 2020, a clip of the popular evangelical leader Francis Chan (whom I appreciate and admire!) was widely circulated and discussed. Speaking about the Eucharist, Chan said,

> I didn't know that for the first 1,500 years of church history, everyone saw it as the literal body and blood of Christ. And it wasn't till 500 years ago that someone popularized the thought that it's just a symbol and nothing more. I didn't

know that. . . . It was at that same time that for the first time someone put a pulpit in front of the gathering. Because before that it was always the body and blood of Christ that was central to their gatherings. For 1,500 years, it was never one guy and his pulpit being the center of the church. It was the body and the blood of Christ—and even the leaders just saw themselves as partakers.[1]

Chan's observation here represents a common way of framing the differences between different Christian traditions. It reinforces the popular perception that, on topics like the Eucharist or worship, Protestantism is an obvious departure from the catholic and historical consensus in the church.

A narrative like this gains traction because it is rhetorically powerful, but it is ultimately unfair and misleading. First, it oversimplifies views on the Eucharist during the first 1,500 years of the church, glossing over both the diversity of the patristic testimony and the turbulence of the medieval development when the Roman Catholic doctrine of transubstantiation officially emerged in the thirteenth century. While some variety of "real presence" is the predominating view of the Eucharist throughout church history, there is unsettledness and diversity within that consensus, and occasional departures from it. In fact, as late as the ninth century there was open debate concerning both whether and how Christ is present in the Eucharistic elements.[2]

Second, the narrative imagined in Chan's remarks misframes where the differences between the Reformers and their opponents actually lie. Most of the Reformers affirmed the real presence of Christ in the Eucharist and opposed transubstantiation on the grounds that it represented a departure not only from Scripture but also from patristic testimony. For example, early Protestants like Peter Martyr Vermigli and Thomas Cranmer argued that for church fathers like Augustine and Theodoret, the bread and wine remained bread and wine in substance while *also* becoming Christ's body and blood.[3] The whole appeal of their Eucharistic theology was a return to catholicity, against the changes introduced by the substance-accidents distinction in the medieval development.[4] It is true that many modern-day evangelicals have adopted more of a symbolic view, but that is by no means representative of Protestantism wholesale.

Third and most egregiously, the idea that the Reformers were intending to replace the Eucharist with a pulpit is quite nearly the opposite of the case. The Protestant effort was to *reclaim* the Eucharist, not replace it. Lay Christians in the late medieval West hardly ever partook of the Eucharist. For most it would have been only once a year, if that, and even then, it was generally in one kind only (the bread, not the wine). For many the Eucharist had become more of a spectacle, and its celebration was plagued by superstitious beliefs. One of the central, animating concerns of the Protestant Reformation was to reestablish for lay Christians a meaningful and frequent participation with the Eucharist in both kinds. Chan's comment that "even the leaders just saw themselves as partakers" is also misleading—the Reformation reduced, rather than increased, the division that had accrued between the clergy and laity in the late medieval West.

There is much more to say about the Eucharist, which I have gone into in online discussions. The point for now is just to see how commonly and easily Protestantism is misrepresented, even by Protestants. It is sadly commonplace for Protestantism to be characterized in terms of the street-level practice at contemporary evangelical churches and ministries, rather than in terms of historic, official, confessional doctrine.

My heart aches for Protestants to understand the riches of their own tradition—especially before they consider leaving it.

The Plan of This Book

Stemming from these four observations, the purpose of this book is to help those navigating ecumenical disagreements by rehabilitating an awareness of historic Protestantism. As you will notice, it is not an exhaustive treatment of Protestant distinctives, and it has a broader and more general scope than an academic book. The goal is simply to convey an overall sense of how Protestantism makes sense and hangs together on its own terms. Thus, this book is *very* far from being comprehensive. But I have felt so burdened about the widespread ignorance of classical Protestant argumentation that I wanted to provide at least a basic introduction. My primary audience is Protestants seeking to understand their own tradition, but I also hope it can be helpful to Christians from other traditions who are open to hearing Protestant arguments, or even those outside the debate looking in.

The book's overarching flow of thought has three basic movements. Part 1 considers Protestantism's relation to catholicity (the wholeness of the church). Chapter 1 suggests Protestantism is a renewal effort *within* the larger church, drawing from the work of the nineteenth-century Protestant historian Philip Schaff. Chapter 2 contrasts this vision of catholicity with that of other traditions, particularly Roman Catholicism and Eastern Orthodoxy, by arguing that the true church cannot be limited to one institution. Chapters 3–4 specify the particular kind of renewal Protestantism occasioned—namely, recovery of the doctrine of justification by faith alone (*sola fide*) as a response to various medieval errors. My hope is that this section of the book would help readers gather an overall sense of the *nature* of Protestantism—as a movement of revitalization, renewal, return, reformation, recentering, recovery. This is the vision of

Protestantism I wish to commend in this book: not an unqualified rejection of the rest of the church, but rather a movement of renewal and reform *within* the church.

Inevitably, debate about Protestantism's position in relation to the broader church boils down to the issue of *authority*: By what standard do we measure authentic renewal movements from spurious counterfeits? Thus, part 2 of the book engages questions of authority, where some of the deepest methodological differences lie between Protestantism and other Christian traditions. Chapters 5–6 commend the Protestant claim that Scripture alone is the infallible rule of faith for the church (*sola Scriptura*), while chapters 7 and 8 consider two alternative proposals of ecclesial authority in the non-Protestant traditions. The goal of this section of the book is to show that the Protestant view of how Christ exercises authority over his church is more plausibly true than the alternatives but also more conducive to the health and vitality of the church.

Part 3 of the book considers Protestantism's relationship to church history. It is commonly argued that Protestantism has no historical basis. Anyone who takes church history seriously, it is claimed, can no longer remain Protestant. After all, the Protestant movement began as late as the sixteenth century. In response, I argue that the Protestant Reformation was not an attempt to create a new church, but rather to reform the historic church of Christ by removing various errors that had gradually developed over time (chapter 9). In the effort, the major Protestant tenets had *strong* historical basis. I then focus on two test cases: the assumption of Mary (chapter 10) and the veneration of icons (chapter 11). These two topics are particularly appropriate examples of the Protestant concern, both because of their historical record as well as the significance attached to them by several of the major non-Protestant traditions. My hope with this section is that a sympathetic reader would not only understand the Protestant position on these specific examples but would also gather an intuition about how Protestants understand their general situatedness within the history of the church—not as a departure from ancient Christianity, but as a return to it by the removal of various innovations or (as I will often call them) *accretions*. A brief conclusion sums up the overall resulting vision of Protestantism and offers practical advice to those facing such questions.

In sum, I commend Protestantism as first, a renewal of the gospel in the church; second, a return to the authority of Scripture; and third, a removal of historical accretions. Or, stated in terms of negations: part 1 opposes the assertion that any one institutional hierarchy comprises the "one true church"; part 2 opposes claims that the postapostolic church can act infallibly; and part 3 opposes the sentiment that Protestantism is a departure from ancient Christianity.

A question some readers might have at the front end is, "Which particular Protestant tradition are you defending in this book?" The answer is none. Although I am baptistic in my theology and ordained in a Congregationalist denomination, in this book I am seeking to commend a *mere Protestantism*, much in the manner that C. S. Lewis sought to defend a *mere Christianity*. Sometimes people criticize me for being a particular kind of Protestant and yet defending Protestantism as a whole. But it is perfectly permissible to defend one's broader level of identity. It would be like a Roman Catholic Christian defending "Christianity" to a Muslim or an Eastern Orthodox Christian defending "religion" to an atheist.

Of course, the differences among Protestant denominations are important, and each of us must consider which particular church we will join. But many people are wondering whether they should be any kind of Protestant, or whether the very *idea* of Protestantism makes sense. It is those kinds of readers whom I hope to help.

A Word to Non-Protestant Readers

Let me say a word to my readers from different Christian traditions. Believe me when I say I understand how frustrating and jarring it can be to patiently listen to the other side. Being on YouTube and seeking to remain irenic in the face of deep disagreements has sensitized me to the intensity of the dynamics of human disagreement. It is one of the driving passions of my life to be a person of charity who sincerely seeks to love and bless (and learn from) the other side amid our conversations and debates.

In my interactions with other Christian traditions through my YouTube ministry, I have frequently reflected on what I regard as the great theme in Harper Lee's novel *To Kill a Mockingbird*: the unmaking of prejudice. Constantly in my process of engaging in non-Protestant views I have thought of Atticus Finch's profound advice to his daughter:

> If you can learn a simple trick, Scout, you'll get along a lot better with all kinds of folks. You never really understand a person until you consider things from his point of view . . . until you climb into his skin and walk around in it.[5]

I believe many (though not all) of the divisions within Christendom result from—or at least are exacerbated by—a failure to employ Atticus's counsel in this passage. There is much prejudice, much pride, much caricature, much tribalism, much aloofness, much unwarranted enmity and distance. None of us are totally above this, so we must seek to listen patiently and really *hear* what the other side is saying. It is a mark of intellectual maturity to lower our guard and sympathetically consider how another person's position makes sense to them. Healthy, God-honoring disagreement, however vigorous, cannot bypass this initial step.

In this vein, I have done everything I can to describe opposing views accurately. I also want to articulate my deep love for my non-Protestant Christian friends at a personal level and my respect for these other traditions at both an intellectual and aesthetic level. The approach I seek in this book and in my YouTube ministry is to encourage candid and robust argumentation about our differences, downplaying or minimizing nothing, while at the same time seeking to maintain a conciliatory relationship. In various videos, I have expressed my appreciation for the wealth of Roman Catholic scholarship and learning, for example, or my admiration for the rich tradition of prayer and spirituality in many Eastern traditions.[6] I could give many other examples of areas of appreciation as well.

Hopefully it is clear that my motive behind this book is not personal animus against anyone. Instead, I write from my sincere conviction before God concerning the truth about our theological differences. These differences are important. They matter profoundly—to the gospel, to the church, and to our mission in this world. We must not and cannot shrug them off as irrelevant or avoid them out of a desire to maintain a superficial "unity." We *should* pray for unity, to be sure, but never at the cost of glossing over important differences concerning the truth.

Ultimately, I am deeply convinced in my conscience that the claims of traditions like Roman Catholicism and Eastern Orthodoxy to be the "one true church" that Jesus founded are wrong. Further, I maintain that the Protestant Reformation represented a genuine recovery of multiple biblical and apostolic truths. I do not maintain that these various non-Protestant traditions have *entirely lost* the gospel, but I do believe, with conviction, that the gospel has been both *obscured* and *added on to* in them. I also maintain, as will become evident, that Protestantism (despite its many imperfections) is best positioned to maintain a truly catholic vision of the church today amid its current fractures and divisions.

In line with that vision, it is my sincere prayer that my case for Protestantism would ultimately serve the unity and welfare of the one true, catholic, and apostolic church founded by Jesus Christ.

Lord Jesus Christ, on your final night in this world, you prayed that all your people would be one. We know that this unity cannot come at the expense of truth, yet we also know that our witness to the world around us depends on our pursuit of it. So we pray for humility and healing amid our often bitter disagreements: that we would better understand your gospel and better love one another in the process. Help us not to shy away from our disagreements in fear, nor reject one another in contempt. Teach us, as we talk to one another, ultimately to look to you. In your holy name, Amen.

PART 1

Protestantism and Catholicity

CHAPTER 1

Protestantism's Core Identity

In the introduction, I mentioned defending *mere Protestantism*. Yet critics of Protestantism sometimes allege that there is no such thing as *mere Protestantism*, since Protestants (it is claimed) agree on nothing except their criticisms of other traditions. Related to this, some fault Protestantism for having a merely *negative* identity—for being constituted only by what it is against, not what it is for.

Now, there are valid criticisms of Protestantism to be made, as we will discuss. But it is not correct or fair to say Protestantism has no core, positive identity. At the heart of the Protestant movement are the five *solae*, particularly *sola fide* and *sola Scriptura* (more on these two doctrines in a bit). Additionally, other doctrines have (with few exceptions) united the various historic Protestant traditions, such as belief in two sacraments, the priesthood of all believers, a shorter Old Testament canon, church discipline as a mark of the church, an emphasis on preaching in worship, a celebration of lay participation in communion in both kinds (both bread and wine), an affirmation of the right of clergy to marry, and many other points. Most of these positions are reflected in the official doctrinal standards of the traditions of magisterial Protestantism, such as the Thirty-Nine Articles (Anglican), the Augsburg Confession (Lutheran), and the various Reformed confessions.

It is true that there are fuzzy edges to how the word "Protestant" is applied—e.g., among the Anglo-Catholics on one side and the Anabaptists on the other. Nonetheless, the essential core of Protestantism is sizeable.

This chapter explores the nature of this core Protestant identity. What, most basically, *is* Protestantism? I propose, drawing from the nineteenth-century historian Philip Schaff, that Protestantism is best understood as *a renewal movement within the one true church.* What emerges from Schaff's vision (considered along the Reformers') is the counterintuitive realization that Protestantism is actually the tradition best positioned to retain and cultivate catholicity (that is, the wholeness of the church throughout space and time).

The Vision of Philip Schaff

I consider Philip Schaff to be for Protestantism what Cardinal John Henry Newman is for Roman Catholicism. A nineteenth-century Protestant historian and pioneering scholar in patristics, Schaff's theological vision (together with that of his colleague John Nevin) is often referenced as "Mercersburg Theology," since both Schaff and Nevin taught at German Reformed Theological Seminary in Mercersburg, Pennsylvania. Like

Cardinal Newman, Schaff was interested in the church's organic development and growth throughout church history—how the true church subsists from one time or place to another.

In 1845, the same year Cardinal John Henry Newman converted to Roman Catholicism, Schaff gave a lecture called *The Principle of Protestantism*, which Nevin subsequently translated. In this lecture, Schaff rooted the church's identity as extending back into the Incarnation, maintained a high view of the sacraments, and advocated for a more generous posture toward non-Protestant churches. Here and elsewhere, Schaff and Nevin offered a vision of Protestantism that is capacious enough to be a rallying cry for catholicity without compromising Protestant principles. He saw Protestantism, fundamentally, as a renewal movement within the church.

It is tragic that many contemporary Christians are unaware of historic articulations of Protestantism like Schaff's and feel they must choose between more sectarian expressions of Protestantism and the non-Protestant options. So here we will work through four principles of Mercersburg Theology that highlight how Protestantism is well positioned to serve catholicity and renewal in the church.

Principle 1: Protestantism Can Affirm the Good in the Pre-Reformation Church and in the Non-Protestant Traditions

For Schaff, construing Protestantism as a renewal of the church in no way entailed that nothing good was happening in the church apart from the Reformation. If that were the case, there would be no church to be *renewed*. Thus, Schaff maintained that prior to (and outside of) the Reformation, Christ was actively building his church. He opens thus:

> We contemplate the Reformation in its strictly historical conditions, its catholic union with the past. This is a vastly important point, which thousands in our day appear to overlook entirely. They see in the 31st of October, 1517, it is true, the birthday of the Evangelical Church, and find her certificate of baptism in the ninety-five theses of Luther; but at the same time cast a deep stain upon the legitimacy of this birth itself, by separating it from all right relation to the time that went before. In this way all interest is renounced in the spiritual wealth of the Middle Ages, which however belongs to us of right, as fully at least as it does to the Church of Rome.[1]

Schaff maintained that the Reformation would be *illegitimate* if it did not stand in organic continuity with the early and medieval church. This continuity, in Schaff's vision, must be rooted in catholicity—as he calls it, "catholic union with the past."

Elsewhere Schaff distinguished the Reformation from both a revolution (which consists in violently overthrowing what came before) as well as a restoration (which consists in a mere repetition of what came before).[2] Instead, he saw Protestantism as a kind of organic outgrowth of what came before, speaking of the medieval era as the "womb" of the Reformation.[3] In other words, Protestantism was new in one sense and ancient in another: It represented a new movement of life in the church, but on the grounds of retrieval and catholicity.

Schaff also stipulated that Protestantism did not consist in a complete negation of other *modern* Christian traditions. On the one hand, Schaff made it clear that he was not calling for a return to Rome. By requiring more and more doctrinal adherence on pain of anathema, the modern Church of Rome had "parted with the character of catholicity."[4] On the other hand, he affirmed the spiritual value and ecclesial status of traditions like Roman Catholicism and Eastern Orthodoxy. Elsewhere, for example, he wrote,

> It is surely an intolerant and narrow imagination, to regard the whole Roman and Greek communions, so far exceeding us as they do in numbers, as out of the Church entirely, and only worthy of course to be blotted out of history altogether as a gigantic spiritual zero.[5]

In Schaff's day, prior to Vatican II, Catholic and Orthodox Christians generally did not reciprocate this generosity. Rather, they typically viewed Protestants as heretics and schismatics, altogether removed from the church and thus from Christ himself. Schaff was aware of this but encouraged a different response: "We may not exclude the Romanists themselves. Let them go on to treat us as lost heretics; we must still return good for evil."[6] He also expressed his hope for *another* reformation within Roman Catholicism, emphasizing the size and value of this particular tradition.

From this it is clear that in Schaff's vision, Protestantism is not a mere assertion of itself over and against the rest of the church; rather, Protestantism takes its peculiar shape and character in order to serve the renewal and betterment of the entire church.

Principle 2: Protestantism Can Acknowledge Its Own Eccentricities, Errors, and Sins

For Schaff, considering Protestantism as a renewal movement did not require seeing it as perfect or completed. He argued that "respect for the Reformation as a divine work in no way forbids the admission that it included some mixture of error and sin; as where God builds a church, the devil erects a chapel by its side."[7] The Reformation did not resolve all errors in the church. To the contrary, Protestant churches have contributed their own errors. For example, Schaff argued that the Puritan stream of Protestantism, while having many admirable qualities, had overreacted to the excesses of the other side, becoming too strict.[8] In the other direction, he criticized Edward Pusey and the Anglo-Catholic movement for being too rigid and not reforming enough.[9]

Schaff was particularly burdened by the sectarian spirit he detected within American Protestantism. He spent many pages railing against what he called the two primary "diseases" of Protestantism: rationalism and sectarianism.[10] He felt that many Protestants, especially in America, had overreacted against the excess of Rome:

> As Catholicism toward the close of the Middle Ages settled into a character of hard, *stiff objectivity*, incompatible with the proper freedom of the individual subject . . . so Protestantism has been carried aside, in later times, into the opposite error of a *loose subjectivity*, which threatens to subvert all regard for church authority.[11]

Nevin held a similar concern. In his introduction to Schaff's lecture, Nevin emphasized that effective reformation had to be careful to honor the good in what is being reformed, lest it go too far. And many Protestants *had* gone too far. The result was that much of modern Protestantism was thin and factional. As he put it, "Ecclesiasticism, as held by Rome and also by Oxford, is indeed a terrible error; but it does not follow that the mere negation of ecclesiasticism is the truth."[12]

While they were willing to acknowledge Protestants' errors, however, both Nevin and Schaff maintained that the proper resources to redress these errors come from within Protestantism itself. They didn't think the answer was to go back to Rome or to one of the Eastern traditions—which would only extend and cement a departure from catholicity. Those traditions are bound to their magisterial pronouncements (and anathemas); thus, only Protestantism even has a *shot* at catholicity. Related to this, Schaff and Nevin argued that sectarian errors were not intrinsic to Protestantism. At one point, Schaff says, "The sect system, like rationalism, is a prostitution and caricature of true Protestantism."[13] Thus, admission of various Protestant errors by no means entailed a refutation of Protestantism as such.

As I've considered this aspect of Schaff's thought, an analogy has helped me conceptualize it. Suppose there is a married couple who, after decades of marriage, while the husband and wife are both around sixty, get a divorce. In the following years, both sides are diminished. The wife's house starts to fall apart slowly. The bushes in the front yard are poking way out into the sidewalk, the air conditioning filters have not been cleaned or replaced in many years, various appliances break down and don't get fixed, and so forth. Also, her finances are in bad shape. She has no savings.

The husband, by contrast, is socially awkward. He is a bad dresser. He has no idea how to get gifts for people. He forgets the grandkids' birthdays. He's lonely.

Recognizing that both sides are diminished by the split doesn't necessarily entail that the blame must be 50/50 or that separation was unjustified. The husband could have been abusive, justifying his wife's departure; or the wife could have been unfaithful, justifying the husband's departure—while both sides would still be ultimately diminished by the resulting split.

Similarly, a Protestant today can maintain that the Reformation was and is justified while also acknowledging various unfortunate tendencies that have characterized much of Protestantism in its overall development and current state. This is actually quite common amid conflict and breakups, when you think about it. In any kind of relational or institutional rupture, it is rare to find that either party is completely unfazed by the incident—including the party that was more in the right. Breakups, more often than not, leave both sides injured.

Thus, a Protestant today can celebrate the doctrinal recoveries that led to separation from Rome while grieving some of the long-term results of this separation and the overall fact of division itself. Further, a Protestant today can work freely and cheerfully toward the renewal and healing of divisions within the church—particularly because we are not bound by dogmatic claims that cement boundaries between different Christian traditions. That leads to the third point.

Principle 3: The Glory and Strength of Protestantism Lies in Continual Reforming

A question arises from the previous two points: If both Protestant and Catholic sides have been diminished from a sixteenth-century division, which side should we join today? Part of the answer results, of course, from which side we think was initially more to blame. But that is not all that is important! The other part of the answer will concern which side we think is best positioned to move forward, to make progress, to seek to heal divisions—or, short of that, to live most peaceably and fruitfully amid divisions.

For Schaff, these kinds of considerations powerfully commend Protestantism. He regards Protestantism as a continual enterprise of reform, an ongoing renewal effort, a dynamic force unfolding throughout church history: "Protestantism is the principle of movement, of progress in the history of the church."[14]

Thus, Protestantism was not consummated in the sixteenth century. It remains *incomplete*. As he puts it, "The present state of Protestantism is interimistic."[15] In other words, Protestantism does not entail that since the Reformation happened, all is well. On the contrary, the whole idea is continual reform.

This is the glory and strength of the Protestant doctrine referenced in the subtitle of this book: *semper reformanda* (always reforming). Protestantism has a built-in capacity for course correction, for fixing errors, for refining practice. To put it colloquially, when you get stuck, you can get unstuck. This opens up pathways for catholicity that are closed for those churches that hold their own pronouncements as infallible, as we will discuss in chapter 2.

Principle 4: The Principles for Reformation Are *Sola Fide* and *Sola Scriptura*

If *semper reformanda* is best pursued on Protestant principles, what precisely are those principles? For Schaff, the heart of Protestant identity lies in two affirmations: justification is by faith alone (*sola fide*), and Holy Scripture is the only infallible rule for the church's faith and practice (*sola Scriptura*). The first of these represents a material component of the apostolic deposit recovered by the Reformation; the second represents a formal principle by which we remain accountable to that apostolic deposit. The way I like to put it is that *sola fide* is the "what" of the Reformation; *sola Scriptura*, the "how." The first is an object, the second a method. The first is a precious jewel; the second, the safe that protects it.

These were not the *only* points the Reformers contended for, but they were at the nerve center of what animated the Protestant movement and gave it shape and positive energy, and also united all the different Protestant traditions together.

Schaff calls justification by faith alone the "life principle" of the Reformation. He denied that this doctrine was new to the Reformation; rather, he argued that it came into greater clarity and apprehension within the church as a result of the Reformation.[16] Schaff was able to outline various points of overlap between the Protestant position and the one adopted at the Council of Trent. Thus, he noted that the Roman Catholic position affirms faith alone for *initial* justification—what he called "the beginning of salvation, the root of justification."[17] However, Schaff faulted the actual practice of the Roman Catholic position for sliding into various kinds of overemphasis on works. For example, he faulted its affirmation of supermeritorious good works that may be deposited into the treasury of merit and deployed by the church to help other Christians or souls in purgatory.[18]

From this system, Schaff argued, sprang the "scandalous trade" of indulgences, in which "the inmost sanctuary of man's life—the pardon of sin and holiness—was put to sale for the most paltry and outward of all interests, money."[19] Schaff called this practice an "abomination," faulting it not merely for giving rise to all manner of corruption and abuse, but more basically for removing from the laity the assurance and peace the gospel is supposed to provide. According to Schaff, the practical result of the Catholic position—both for its overemphasis on works as well as for its financial and commercial legalism—is "an entire want of evangelical freedom and assurance."[20] The recovery of *sola fide* in the sixteenth century therefore had the effect of returning to the laity a meaningful experience of their forgiven status and good standing in the sight of heaven.

Schaff also construed *sola Scriptura* as an impetus for renewal. For him, this doctrine was in no way at odds with tradition. On the contrary, tradition is the necessary context and correlate for

Scripture because Scripture "flows forward in the church, and comes there continually to clearer and deeper consciousness."[21] Nonetheless, Scripture held priority over tradition as the *greater* authority. The Roman Catholic position defined at Trent, by placing Scripture and tradition in theoretically parallel placement, and taking unto herself the role of interpretation, has had the overall practical effect of placing the church *over* Scripture:

> The whole tendency of the Roman Catholic Church has for its object to subordinate the Bible to tradition, and then to make itself the infallible judge of both, with power to determine at pleasure what is God's word and the doctrine of the church, and to anathematize everything that may go beyond its past decisions.[22]

Schaff thus argued that the Council of Trent ultimately represented a departure from catholicity. By making herself the final arbiter of Scripture and tradition, the Church of Rome not only blocked communion with any and all Christian traditions dissenting from her pronouncements, but also removed the possibility of any meaningful internal reform of her own prior magisterial teaching. It gave her the power to yoke the consciences of the laity to error, effectively removing them from meaningful accountability to Scripture (and, Schaff noted, sometimes even blocking their *possession* of Scripture): "The Church of Rome under the credit of apostolical tradition had smuggled into her communion the most shocking errors, and brought the word of God almost entirely into oblivion, had repeatedly prohibited it to the laity indeed in express terms."[23] Thus, *sola Scriptura* brought both a renewed contact between the Bible and laity as well as the possibility of ongoing accountability and reform in the church according to the Word of God.

We will return to both *sola fide* and *sola Scriptura* later in subsequent chapters; the point for now is simply to see that, for Schaff, these doctrines ultimately served the larger purpose of the renewal and ongoing reformation of the whole church. Imbedded at the very heart of Protestantism lay an instinct toward revitalization and catholicity.

Was Schaff's Vision of Protestantism Unusual?

The Mercersburg vision of Protestantism is by no means representative of all Protestants. In his own day, as we have seen, it stood between the stricter Puritans and the Anglo-Catholics. It also differs from many more sectarian attitudes among Protestants today.

Nonetheless, Schaff's overall vision of Protestantism as a renewal movement within the church has much resonance with the perspective of the Reformers. In part 3 we will consider the Reformers' posture toward earlier church history, especially the church fathers. Here we note the Reformers' recognition of the true church outside of Protestantism *even in their own day*. Martin Luther, for example, commenting in the 1530s on Paul's characterization of the Galatian churches as true churches (Gal. 1:2) despite their compromise of the gospel (Gal. 1:6), drew a comparison with the Church of Rome. On the one hand, the Church of Rome was "worse than Sodom and Gomorrah" because of her doctrinal and spiritual corruption. On the other hand, Luther stipulated that "today we still call the Church of Rome holy and all its sees holy, even though they have been undermined and their ministers are ungodly."[24] This is because, Luther maintained, the Church of Rome still possesses "Baptism, the Sacrament, the voice and text of the Gospel, the Sacred Scriptures, the ministries, the name of Christ, and the name of God."[25] The comparison to the Galatian churches, the use of the term "holy," and the reference to valid sacraments and ministry—all this indicates that Luther, for all his strident criticism of papal abuses, did not deny the ecclesial status of the Church of Rome.

Another episode a few years earlier reveals Luther's position even more transparently. Responding to an inquiry about baptism from two pastors, Luther critiqued the Anabaptist practice of rebaptism. His rationale for this position reveals his view of the status of the Church of Rome:

> There is much that is Christian and good under the papacy. . . . In the papal church there are the true holy Scriptures, true baptism, the true sacrament of the altar, the true keys to the forgiveness of sins, the true office of the ministry, the true catechism in the form of the Lord's Prayer, the Ten Commandments, and the articles of the creed.[26]

From this language it is clear that Luther regarded the Church of Rome as a genuine church. He then makes this point explicitly: "In the papacy there is true Christianity, even the right kind of Christianity and many great and devoted saints. . . . The Christendom that is now under the papacy is truly the body of Christ and a member of it."[27]

John Calvin held a similar view. In his reply to Sadoleto, he called the Roman hierarchy ravenous wolves, yet he also maintained that "those over which you preside are Churches of Christ."[28] Elsewhere Calvin bewailed the rampant idolatry, superstition, and error in the Church of Rome in his day but then qualified his critique: "When we categorically deny to the papists the title of *the* church, we do not for this reason impugn the existence of churches among them."[29] He compared these true churches to a scattered remnant, and the general status of the Church of Rome to a half-demolished building.[30] These statements are representative of the general perspective of the magisterial Reformers—the Church of Rome had fallen into gross sin and error, but *she was still a church.*

After the Council of Trent, Protestant evaluation of the Church of Rome continued to reflect this balance of strident censure mixed with a qualified affirmation of her ecclesial status. Francis Turretin distinguished between two ways the Church of Rome could be considered a church: first, "as it is Christian, with regard to the profession of Christianity and of gospel truth which it retains"; second, according to its subjection to the pope and the errors it has intermingled with the truth. Considered in terms of the latter, the Church of Rome was "AntiChristian and apostate,"[31] but in terms of the former, the Church of Rome ought to be considered a church for three reasons: (1) there were Christians within her, (2) she retained the Word and sacraments, however corrupted or neglected they may be, and (3) she maintained "Christian and evangelical truths concerning the one and triune God, Christ the God-man Mediator, his incarnation, death and resurrection and other heads of doctrine by which she is distinguished from assemblies of pagans and infidels."[32] To summarize Turretin's view: the Church of Rome is a true Christian church insofar as she has Christian people, Christian sacraments, and Christian doctrines.

In the Anglican tradition, Richard Hooker held that separation from Rome was necessary because of her "gross and grievous abominations," yet he also maintained that

> touching those main parts of Christian truth wherein they constantly still persist, we gladly acknowledge them to be of the family of Jesus Christ; and our hearty prayer unto God

Almighty is, that being conjoined so far forth with them, they may at the length (if it be his will) so yield to frame and reform themselves, that no distraction remain in any thing, but that we "all may with one heart and one mouth glorify God the Father of our Lord and Saviour," whose Church we are.[33]

Hooker's perspective is remarkably generous for his historical context in sixteenth-century England, where brutal violence between Catholics and Protestants was sadly common.

What about the Protestant attitude toward other traditions, such as Eastern Orthodoxy? Strikingly, both Calvin and Luther rejected the Roman Catholic claim that the "Greek Church" (as Calvin and Luther called it) had lapsed from the faith and was damned. Calvin opined, "They make the Greeks schismatics: with what right? Because in withdrawing from the apostolic see they lost their privilege. What? Would not they who fall away from Christ deserve to lose it much more?"[34] John McNeill, editing this passage in Calvin, notes that Luther's expression of the same opinion was typically colorful: "Luther, as early as 1519, in his Leipzig Disputation, soundly condemned the view expressed by Eck that by separation from Rome the Greeks had lapsed from the faith and were damned: 'nothing more detestable than this blasphemy could be spoken.'"[35] The point here is not that the Reformers were in agreement with Orthodoxy (they were not, though they were arguably closer to it than they were to Rome), but simply that they rejected Rome's condemnation of Orthodoxy as outside the church.

Later in the sixteenth century, a group of Lutheran theologians wrote to Jeremiah II, Ecumenical Patriarch of Constantinople, to send him a copy of the Augsburg Confession and engage in theological correspondence. The Lutherans treated Jeremiah respectfully, addressing him with titles like "the

Most Honorable Lord," "the All-Holy Ecumenical Patriarch," and "God-Beloved Sir."[36] The Lutherans opened the dialogue with an assertion that Eastern Orthodox Christians possessed a common salvation in Christ and expressed their earnest desire for a closer unity with the Orthodox Church.[37]

The subsequent interaction (three letters each way) revealed an enormous amount of agreement on matters such as the truth and inspiration of Scriptures, the doctrine of God, the Trinity, the two natures of Christ, the nature of evil, the saving office of Christ in his death and resurrection, the future second coming of Christ, and much more. They also shared many points of doctrine over and against the Western Roman Catholic church: for example, affirmation of communion in two kinds and rejection of indulgences, the papacy, and purgatory. Nonetheless, disagreement persisted between the Lutherans and the Orthodox on topics like the *filioque* (the affirmation among Western Christians that the Holy Spirit proceeds from the Son as well as the Father), free will, justification, the number of sacraments, invocation of the saints, icons, relics, and a few other matters.[38]

Jeremiah's responses were initially warm but perhaps condescending—his opening letter addressed them "with the cheerfulness of a father to his children."[39] At the end of his second reply, Jeremiah noted that "we have agreed on almost all of the main subjects," but noted areas of difference pertaining to the interpretation of Scripture.[40] He enjoined the Lutherans to put aside these "irrational innovations" and enter the Eastern Orthodox Church, "for nothing else is the cause of dissension than this and only this, which when you correct it, we will be, with the grace of God, in agreement."[41] Yet in his third letter, when it had become evident the Lutherans were not yielding on their points of difference, Jeremiah took a more upbraiding tone, at one point sarcastically exclaiming, "You call yourself theologians!"[42] At this point he ultimately brought the dialogue to an end:

> We request that from henceforth you do not cause us more grief, nor write to us on the same subject if you should wish to treat these luminaries and theologians of the Church in a different manner. . . . Thus, as for you, please release us from these cares. Therefore, going about your own ways, write no longer concerning dogmas; but if you do, write only for friendship's sake. Farewell.[43]

For their part, the Lutherans decried the charge that they had strayed from the ancient and catholic faith: "We cannot bear to be called heretics. . . . Indeed, we embrace all the articles of the catholic faith, rejecting absolutely none of them, and we respectfully make use of the sacraments which were instituted by Christ."[44] Repeatedly they stressed that their doctrine was *not* new. On the contrary, it was founded upon the Word of God. They acknowledged Jeremiah's request to stop writing, but expressed their hope that the matters under discussion would be reconsidered in due time. In the meantime, they offered their friendship and good wishes to the Patriarch:

> Therefore, standing together with Your Holiness, Patriarch and Most Reverent Sir, we offer to the God of all, our true friendship which we have shown to you and which we will continuously afterwards keep. We wish Your Holiness, with all our heart, all that is best and a prayerful wish for salvation, and above all this, that the Holy Spirit will lead all the activities of Your Holiness, the honor of God, and the salvation of His Church, Amen.[45]

From this interchange are evident two vastly different visions of catholicity. For Jeremiah, unity with the Lutherans necessarily involved institutional incorporation within the Eastern Orthodox Church. For the Lutherans, by contrast, the criterion for unity was adherence to the gospel of Christ, as held forth in the Scriptures. Here, for instance, is how they made their appeal:

> We desire from the bottom of our hearts to preserve a God-pleasing peace with all who love the Gospel of Christ, who hold the right interpretation of Christ, the unique teacher (who speaks to us through the words of the Old as well as the New [Testaments]). We do not innovate in any matters of faith.[46]

Now, many Protestants have not shared the spirit of catholicity reflected by these Lutheran theologians. Sectarianism can be found in all traditions and is common in many contemporary Protestant circles. Nonetheless, none of the major historical Protestant traditions have claimed to be the only church or the only true church. Thus, for example, the Lutheran theologians were not compromising any official historic Lutheran standard in engaging Jeremiah II as a Christian person within the Christian church, to whom Christian obligations and love are in order. Nor are contemporary Protestants compromising in acknowledging true Christians and true churches outside of Protestantism. This is because Protestantism does not restrict the church to one institution. In this posture of institutional inclusivism, as we will see in the next chapter, Protestantism is rather unique.

CHAPTER 2

"The One True Church"

T he major Christian traditions outside of Protestantism—
Roman Catholicism, Eastern Orthodoxy, Oriental
Orthodoxy, and the Assyrian Church of the East—all
claim to be the "one true church." Each of these churches sees
itself, to the exclusion of the others, as the original church
Christ founded. There are variations in how this is articulated
and what implications are drawn from it (for example, which
church will consider other churches to have valid sacraments,
how Christians in other churches can be saved, and more), but
the core idea of institutional exclusivism—that the real church
is Christ is restricted to one visible, institutional church with its
own unique hierarchical structure—permeates all of them. The
highly institutional character of each of these churches developed in large measure in the context of union with the Roman
(and later Byzantine) Empire, starting in the fourth century.

Protestantism represents a different approach to discerning the true church. It is not that Protestants deny that the church is *visible*. This is a common misunderstanding. Historically, Protestants have distinguished between the visible and invisible church, drawing from St. Augustine—but this distinction does not entail a *denial* of the visible church.[1] It is simply a distinction, making a modest point: We can count the number of baptized Christians (the visible church), but only God knows who is truly united to Christ (the invisible church). For example, Judas Iscariot was a member of Christ's church in one sense, but not in another sense. What distinguishes the Protestant view of the church is not a denial of the visible church but rather *the claim that this visible church coheres within multiple institutions.* To put it negatively, Protestantism denies the claim that any one institutional hierarchy constitutes the "one true church."

"No Salvation outside the Church" in Eastern Orthodoxy

Today, many Christians in these traditions recognize that there can be true Christians outside of their ranks and have found various ways to articulate that. Similarly, in the early church there was more openness as to how a person could be united to the body of Christ without having explicit faith or being formally in the church. For example, early Christians like Justin Martyr developed ways of explaining how pagans who lived justly could be members of the body of Christ.[2] At the same time, most of these statements were made with reference to those who lived prior to the time of Christ. As early as the third century, Cyprian of Carthage articulated the doctrine that there is "no salvation outside the church." In Cyprian's context, however, these statements were applied to heretical groups like the Marcionites and Gnostics at a time when the church was a persecuted minority.[3]

Eventually, particularly after the union of church and empire in the fourth century, the doctrine of "no salvation outside the church" came to be applied more absolutely and more restrictively. Thus, after the great schism of the eleventh century, each side seems to have regarded the other as having departed from both church and salvation. The same general stakes seem to be at play in the fifth-century christological schisms. For example, Pope Dioscorus I of Alexandria, considered a saint by several of the Oriental Orthodox Churches, was anathematized at the Council of Chalcedon, while for their part the non-Chalcedonians anathematized several of the prominent Chalcedonian leaders, such as Pope Leo of Rome.

Prior to a debate I had with an Eastern Orthodox priest, I combed through everything I could find in the Eastern Orthodox tradition concerning the status of non-Orthodox Christians (such as Roman Catholics) from the 1054 split (and a bit before, as conflict was setting in) up through modern times. I was not able to find *any* affirmations that non-Orthodox Christians like Roman Catholics or Protestants could be saved until the nineteenth century, where they were rare, and then more in the twentieth century, where they were still tentative and controversial. I have asked numerous times for people to share with me if they find any examples I am not aware of, and I have not yet had anyone produce anything that alters this picture.

Essentially, the historic Eastern Orthodox position is that perceived Western innovations such as the *filioque* are heresy and that heresy places you outside the canonical boundaries of the Orthodox Church. To be outside the church is to be cut off from the grace of the Holy Spirit given in the sacraments and therefore cut off from salvation. The basis for this claim is rooted in a particular construal of the unity of the church: Orthodox ecclesiologists taught that the church is ontologically one such that there are no schisms *in* the church, only schisms *from* her.[4] A common metaphor is the ark of Noah: If you are outside of the "one true church," you are drowning in the waters of sin and cut off from salvation.

A good representative portrait of historic Orthodox thought can be found in the eighteenth-century Orthodox monk and theologian Paisius Velichkovsky's categorization of the *filioque*. Responding to an inquiring priest, Velichkovsky referred to the *filioque* as "the first and most important of all the heresies."[5] According to Velichkovsky, rejection of the *filioque* was the unanimous consensus of the church, such that all those embracing it had no hope of salvation:

> All the holy ecumenical teachers who have interpreted the Scripture as if with one mouth say that the Holy Spirit proceeds from the Father, and nowhere have they written that he proceeds from the Son also. Thus, if Uniates think exactly like the Romans in such a serious heresy, what hope do they have for salvation, unless they openly renounce this Spirit-fighting heresy and become united again with the Holy Orthodox Eastern Church?[6]

"Uniate" Churches are Eastern churches (often historically Eastern Orthodox or Oriental Orthodox) that are in full communion with the Church of Rome while retaining their own liturgy. Velichkovsky made it clear that to be among such churches is to be without hope of salvation: "Depart and flee from the Unia as speedily as possible, lest death overtake you in it and you be numbered among the heretics and not among the Christians."[7]

Someone might object that Velichkovsky is just one theologian, but his perspective is representative of premodern Orthodox thought. Thus, in the seventeenth century, something like a crisis emerged in the Eastern Orthodox church when Cyril Lucaris (the Patriarch of Constantinople) advanced various teachings that had points of similarity to Protestant, and especially Calvinist, views. In response, the 1672 Synod of Jerusalem met to condemn these doctrines, producing the Confession of Dositheus (Patriarch of Jerusalem), an official and formally approved statement of Orthodox belief. The Confession repeatedly refers to Protestants as wicked heretics and Protestant teachings as heretical.[8] In the context of opposing the idea that the offices of priest and bishop are the same, it stipulates that "the dignity of the bishop is so necessary in the Church, that without him, neither Church nor Christian could either be or be spoken of. . . . He is, we affirm, as necessary to the Church as breath is to man, or the sun to the world."[9] Those outside the church are therefore regarded as forsaken by the Holy Spirit: "When these forsake the Church, they are forsaken by the Holy Spirit, and there remains in them neither understanding nor light, but only darkness and blindness."[10] The Synod also formally approved of Jeremiah II's replies to the Lutherans.

The 1848 Encyclical of the Eastern Patriarchs, a letter issued by the four Eastern Patriarchs in response to Pope Pius IX's "Epistle to the Easterners" earlier that year, maintained the traditional identification of the *filioque* as damnable heresy, ranking alongside Arianism and the papacy. It repeatedly refers to the Roman Catholic Church as apostate and heretical. Here is a flavor:

> The One, Holy, Catholic, and Apostolic Church, following
> in the steps of the holy Fathers, both Eastern and Western,
> proclaimed of old to our progenitors and again teaches today

synodically, that the said novel doctrine of the Holy Ghost proceeding from the Father and the Son is essentially heresy, and its maintainers, whoever they be, are heretics, according to the sentence of Pope St. Damasus, and that the congregations of such are also heretical, and that all spiritual communion in worship of the orthodox sons of the Catholic Church with such is unlawful.[11]

Bear in mind that "Catholic" here does not mean Roman Catholic; historically, the Eastern Orthodox Church has referred to itself as the Catholic church. Later in the nineteenth century, the Patriarchal Encyclical of 1895, responding to Pope Leo XIII's invitation to unity with Rome, maintained the same position that Roman Catholicism is heretical and didn't hesitate to draw implications for salvation:

> But, as has been said before, the Western Church, from the tenth century downwards, has privily brought into herself through the papacy various and strange and heretical doctrines and innovations, and so she has been torn away and removed far from the true and orthodox Church of Christ. How necessary, then, it is for you to come back and return to the ancient and unadulterated doctrines of the Church in order to attain the salvation in Christ after which you press.[12]

The Longer Catechism of Saint Philaret (a significant nineteenth-century Metropolitan of Moscow) referenced the familiar imagery of Noah's ark and then stipulated, "to have part in [Christ's] salvation, we must necessarily be members of his body, that is, of the Catholic church."[13] At this time there seems to be no conception of an "invisible connection to the visible church," as is sometimes suggested today. I could keep providing examples, but hopefully the main point is clear.[14] Again, I have not been able to find any exceptions to this exclusivism until the most recent centuries.

Today, one finds a multiplicity of views within Eastern Orthodoxy concerning the ultimate fate of the non-Orthodox. Timothy Ware represents a moderate Orthodox view when he writes, "There is no division between a 'visible' and an 'invisible Church', yet there may be members of the Church who are not visibly such, but whose membership is known to God alone."[15] On the other hand, it is not hard to find the traditional view represented today (I have been told in multiple debates/dialogues by Eastern Orthodox Christians that I am going to hell unless I convert to Orthodoxy). One can also find arch-traditionalist Orthodox groups like the True Orthodox Church (or Genuine Orthodoxy) that have severed communion with mainstream Orthodoxy, claiming it has been corrupted by heresy no less than the Catholics, Protestants, and others. Current changes in how "no salvation outside the church" is understood within Eastern Orthodoxy are one example of how Orthodoxy's claim to be the "unchanged church" that represents the consensus of the fathers is ultimately unconvincing.

"No Salvation outside the Church" in Roman Catholicism

The Roman Catholic Church currently has a more inclusive posture toward non-Catholics, especially since the Second Vatican Council in the 1960s. Thus, the Catechism of the Catholic Church clarifies that the "outside the church there is no salvation" principle is not aimed at "those who, through no fault of their own, do not know Christ and his Church."[16] It also speaks of Jews and Muslims being included in the plan of salvation in some sense.[17] One can still find more restrictive views, especially among traditionalist groups, but most Catholics today claim that although the Roman Catholic Church is the one true church, there can be true Christians outside of her.

However, this is not the historical Roman Catholic view. Historically, Roman Catholics regarded the Eastern Orthodox in the same way the Eastern Orthodox regarded them: They are off Noah's ark and therefore drowning in the floodwaters of sin. Both sides used this same imagery, and both drew from the patristic idea that "outside the Church there is no salvation." For example, Unam Sanctam was an early fourteenth-century Bull on papal supremacy issued by Boniface VIII related to a dispute he was having with a king of France. Drawing from the ark imagery for the true church, it restricted salvation to those in submission to the pope: "Now, therefore, we declare, say, determine and pronounce that for every human creature it is necessary for salvation to be subject to the authority of the Roman pontiff."[18]

This assertion is generally regarded as magisterial—and therefore irreformable—teaching. Thus, to reconcile this assertion with Vatican II, contemporary Roman Catholics will sometimes claim that it does not rule out *implicit* subjection to the pope. But this is an artificial reading of Unam Sanctam that lacks any historical precedent from the time in question. It is true that exceptions were made for catechumens awaiting baptism and that a few Jesuit theologians in the early modern era (controversially) extended the principle of *implicit faith* more widely. Still, virtually *no one* in the medieval church interpreted Unam Sanctam like post-Vatican II Catholics do today. As the Roman Catholic scholar Francis Sullivan notes, "The teaching of St. Thomas and the whole medieval tradition . . . required explicit Christian faith for the salvation of everyone in the Christian era. After the suppression of the Jesuit order, hardly any Catholic theologians dared to question the traditional teaching on this point."[19] Only in the modern era has the picture changed.

Consider, as another example of the medieval outlook that found its way into magisterial (allegedly infallible) teaching, the following passage from Cantate Domino (or "the Bull of Union with the Copts") promulgated by Pope Eugene IV at the Council of Florence in the fifteenth century:

> [The Roman Catholic Church] firmly believes, professes and preaches that all those who are outside the catholic church, not only pagans but also Jews or heretics and schismatics, cannot share in eternal life and will go into the everlasting fire which was prepared for the devil and his angels, unless they are joined to the catholic church before the end of their lives.[20]

You wonder, how could it be clearer? If the Roman Catholic Church had wished to teach that all outside of her bounds would be damned, how *could* they have done so, if not with a statement like this?

Some argue that because the Church of Rome recognized the validity of some sacraments performed by other churches, they implicitly recognized salvation as a possibility as well. But note how the passage continues: "The unity of the ecclesiastical body is of such importance that *only for those who abide in it do the Church's sacraments contribute to salvation*."[21] Thus, the fact that a baptism could be valid for those entering Rome did not necessarily mean it was salvific for those remaining without. The passage proceeds to assert that even extravagant almsgiving and martyrdom are useless unless you are Roman Catholic: "Nobody can be saved, no matter how much he has given away in alms and even if he has shed his blood in the name of Christ, unless he has persevered in the bosom and the unity of the Catholic Church."[22]

Again, post–Vatican II Roman Catholics have to interpret this passage differently from the way virtually everyone interpreted it when it was written. For example, people will speak of being *unknowingly* within the church. But medieval Christians had no more conception of the possibility of being *unknowingly* in the true church than they did that those drowning in the flood could be unknowingly on the ark of Noah. If hardly any Roman Catholic Christians held this view prior to the modern era, why should it be allowed as an authentic interpretation of the doctrine "no salvation outside the church," rather than a change in its meaning? This is a significant problem with the Roman Catholic notion of doctrinal development: its tendency to move the goalposts in order to make the goal.

Besides representing a potential falsification of the Roman Catholic claim of infallibility, changes in the "no salvation outside the church" doctrine raise a practical concern about the actual value of an allegedly infallible magisterium. For example, we are often told we need an infallible magisterium to interpret the Bible, but much less appreciated are the intractable problems of interpreting the magisterium *itself.* Is such an entity really the solution to division and confusion if nearly everyone can misunderstand it for six hundred years? How do we know that current universal understanding of magisterial teaching won't be similarly overturned in another six hundred years?

What Constitutes a "Valid Church"?

Beyond questions of salvation, there are other consequences of the "one truth church" claims. For example, the Roman Catholic Church regards Protestant churches as "ecclesial communities" but not churches and denies that they enjoy a valid Eucharist, since they allegedly lack valid holy orders (valid ordained ministry). Even the Anglicans do not have a valid Eucharist, despite holding to apostolic succession, since their episcopal succession is considered null and void. By contrast, the Roman Catholic Church recognizes the validity of Eastern Orthodox and Oriental Orthodox sacraments, and generally recognizes the validity of all Trinitarian baptisms.

The historic Eastern Orthodox position on valid Eucharists was addressed in the Confession of Dositheus:

> This Mystery of the Sacred Eucharist can be performed by none other, except only by an Orthodox Priest, who has received his priesthood from an Orthodox and Canonical Bishop, in accordance with the teaching of the Eastern Church. This is compendiously the doctrine, and true confession, and most ancient tradition of the Catholic Church concerning this Mystery; which must not be departed from in any way by such as would be Orthodox and who reject the novelties and profane vanities of heretics. But necessarily the tradition of the institution must be kept whole and unimpaired. For those that transgress, the catholic Church of Christ rejects and anathematises.[23]

One can find a mixture of views among contemporary Eastern Orthodox Christians concerning the validity of a Roman Catholic or Oriental Orthodox Eucharist, but the nullity of Protestant Eucharists is the standard view.

By contrast, a Protestant can recognize a true church wherever Christ is present in Word and sacrament—and wherever such a church exists, there is the potential for a valid Eucharist. Imagine a remote village in the Middle East where a number of Muslims begin having dreams in which Jesus appears to them and reveals himself as Lord. They respond with repentance and baptism, and a small community of worshiping Christians is formed. Is this a valid church, and do they have a valid Eucharist? While some in the non-Protestant traditions may want to make such allowances, this generosity is not consistent with their churches' historical teaching. On Protestant principles, by contrast, the converted Muslim community is a fully valid church with a fully valid Eucharist. No qualifications, conceptual gymnastics, or revisionist readings of historical standards are needed to explain this phenomenon. It is simply Christ the Lord building his empire.

In short, Protestantism has a superior orientation toward catholicity than its rivals because it lacks their institutional exclusivism. Protestantism acknowledges true churches within multiple institutions. This does not mean Protestants are universalists. The vast majority of Protestants are exclusivists in the sense of believing there are boundaries to the church; not everyone is within it; and not everyone will be saved. The point is they are not *institutional* exclusivists: They do not restrict the "one true church" to a single, visible hierarchy.

Now we can ask: Which view better accords with the New Testament? Does institutional exclusivism reflect the kind of church Jesus and the apostles founded?

Institutional Exclusivism and New Testament Ecclesiology

As we look at the church today, we cannot help but see the fruits of the church in multiple institutional expressions of the church. Glory unto the Trinity, glory unto the name of Jesus Christ, spiritual fruit and virtue wrought by the Holy Spirit, the pushing back of demonic powers, and the saving knowledge of the true God—all this occurs in more than one institution. We see saints in the medieval East and saints in the medieval West. We have exorcisms in Roman Catholic contexts and exorcisms in Pentecostal contexts. We find testimonies of spiritual transformation in the name of Christ in Congregationalist churches, and we find the same in Coptic churches.

What are we to make of this? How does the New Testament teach us to discern the work and presence of Christ?

In Matthew 7:15–20, Jesus gives a criterion by which to determine true and false prophets:

> Beware of false prophets, who come to you in sheep's clothing but inwardly are ravenous wolves. You will recognize them by their fruits. Are grapes gathered from thornbushes, or figs from thistles? So, every healthy tree bears good fruit, but the diseased tree bears bad fruit. A healthy tree cannot bear bad fruit, nor can a diseased tree bear good fruit. Every tree that does not bear good fruit is cut down and thrown into the fire. Thus you will recognize them by their fruits.

Here Jesus articulates not merely that good fruit is more likely to come from a good tree. He claims that a bad tree *cannot* bear good fruit (v. 18). Therefore, if we have good fruit, we know we have a good tree. Jesus gave us this teaching because he expected us to put it into practice. He expected us to distinguish true and false prophets on the basis of their fruit.

When I have made this point in YouTube videos, critics often respond by asking if this means Buddhists or Mormons who have positive religious experiences are saved. This objection misses the point: We are seeking to obey the command of Christ, and Christ was not advancing religious pluralism or playing on our sentimentality. By the word "fruit," Christ did not mean generic religious experience but the spiritual result of the

Holy Spirit's work in and through the Christian gospel. This is the same word used in Matthew 3:8, "Bear fruit in keeping with repentance," and John 15:5, "Whoever abides in me and I in him, he it is that bears much fruit." Paul uses this term to refer to the virtues wrought in a believer by the Holy Spirit: "love, joy, peace, patience, kindness, goodness, faithfulness, gentleness, self-control" (Gal. 5:22–23). In its usage in the New Testament, this term refers to spiritual good wrought by the Holy Spirit in the lives of those responding to the gospel of Christ and being incorporated into his kingdom.

It is this understanding of "fruit" that Jesus commands us to consider in practicing spiritual discernment. This does not mean there will be no fake miracles or exorcisms, as Jesus also warns in the immediately following verses (Matt. 7:21–23). Satan can occasionally work miracles, as we see with Pharaoh's sorcerers (Ex. 7:11), and as Jesus warns concerning false Christs and false prophets (Matt. 24:24). But Satan cannot produce virtues. He is incapable of producing joy, peace, goodness, kindness, love for Christ, love for God, love for the Holy Spirit, love for the Scripture, love for truth. Only Christ produces these things. Therefore, such fruit testifies to the genuine work of Christ.

Even exorcisms can provide a generally reliable criterion for discerning the work of Christ. For example, a few chapters later in Matthew, Jesus heals a demon-possessed man who was blind and mute. When the Pharisees respond by speculating that he casts out demons by Beelzebub, Jesus responds, "Every kingdom divided against itself is laid waste, and no city or house divided against itself will stand. And if Satan casts out Satan, he is divided against himself. How then will his kingdom stand?" (Matt. 12:25–26). Thus, Jesus holds the Pharisees accountable to judge that an exorcism should not be attributed to Satan. It is in this context that Jesus warns about blasphemy against the Holy

Spirit and then again stipulates a criterion for spiritual discernment: "Either make the tree good and its fruit good, or make the tree bad and its fruit bad, for the tree is known by its fruit" (Matt. 12:33). From this it is evident that exorcisms generally constitute positive spiritual fruit that reveal the genuine advance of God's kingdom.

In Mark 9:38–40, Jesus offers an even more expansive principle of discernment based on another exorcism:

> John said to him, "Teacher, we saw someone casting out demons in your name, and we tried to stop him, because he was not following us." But Jesus said, "Do not stop him, for no one who does a mighty work in my name will be able soon afterward to speak evil of me. For the one who is not against us is for us."

It is significant here that, according to John's report, this exorcist was casting out demons *in Jesus's name*. He was not a member of a different religion. John's rationale for attempting to stop him concerned not the exorcist's orientation to Christ but his orientation to the disciples: "He was not following *us*."

Thus, on one level, it is scandalous that the disciples would actually try to *stop* an exorcism. Imagine how that must have felt to the man possessed by the demon! But their attitude is more understandable (though still wrong) when you remember they had been unable to cast out a demon earlier in the chapter (Mark 9:18). They must have felt threatened by this other exorcist, whose power undermined their sense of exclusivity and privilege.

Oh, how easy it is for the church today to fall into the disciples' error here! All we need to do is feel threatened by another Christian who has some gift or calling that we do not. Every church today, and every Christian today, needs to carefully heed the rebuke of Christ in this passage: "No one who does a mighty work in my name will be able soon afterward to speak evil of me. For *the one who is not against us is for us*" (vv. 39–40, italics mine). Do we heed Christ's warning here? Our Savior commands us to regard those who do mighty works in his name as for us, not against us. This is an exclusivism, but it is a radically *Christocentric* exclusivism. It is not an institutional exclusivism or an exclusivism based on human distinction or pride. That is the kind of exclusivism reflected, sadly, in John's comment in Mark 9:38.

Another principle for discerning the work of Christ is given to us by Paul in 1 Corinthians 12:3: "No one speaking in the Spirit of God ever says 'Jesus is accursed!' and no one can say 'Jesus is Lord' except in the Holy Spirit." This test is both spiritual and doctrinal—we are commanded to discern the work of the Holy Spirit based on the fact that it results in an affirmation of the lordship of Christ. Once again, this is an exclusivism, but it's a Christocentric exclusivism. Both a Roman Catholic and a Calvinist could pass the test, but a Buddhist or a Mormon could not, since neither would affirm that Jesus is Lord as Paul understands and teaches in his letters.

So consider the following scenario. The gospel comes to a remote village through the advance of the internet. People start reading the Gospel of John online and come to believe in Jesus as the Son of God and Savior of the world. The gospel message about Jesus's death and resurrection for our forgiveness and reconciliation to God spreads throughout the village. The whole community is baptized and confesses the name of Christ. In response, the witch doctors lose their power, the sorcerers burn their magic books, and the demons leave the village. The people start devouring the New Testament, and some even begin spreading the gospel message to neighboring villages. Sick

people are healed in the name of Christ, and practices like polyg-
amy and slavery gradually cease through the gospel's influence.
The community eventually discovers the Apostles' Creed and
recites it every Sunday during their worship celebration. Their
celebration of the Eucharist is marked by tears of joy.

Considering the principles of Matthew 7, 12, Mark 9, and
1 Corinthians 12, are we not to suppose this is Christ advancing
his Church? Do they not have a valid Eucharist?

It is true they have no formal, continuous succession of bishops back to apostolic ministry via the laying on of hands. They
don't have "a bishop" at all, in the sense of an office distinct from
presbyter. So what? They have Christ. They have the Spirit.
They have faith. They have the gospel.

We should tremble to reject them from full membership,
full participation, in the true church of Christ! Do we not fear
blaspheming the Spirit? Are we not commanded to infer a good
tree from the good fruit? Satan doesn't cast out demons, convict
sorcerers, convert idolators to the true God, or glorify the name
of Jesus Christ. A kingdom divided against itself cannot stand.
What is happening in this village must be recognized as the true
work of Christ in advancing and building his church.

The point of this chapter has been to demonstrate that a
Protestant ecclesiology is better equipped to allow for judgments of this kind. Because it does not claim to be the "one
true church" but instead positions itself as a renewal movement
within her, Protestantism is prepared to discern the true church
wherever Christ is present in word and sacrament. Therefore, for
Christians seeking to recognize the church in her fullness as we
move into the middle of the twenty-first century and beyond,
awaiting the return of Christ, Protestantism offers the most
promising pathways by which to cultivate and pursue catholicity.

CHAPTER 3

Catalysts for Reformation

We have argued that Protestantism is a movement of renewal within the church. In the next two chapters we ask about the nature of this renewal. What, specifically, needed to be renewed?

It is not the Protestant position that the church had died and needed to be reborn. That is a caricature, as we will explain more fully in part 3 of this book. Rather, Protestants claim that the gracious character of God revealed in the gospel had been obscured and diminished in the late medieval Western church and was rediscovered and revitalized during the Reformation, particularly through the recovery of the Pauline teaching of justification by faith alone (*sola fide*).

But the doctrine of justification does not function in a vacuum. To tell the story of the sixteenth-century renewal of the gospel, we must first understand the abuses that provoked it. In this chapter we examine two aspects of spiritual life in the late medieval West that demanded Reformation: indulgences and persecution.

Indulgences: The Spark of the Reformation

In Roman Catholic theology, an indulgence is the remission of the *temporal punishment* for sin, given in certain conditions by the Church to Christians. Whereas eternal punishment involves the ultimate consequences of sin in hell, temporal punishment has to do with the process of being purified from sin, which happens in this life and potentially in purgatory. Indulgences are possible because of *the treasury of merit*, the supposed infinite storehouse of the merits of Christ, Mary, and the saints that the church can apply to Christians on earth or in purgatory. The Council of Trent opposed abuses in the practice of indulgences but affirmed indulgences as such, and in fact pronounced an anathema on anyone who denies their power or validity:

> The sacred holy Synod teaches, and enjoins, that the use of Indulgences, for the Christian people most salutary, and approved of by the authority of sacred Councils, is to be retained in the Church; and It condemns with anathema those who either assert, that they are useless; or who deny that there is in the Church the power of granting them.[1]

It is both fair and necessary to give consideration to medieval indulgences here. *Sola fide* must be understood in historical context. Protestantism was a renewal of the gospel not in recovering a bare doctrinal formula or slogan, but in upturning and opposing the legalism, superstition, and financial abuse of the laity that sadly characterized much of European spirituality in the late medieval era.

The immediate cause of the Reformation was the preaching of indulgences by the Dominican friar Johan Tetzel, who had been appointed by Archbishop Albert of Brandenburg. The Catholic Encyclopedia, a work of early twentieth century Catholic scholarship, explains how funds raised by Tetzel were used:

> Albert of Brandenburg, already Archbishop of Magdeburg, received in addition the Archbishopric of Mainz and the Bishopric of Hallerstadt, but in return was obliged to collect 10,000 ducats, which he was taxed over and above the usual confirmation fees. To indemnify him, and to make it possible to discharge these obligations Rome permitted him to have preached in his territory the plenary indulgence promised all those who contributed to the new St. Peter's; he was allowed to keep one half the returns, a transaction which brought dishonour on all concerned in it.[2]

Now just imagine this. You are a lay Christian in Germany in the early 1500s. Your mother has recently died. You are told that giving money to the church will not only release her from thousands of years in agonizing fire in purgatory (perhaps even tens of thousands) but will also go to fund the reconstruction of St. Peter's Basilica in Rome. Who, put in this position, wouldn't be motivated to give whatever was asked? Meanwhile, half of the money is actually going to Archbishop Albert to pay off the massive debts he owed for buying his archbishopric (despite already holding other offices, contrary to canon law). Who cannot feel indignant in considering such a scenario?

What must be appreciated is how *common* it was for indulgences to fund simony (the buying or selling of ecclesiastical privileges), as well as other clerical abuses. At the turn of the sixteenth century, indulgences were a booming industry. To give some immediate context, Raymond Peraudi, who collected funds for indulgences throughout Germany just prior to Tetzel, was able to raise more than half a million guilders (the basic monetary unit in that place) between 1486 and 1503 to support crusades.[3] Throughout the fourteenth and fifteenth centuries, indulgences also funded the luxurious living of the Catholic hierarchy, many of whom lived in open concubinage and sexual immorality.[4] In the year 1500, Isabella of Castile, a Roman Catholic Queen famous for her role in expelling Jews from Spain and supporting the Inquisition, recounted that not only did the *majority* of her bishops live in open concubinage, but they armed themselves to oppose efforts at discipline.[5]

In his *Examination of the Council of Trent*, Martin Chemnitz documents indulgences offered throughout churches in the city of Rome in the year 1475 to give his readers a flavor of how the practice functioned.[6] In the Lateran Church, for example, there was a chapel with twenty-eight steps. Whoever ascended those steps with devotion, Chemnitz noted, received nine years of indulgences; whoever did so on their knees released one soul from purgatory. Whenever the heads of Peter and Paul were shown there, the Romans received three thousand years of indulgences, their neighbors received six thousand, and those who have travelled from afar received twelve thousand.[7] Chemnitz proceeds with page after page of descriptions like this and then notes,

> The quaestors of the Hospital of the Holy Spirit in the city of Rome undertook a reckoning, and found that the indulgences of all the stations in the city of Rome come to a total of more than a million years and more than 42 plenary indulgences, besides the souls which are liberated from purgatory![8]

Now, some might argue that this was all just a sudden, terrible left turn in the late fifteenth and early sixteenth centuries. In reality, indulgences had a long history. Indulgences as such began in the eleventh century with the concept of reduced temporal punishment apart from the process of sacramental discipline. But this idea was an extension out of various penitential processes going back much further. The most influential study of the historical development of indulgences is generally regarded to be the German Roman Catholic priest Nikolaus Paulus's work in the 1920s, which the subsequent scholarship has followed in broad form, and which I will recount the broad counters of here.[9]

In the early church, various forms of penance developed for dealing with those who had sinned in a particularly serious way (and for those who had renounced the faith under persecution). Standards for readmittance were rigorous. For example, the canons at the Synod of Ancyra in 314 stipulate that someone could be a penitent for twenty or thirty years; in some cases (as with willful murder) they could be readmitted to communion only at the end of their life.[10]

Over time the church developed various ways of relaxing the stated canonical punishment for a given sin. Such reductions gradually became more common and more transactional. For example, whereas in the early church, penitents could be readmitted to the church in the context of persecution or when martyrdom was expected, later simpler virtuous acts like fasting, almsgiving, or pilgrimages came to function as substitutions for penitential requirements.[11] Paulus calls these lesser forms of penance "redemptions" or "ransoms," tracing their origins to the middle of the seventh century in Ireland and England, from where they spread throughout Europe.[12] The practice slowly evolved. At the Council of Chalon in 813, canons were developed against clergy who thought they could make up for negligent living through pilgrimages to Rome, Tours, or other places of prayer.[13] But all this was still connected to the process of sacramental discipline. The Roman Catholic theologian Enrico dal Covolo describes the transition to indulgences proper:

> Finally—beginning again in the 11th century—the possibility of providing for the multiple works of piety through the imposition of a donation as a condition for the remission of punishment, *even outside the sacrament*, led the way to indulgences in the strict sense of the term, i.e., apart from sacramental penance.[14]

In the subsequent medieval development, indulgences became interconnected with the crusades, the expansion of papal power, and the financial revenue of the Roman Catholic Church. The first documented plenary indulgence—a remission of *all* temporal punishment for sin—was probably offered in 1095 by Pope Urban II for those taking part in the First Crusade. Pope Eugene III's offer of indulgences for participation in the second crusade went further, extending indulgences for the remission of temporal punishment not only in this life but also in purgatory.[15]

In the early thirteenth century, the concept of the "treasury of merit" was first articulated, and by the middle of the thirteenth century, it became the dominant theological rationale for indulgences.[16] This concept both accelerated the usage of indulgences and further concentrated them within the powers of the Pope.[17] In the year 1300, Pope Boniface VIII declared the first "jubilee indulgence," promising full forgiveness for all who were penitent for their sins and visited the basilicas of St. Peter and St. Paul in Rome under certain conditions. This began a tradition of jubilee years observed in 1350, 1390, and then regularly throughout the fifteenth century up to the present day.[18] In the thirteenth and fourteenth centuries, the practice of indulgences on behalf of deceased Christians in purgatory emerged and then expanded greatly, though it was controversial and rejected by some theologians. Shirrmacher, observing how the practice of indulgences preceded the theology of indulgences at virtually every point, notes that "the first certain attestation of papal approval of indulgences for the deceased (there are numerous falsified documents) comes from Calixtus III (+ 1458)."[19]

This general timeline—an eleventh-century emergence of indulgences proper (as distinct from prior penitential reductions), with aggressive expansion and development over the next four centuries—is the common narrative represented in the scholarship, including among Roman Catholic historians. The German Anglican theologian Thomas Schirrmacher, who wrote an analysis of the history of indulgence and purgatory, provides a battery of quotations from Roman Catholic scholars all following the same basic historical outline.[20] Here is how he notes Gerhard Ludwig Müller, a Cardinal in the Roman Catholic Church, put it: "The indulgence has neither a model in the New Testament nor in public church penance found in the first millennium, be it in practice or insofar as theological grounds are concerned."[21]

Sometimes it is difficult for modern readers to accept just how scandalous the history of indulgences is. So here is my challenge to anyone who would like to have confidence about the truth of this matter: Don't take my word for it. Look into the historical sources about medieval indulgences for yourself. You will not be underwhelmed.

Persecution: Resistance to Reformation

One question that might arise from the preceding narrative is, "If things were really that bad, why did no one notice and object?"

The answer is that they did, but they often got slaughtered for it. The Protestants Reformers, far from being original dissenters, were the inheritors of a long and bloody tradition of protest.

We must be careful not to exaggerate the extent of medieval persecution, as some Protestants polemicists have done. But there a danger in the opposite direction: downplaying it. It is often hard for modern readers to take in how bad things got. Some of the medieval crusades classify as genocide.[22] As painful as it is to come to terms with the gratuity and scale of violence in church history, it is absolutely essential to appreciate the context of the Reformation. Protestantism cannot be understood apart from it.

Now, it is true that Protestants persecuted others as well (especially the Anabaptists). As a Baptist committed to nonviolence within the church and the separation of church and state, I have no hesitation faulting the Reformers for wherever and however they sinned against these values. On the one hand, early in his career Luther protested mistreatment of Anabaptists (while condemning their theology): "still, it is not right, and I truly grieve, that these miserable folk should be so lamentably murdered, burned, and tormented to death. We should allow everyone to believe what he wills."[23] Furthermore, as is commonly discussed, one of the statements for which Luther was opposed by the Catholic Church is his claim that "the burning of heretics is contrary to the will of the Spirit." On the other hand, Luther did approve of the death penalty for sedition and blasphemy, and his mentality hardened over his career in terms of how this should be applied. His terrible statements about the Jews are well documented, as is Calvin's involvement in the death of Michael Servetus, and Zwingli's participation in the drowning of Anabaptists. All of this is wrong.

At the same time, it is *also* wrong to attempt to equalize the blame on both sides when they are not to scale. There is simply nothing on the Protestant side that compares to the quantity and organization of late medieval Roman Catholic violence. Saying, "Yes, Roman Catholic persecution of dissident groups was bad, but Protestants persecuted others, too!" is like saying, "Yes, Texas may be large, but so is Rhode Island!" Even more importantly, when Protestants tolerated or supported violence, they did not do so within allegedly magisterial teaching. As we will see, medieval persecution resulted from theology promulgated by the highest levels of authority within the Roman Catholic Church, including *ex cathedra* statements from popes (more on this in a bit). This is why it is so important for understanding the context of the Reformation—we will never grasp why the Reformation was good news for Christian laity in the 1400s and 1500s unless we appreciate what they were up against.

The Bohemian priest and Reformer Jan Hus provides a good window into the state of the church just prior to the Reformation. Hus was tried and executed at the Council of Constance (1414–1418), the sixteenth ecumenical council of the Roman Catholic Church, just over 100 years before Luther produced his famous Ninety-Five Theses that sparked the Reformation. The previous fall, Hus had been promised safe conduct to Constance but was imprisoned not long after his arrival. The following summer, his trial began, and he was publicly burned at the stake on July 6, 1415.

Thomas Fudge is perhaps the greatest living expert on Hus (and the Bohemian Reformation generally), having written nearly a dozen books in the field. Fudge notes he has been accused of being a "right-wing Roman Catholic" for his refusal to demonize Hus's opponents,[24] his defense of the legality of Hus's trial despite "irregularities,"[25] and his conviction that Hus was indeed a heretic.[26] (Others, Fudge notes, point to canonical infractions, bribery, and false testimony as evidence of the trial's invalidity.)[27] Nonetheless, even Fudge acknowledges that "Hus was a good man, a person of virtue and integrity, a faithful priest who strove for honesty, conviction, and truth in the practice of his faith."[28]

Similarly, Pope John Paul II in 1999 praised Hus as a "remarkable man" with "moral courage," expressing "deep regret for the cruel death" inflicted upon him.[29] Meanwhile, it is extremely hard to deny that his opponents were scheming and treacherous. Again, the even-handed Fudge states plainly,

> The portrayal of the men of the Council in some of the more fulsome accounts of the Hus trial in its final stages, where they appear as bitter and hateful men quite unconcerned with issues of truth and justice, is a portrait accepted by leading scholars as altogether accurate. . . . Hus was condemned not by the worst men at Constance but by the best. The picture is sobering.[30]

Fudge's reconstruction of the final stages of Hus's sentencing and execution is worth quoting at length:

> The accused was placed on an elevated chair for all to see, and we hear judges instructing guards to force the prisoner to maintain silence. The emperor sits in some splendor. A German military governor bears the imperial mace. A Bavarian prince holds the gold crown. A Hungarian knight wields the royal sword. We read of fervent prayers and details of the defendant crying out in despair of justice. There are accusations and arguments. We read of jeers from the men whom the prisoner forgives. We listen as an archbishop mounts the pulpit and delivers a bombastic sermon against the accused, insisting that the body of sin must be eradicated

without delay. An old, bald auditor reads the official verdict. When the man who is about to die turns to look at the king, we are told that the embarrassed monarch 'blushed deeply and turned red' but never uttered a word.[31]

This monarch was King Sigismund of Luxembourg (then king and later Holy Roman Emperor). He was embarrassed because he had offered safe conduct to Hus. We read here of an archbishop but never a pope because this is during the Western Schism, during which three bishops all claimed to be the pope. John XXIII, one of these individuals, had already fled Constance by this point. Fudge continues:

> The defendant is defrocked in an elaborate ceremony of degra-dation. He holds a chalice, which is taken from his hands as he is cursed and given the moniker Judas. The stole is removed. Then the chasuble. Then the rest of the priestly vestments are stripped from the prisoner. As each item is removed, an appropriate curse is intoned. We find the man weeping, and there are disagreements over how best to obliterate his tonsure. The humiliation continues as the ex-priest is forced . . . to wear a paper miter adorned with demons and bearing letters indi-cating his crime, while formal maledictions are pronounced by seven bishops over the condemned man.[32]

In his older biography, David Schaff (son of Philip Schaff) also cites historical sources noting that during Hus's ceremony of ministerial degradation, these seven Catholic bishops and archbishops (the number is disputed) cut his hair unevenly to disfigure his tonsure.[33] After this, Hus was led outside, past a roaring fire into which his books were being thrown, to a meadow just outside the city gate. A huge crowd had gathered.

Hus protested his innocence to the crowd and thanked his prison guards for their humanity to him. There are numerous reports of Hus forgiving his enemies. Then the dreadful end comes:

> We witness the stripping of the prisoner. Wearing only a gown, he has his hands tied behind his back, his neck fastened to the stake with a "sooty chain," one foot shackled. He is made to stand on a stool so that wood can be placed under his feet and the gathered multitudes can better see a man dying in the fire. An eyewitness notes that the condemned man is still wearing his shoes as the executioner's assistants unload two wagons filled with wood and pile the faggots to his chin. Straw and some pitch are added, and the moment of truth arrives. Two men, one of them the imperial marshal, implore the convicted prisoner to reconsider his position. We note a final opportunity to save his life extended to the man about to die. We listen to his poignant refusal. Onlookers marvel at his pious words. We read of a futile attempt to deliver one last sermon from inside the woodpile. The marshal claps his hands, and the executioner takes the torch. Then come the flames, and the "worst stench arose that one could smell" on account of a mule's carcass recently buried beneath the pyre. As the inferno roars, we hear the convict break forth in screams and song: "Christ, son of the living God, have mercy on me."[34]

After his death, though Hus had preached against relics, his opponents took no chances. His heart was smashed with clubs, his heart was roasted on the end of a stick in the flames, and all his personal effects were burned. His ashes were then carefully loaded into a cart and dumped into a river.[35]

What are we to make of Hus's death? On the one hand, we should not exploit the grisly nature of Hus's death for rhetorical purposes. But again, there is a temptation in the opposite direction: to downplay or minimize what happened to Hus (or, perhaps, simply to ignore it altogether). Hus's death is crucial to consider because it represents an illuminating vignette into the larger world of late medieval Western Europe. Why did the Protestant Reformation represent, for so many, a breakthrough and renewal in the understanding of the gospel? The answer is not only that the gospel had been obscured by the financial scandal of ever-expanding indulgences but also that opposition to this abusive practice was viciously persecuted by the highest levels of leadership within the Church of Rome.

What must be grasped is that Hus's execution was not a violation of medieval Roman Catholic theology, but its expression. This sounds shocking to modern ears, but it is true to history. The medieval Roman Catholic Church claimed the authority to exterminate heretics, and to do so through the secular authority, over which she claimed jurisdiction.[36] Boniface VIII's 1302 bull *Unam Sanctam*, for example, distinguished between the "temporal sword" (wielded by the secular authority) and the "spiritual sword" (wielded by the church), insisting that the temporal is subject to the spiritual:

> Both, therefore, are in the power of the Church, that is to say, the spiritual and the material sword, but the former is to be administered for the Church but the latter by the Church; the former in the hands of the priest; the latter by the hands of kings and soldiers, *but at the will and sufferance of the priest.* However, one sword ought to be subordinated to the other and temporal authority, subjected to spiritual power.[37]

The important point to note is that in the "two swords" theological framework, although the church does not herself wield the temporal sword, the civil authority does so at the church's discretion ("at the will and sufferance of the priest"). Thus, Canon 3 of the Fourth Lateran Council in 1215 threatened civil authorities with excommunication if they neglected their responsibility: "If however a temporal lord, required and instructed by the church, neglects to cleanse his territory of this heretical filth, he shall be bound with the bond of excommunication by the metropolitan and other bishops of the province."[38] Similarly, Pope Innocent IV's 1252 bull *Ad Extirpanda* threatened secular leaders with various penalties if they allowed themselves to become "protectors of heretics." Elsewhere it states that heretics "are to be coerced—as are thieves and bandits—into confessing their errors and accusing others, although one must stop short of danger to life or limb."[39]

This is why it is so offensive and wrong when people claim it was secular authorities rather than the Roman Catholic Church who killed Hus. Roman Catholic prelates jailed Hus, tried him for heresy (at an ecumenical council), and then handed him over for execution in consequence of their guilty verdict. On the day of Hus's sentence, the proceedings opened with a sermon from the bishop of Lodi, who preached from Romans 6:6, "that the body of sin must be done away," in which the bishop proclaimed—using lurid imagery like rotting flesh, cancer, and poison—that the extermination of heretics was pleasing to God.[40]

I find attempts to minimize the significance of Hus's death distressing because Hus is a hero of mine. I have often put myself in Hus's shoes. Would I have had his courage? I hope so. In my imagination, the worst part of the whole ordeal relates to the simple fact that Hus was not informed when his execution would be. From the conclusion of his trial on June 8 till his execution on July 6, he waited. For some reason, this little detail niggles in my mind. It's one thing to steel yourself to prepare for a dreaded day, but imagine waking up every morning knowing that at any moment you might face the flames!

What was the truth Hus proclaimed that led to his conflict with Roman Catholic hierarchy? Hus's deepest grievances were ecclesiological and moral. He was horrified by ungodliness in the clergy, especially the rampant practice of simony, the tendency of priests to have mistresses, and the use of indulgences to motivate military action. Hus also opposed the theology of exterminating heretics, appealing to Augustine to argue that heretics should be appealed to with Scripture and reason. From the pulpit, Hus railed against these practices, proclaiming that we must bless our enemies rather than kill them and that money cannot procure forgiveness.[41]

Hus's criticisms also touched on the authority and nature of the church. Toward the end of Hus's trial, thirty-nine articles summarizing his beliefs and teachings were put into evidence. Two prominent themes can be drawn out: First, Hus defined the church as all the elect; second, Hus maintained that ecclesiastical authorities must not be followed when they depart from Scripture.[42] For Hus, this latter principle applied to the pope as well—he insisted that all the apostles had equal right of binding and loosing, and that when the pope departs from the law of Christ, his authority is null and void. Hus's position on this latter point can be seen in his opposition to the papal bull of John XXIII (now recognized as an antipope) offering indulgences for a military campaign against Ladislaus the Magnanimous, the king of Naples. For his opposition to this practice, Hus was summoned to meet with papal delegates, to whom Hus declared his intention to obey the "Apostolic mandates." When this was interpreted as an intention to submit to the pope, Hus clarified,

My lords, understand me; I said that with my whole heart I am minded to obey the Apostolic mandates and to obey them in all points, but what I call the Apostolic mandates are the doctrines of Christ's Apostles, and so far as the mandates of the Roman pontiff are in accord with the Apostolic mandates and doctrine, that is, according to the rule of Christ, so far I intend most certainly to obey them. But, if I find them to be at variance, I will not obey them even if you put before my eyes fire for the burning of my body.[43]

This is at the nerve center of what got Hus into trouble: the question of authority. Like Luther after him, Hus insisted that popes and councils were fallible and thus subordinate to Scripture. Scripture was the highest authority. Hus also insisted that the Bible should be translated into the vernacular language for the laity to read.

There is much more that could be said about Hus, but the important point to recognize at the moment is simply this: as an example of what happened to those who opposed indulgences and ecclesiastical abuse in late medieval Roman Catholicism, *Hus is not rare.* We are focusing on him as representative of the larger world he inhabited. Many of Hus's followers, such as Jerome of Prague, were burned at the stake in a very similar manner.[44] The Roman Catholic Church waged a total of five crusades *against the Hussites alone*, starting in 1420 and continuing on for nearly two decades.[45] We typically think of crusades as being waged against Muslims, but they were also waged against separatist groups like the Hussites and many others. Some were less orthodox, like the Cathars (or Albigensians); others were more orthodox, like the Waldensians (a proto-Protestant group that eventually united with the Reformed Church).

Opposition to indulgences and financial excess in the church was a common tenet among these separatist groups. The Waldensians opposed indulgences and denied the existence of purgatory; they were charged with maintaining that "offerings for the dead benefit the clerics who devour them, not the souls who do not need them."[46] Like Hus, they also opposed ungodliness among clergy, claiming that their spiritual authority was forfeited by ungodliness.[47] In 1487, four years after the birth of Martin Luther, Pope Innocent VIII issued a bull calling for the extermination of the Waldensians and offering a plenary indulgence to all who should engage in a crusade against them.[48] I won't outline here the repeated massacres of the Waldensians the following year and continuing sporadically across the next several centuries, but if you are interested, google "1655 Piedmont massacre." Just be warned, it's nightmarish.

In his history of indulgences, Henry Lea recounts various other groups persecuted for their opposition to indulgences: the group of Fraticelli or Spiritual Franciscans tortured in Rome in 1466;[49] the eighty "flagellants" and followers of Konrad Schmid who burned alive in Germany in 1414, as well as the three hundred who were also burned alive in 1416;[50] and Pietro Bernardino (a follower of Girolamo Savonarola) and his followers, who were burned alive in Italy in 1502.[51] He also discusses the role of the reintroduction of the Inquisition in the mid-fifteenth century to suppress various clergy who spoke against indulgences in France, Bergundy, and Germany—notably including Johann von Wesel, a German scholastic theologian imprisoned for his treatise against indulgences.[52] Opposition to indulgences was a nearly universal theme among various proto-Protestant groups, with perhaps the only major exceptions being the earlier groups who lived prior to the worst abuses, such as the Henricans (followers of Henry of Lausanne) and the Petrobrussians (followers of Peter of Bruys), both of which were proto-Protestants groups in France in the twelfth century.

Now, the mere fact of historical persecution does not itself disprove that the Roman Catholic Church is the one true church of Christ. Great sins are committed by true Christians and true churches. And again, certain Protestant groups have engaged in terrible persecution as well—though not on the scale of medieval Roman Catholicism, and not with the "two swords" theological framework. Nonetheless, late medieval abuses—both financial and physical—help explain why renewal in the church could come only in the form of protest.

CHAPTER 4

The Recovery of *Sola Fide*

I t is against this historical backdrop—ever-expanding indulgences and persecution of those opposed to the practice—that Luther's articulation of justification by faith alone must be understood. In no small measure, Luther championed *sola fide* specifically *in response* to this commercial and ecclesiastical system. Consider the first of his 95 theses: "When our Lord and Master Jesus Christ said, 'Repent' (Mt 4:17), he willed the entire life of believers to be one of repentance."[1]

This may initially read like a generic affirmation of the need for ongoing repentance, but in historical context, it was a protest against the financial system that had mangled and obscured the gospel's call for repentance. For example, Luther's colleague Friedrich Myconius described how Luther's own parishioners came to him with letters of indulgence from Tetzel, complaining that he would not absolve them because they "did not want to desist from adultery, whoredom, usury, unjust goods, and such sins and evil."[2] From this it is evident how indulgences had commonly come to function as a substitute for repentance.

Ultimately, Luther's concern with indulgences was not just about financial abuse but also about a distortion of the gospel itself. The practical effect of indulgences in the everyday life of the laity had diminished not only the need for genuine repentance but also the comfort and consolation that the gospel is designed to give to the penitent believer.

This was the consolation Luther had discovered in his own experience. As a young monk, Luther had lived in dread fear before God: "Though I lived as a monk without reproach, I felt that I was a sinner before God with an extremely disturbed conscience. I could not believe that he was placated by my satisfaction."[3] After much struggle with Paul's epistle to the Romans, particularly the phrase "the righteousness of God" in Romans 1:17, Luther came to a breakthrough in understanding the most wonderful secret in the universe: *the grace of God*. He described this experience as follows:

> At last, by the mercy of God, meditating day and night, I gave heed to the context of the words, namely, "In it the righteousness of God is revealed, as it is written, 'He who through faith is righteous shall live.'" There I began to understand that the righteousness of God is that by which the righteous lives by a gift of God, namely by faith. And this is the meaning: the righteousness of God is revealed by the gospel, namely, the passive righteousness with which merciful God justifies us by faith, as it is written, "He who through faith is righteous shall live." Here I felt that I was altogether born again and had entered paradise itself through open gates.[4]

Luther's personal testimony here highlights how Protestantism as a whole served the renewal of the gospel in the sixteenth century. His imagery—the gates of paradise being thrown open—conveys the consolation offered in the gospel, which later texts in Romans identify as "peace with God" (Rom. 5:1) and "no condemnation" (Rom. 8:1). In Luther's former state, the murmuring monk unable to placate a troubled conscience, we get a window into the malaise and anxiety characteristic of the spiritual experience of so many in his day. In the context of this dark, cloudy uncertainty, *sola fide* was good news.

A good example can be found in Catherine Parr, the final of Henry VIII's wives, who was raised as a Roman Catholic but developed Protestant sympathies and eventually published a work promoting *sola fide*. Commenting on Matthew 11:28, she wrote,

> "Come to me all you that labor and are burdened, and I shall refresh you." What gentle, merciful, and comfortable words are these to all sinners? . . . What a most gracious comfortable, and gentle saying was this, with such pleasant and sweet words to allure his enemies to come to him? . . . When I behold the beneficence, liberality, mercy and goodness of the Lord, I am encouraged, emboldened and stirred to ask for such a gift as living faith. . . . By this faith I am assured: and by this assurance I feel the remission of my sins. This is it that maketh me bold. This is it that comforteth me. This is it that quencheth all despair. . . . Thus, I feel myself to come, as it were, in a new garment before God, and now by his mercy, to be taken as just and righteous.[5]

Gentle. Gracious. Pleasant. Sweet. Encouraged. Emboldened. Assured. Comfort. Assurance. These are the words employed by a heart that has been touched by the gospel! In my online ministry

I encounter people over and over who are drowning in anxiety about their spiritual status before God. My heart aches for them to know the peace and comfort that Parr describes here!

This experience stood behind Luther's articulation of *sola fide*. The doctrine does not deny the necessity of good works, as it is often caricatured. Luther insisted that good works will issue forth from a genuine faith. But he also maintained that good works contribute nothing to how a sinner is actually made right in the sight of a holy God. Justification was, for Luther, a forensic declaration of our status before God, grounded solely on the imputed righteousness of Christ, received by the empty hands of faith.[6]

This is the wonderful simplicity of the gospel, recaptured and recentered in the Protestant movement: We are made right with God simply by repenting and receiving the gospel. There are no additional offerings or sacrifices to be made (least of all through money), no further punishments to be meted out through purgatorial fire, and no other rites to be performed. All you must do is turn away from sin and cleave unto Christ with all your heart, and you will be welcomed into citizenship in heaven, cleansed of all sin, adopted as the child of God, indwelt by his Spirit, and united to Christ. The thief on the cross is paradigmatic, not exceptional. All this is grounded in the promise of Christ himself: "Truly, truly, I say to you, whoever hears my word and believes him who sent me has eternal life. He does not come into judgment, but has passed from death to life" (John 5:24).

Justification Today

Catholic and Protestant dialogue on justification has made much progress since the Reformation.[7] Part of the progress has resulted from greater clarity that we are using terminology differently.

If we don't understand these differences, it is like an American and Brit arguing whether "football" is the greatest sport, without realizing they are using the same word to refer to different realities. For example, in Roman Catholic theology, *justification* means "making righteous." It thereby includes what Protestants think of as sanctification. As the Catechism puts it, "Justification is not only the remission of sins, but also the sanctification and renewal of the interior man."[8] Roman Catholic theology also distinguishes between initial justification and ongoing justification. Thus, good works are not necessary to come into an *initial* state of reconciliation with God.

In Protestant theology, *justification* means "declaring righteous." It refers to the forensic act by which we enter into right standing in God's sight, distinct from our subsequent moral transformation (what we call sanctification). However, though Protestants distinguish between justification and sanctification, they also insist that they are inseparable. Michael Horton notes that in defining justification as a free gift of God's grace, "the Reformers did not thereby exclude the process of becoming holy. Rather, they argued that through union with Christ we receive both justification and sanctification, and these distinct acts must never be confused or separated."[9] Thus, the historic Protestant position is that good works are necessary for salvation as the fruit of a true saving faith. As Calvin put it, "It is therefore faith alone which justifies, and yet the faith which justifies is not alone: just as it is the heat alone of the sun which warms the earth, and yet in the sun it is not alone, because it is constantly conjoined with light."[10]

Already it is evident that the two positions have a great deal more overlap than is often recognized. After all, both systems speak of an initial change by grace and then a subsequent process requiring works. On this basis, the Roman Catholic theologian Hans Küng, in his influential engagement with Karl Barth's doctrine of justification, went so far as to assert that the remaining differences are only imaginary: "Protestants speak of a declaration of justice and Catholics of a making just. But Protestants speak of a declaring just which includes a making just; and Catholics of a making just which supposes a declaring just. Is it not time to stop arguing about imaginary differences?"[11]

It is good to celebrate areas of agreement, and such areas are real and considerable. However, there remain areas of difference, and these are not imaginary. Take the matter of the formal cause of justification, for example. Historically, Protestants and Roman Catholics have generally agreed that the *meritorious* cause of justification is the saving work of Christ, the *efficient* cause is the mercy of God, and the *final* cause is the glory of God (these terms draw from Aristotle's identification of four different kinds of causation[12]). However, Protestants have insisted that the *formal* cause of justification—that is, the intrinsic component of our justification that it essentially consists of—must be identified as the imputed righteousness of Christ, as opposed to infused or inherent righteousness wrought within us. Simply put, our legal standing before God is not ultimately based on anything within us, but on the external, alien, perfect righteousness of Jesus Christ.

For Protestants, such an account is necessitated by Paul's teaching on justification, particularly in Galatians and Romans. For example, Paul teaches that righteousness is "credited" to those who do *not* work but rather have faith: "to the one who does not work but believes in him who justifies the ungodly, his faith is counted as righteousness" (Rom. 4:5). The word "counted" here (and later in Rom. 4:23–24) can also be translated as reckoned, credited, or imputed. For Protestants, this understanding of justification is necessary for assurance of salvation since an infused righteousness within us can never be the basis for our standing before a holy God.[13]

The matter of the formal cause of justification can seem like a technicality, but it is foundational—it bears upon the question of how we are actually acceptable to God. Historically, it has been seen as a fault line of difference. Thus, various anathemas were directed at the Protestant position at the Council of Trent. Even more ecumenically minded interpreters often acknowledge that the 1999 *Joint Declaration on the Doctrine of Justification* between the Lutheran and Catholic Churches, for all the helpful progress that this document does reflect, did not fully resolve this issue. As we continue to seek to understand one another's positions, areas like this must not be brushed over.

More practically, important differences remain in the broader soteriological and ecclesiological context in which justification functions. What is the role of baptism, penance, and indulgences with respect to justification? On what basis are we accepted as righteous in God's sight after our initial justification? What about purgatory, after this life is over?

These kinds of differences are far from trivial. In Roman Catholic theology, for example, if you commit a mortal sin and die prior to confession, you go to hell. Not just purgatory; *hell*. What exactly constitutes a mortal sin? The very ambiguity involved in such a determination in real life cases is part of the dilemma. But the misuse of sexual faculties—say, masturbation or using contraception—is typically regarded as a mortal sin. It doesn't require much imagination or sympathy to start pondering the pastoral implications of such a system of theology for the actual experience of justification for Christian laypeople—for their sense of security in having obtained good standing within God's favor, for their felt experience of the love of God in real time, and for their preparedness for death and eternity.

Protestants today can happily recognize many justified brothers and sisters within the Roman Catholic Church. As J. I. Packer emphasizes, we are not justified by our theology of justification, but by genuine trust in Christ and his saving work, which both sides affirm.[14] And we can rejoice in the progress that has been made, which is considerable. We should also remain open and eager for further progress. At the same time, sober honesty requires us to acknowledge that the remaining differences about justification—especially as they play out concerning assurance of salvation—are poignant, unavoidable, and possibly irresolvable.

Objections to *Sola Fide*

A frequent criticism of *sola fide* is that it is inconsistent with James 2:14–26. But here again, carefulness about terminology is important. In Protestant theology, "faith" does not mean bare intellectual assent. That appears to be how James is using the term; otherwise he could not state that "even the demons believe" (James 2:19). But for the Reformers, faith meant a disposition of trusting assent and consecration. It is typified by the tax collector in Luke 18 beating his breast and saying, "God, be merciful to me, a sinner" (v. 13). Historically, the Reformers spoke of faith as expressing itself through love, following the language of Galatians 5:6. Thus Calvin: "We confess with Paul that no other faith justifies 'but faith working through love' [Gal. 5:6]."[15] Further, as we have seen, while the Protestant position maintains that this kind of faith is the instrumental means by which we are actually made righteous in God's sight, it also holds that good works must follow as the fruit of that faith. So the Protestant position is not what is being targeted by James.

Another criticism of the Protestant position on justification is that it has no historical precedent. It is true that Augustine's use of the term *justification* to mean "making righteous" had come to predominate in the medieval tradition.[16] However, though the Reformers' articulation of justification and sanctification as distinct was fresh, this basic distinction is implicit in the prior tradition (indeed, it seems entailed by the very nature of forgiveness).[17] Again, different terminology can conceal the substantial conceptual overlap here. Further, the Protestant emphasis on *sola fide* as the means of justification has wide attestation prior to the Reformation. In John Chrysostom's homilies on the epistles of Paul, for example, one finds a clear articulation of justification by faith alone, apart from works, in ways that don't seem to cohere with an initial/final justification distinction—they seem to be talking about a status rather than a transformative process.

For example, in explicating the meaning of the phrase "the righteousness of God" in 2 Corinthians 5:21, Chrysostom stipulates,

> For this is the righteousness of God, when we are justified not by works, in which case it would be necessary that not even a spot should be found, but by grace, in which case all sin is done away. And this, at the time that it does not allow us to be lifted up, for it is entirely the free gift of God, teaches us also the greatness of what is given.[18]

Chrysostom seems to presume that if justification *were* by works, it would be necessary to be completely righteous (not even a spot). Further, he contrasts that kind of righteousness with a righteousness given entirely as a free gift of grace, in which all sin is done away. When it comes to the phrase "the declaring of righteousness," as Chrysostom says of Romans 3:24–25, he stipulates,

> The declaring of His righteousness [is] not only that He is
> Himself righteous, but that He does also make them that are
> filled with the putrefying sores of sin suddenly righteous. . . .
> Doubt not then: for it is not of works, but of faith: and shun
> not the righteousness of God, for it is a blessing in two ways;
> because it is easy, and also open to all men.[19]

Here Chrysostom situates "making" righteous and "declaring" righteous in parallel placement, describing this process as "sudden," as well as "easy" and "open to all men." Further, he explicitly asserts that the means by which we are made righteous is "not of works, but of faith." There is no indication here or in the surrounding context that he has any conception of a final justification, distinct from the reality he outlines here.

Rather, all throughout his Romans homilies, Chrysostom repeatedly uses adverbs to express the immediacy of this declaration of righteousness. Commenting on Romans 3:31, he says, "For when a man is once a believer, he is straightway justified. . . . But since after this grace, whereby we were justified, there is need also of a life suited to it, let us show an earnestness worthy the gift."[20] He appears to be conceiving of justification as a gift given immediately ("straightway") upon belief, with good works then subsequently following it as a *response* to this gift ("a life suited to it"). Preaching later on Romans 4:5, Chrysostom writes, "God is able on a sudden not to free a man who has lived in impiety from punishment only, but even to make him just, and to count him worthy of those immortal honors."[21] Again, the adverbial phrase "on a sudden" suggests that he is envisioning justification as a declaration of status more than an ongoing transformative process. Further, this *making just* results in an immediate change from a life of impiety to being worthy of immortal honors. He nowhere qualifies this gift as simply referring to initial justification. On the contrary, he speaks of good works as in response to the gift of justification.

Many more such passages could be adduced in John Chrysostom and in other church fathers.[22] At the same time, one can find in the early and medieval church many accounts of justification that speak of justification as a process and particularly emphasize the role of works in the process. The pre-Reformation church did not speak with one voice about justification. Thus, both Roman Catholic and Protestant positions can find precedent in the pre-Reformation church. Here is how the eminent church historian Jaroslav Pelikan summarized it:

> Every major tenet of the Reformation had considerable support in the catholic tradition. That was eminently true of the central Reformation teaching of justification by faith alone. . . . The Council of Trent selected and elevated to official status the notion of justification by faith plus works, which was only one of the doctrines of justification in the medieval theologians and ancient fathers. When the reformers attacked this notion in the name of the doctrine of justification by faith alone—a doctrine also attested to by some medieval theologians and ancient fathers—Rome reacted by canonizing one trend in preference to all the others. What had previously been permitted also (justification by faith alone), now became forbidden. In condemning the Protestant Reformation, the Council of Trent condemned part of its own catholic tradition.[23]

Conclusion

There is much more to say about justification. The purpose of this chapter has simply been to offer a brief chronicle of how its recovery in the sixteenth century functioned as a stimulus for renewal and revitalization within the Christian church. Martin Luther's experience of the "righteousness of God" in Romans 1:17 represented a genuine encounter with the grace of God and a valid insight into the entirely gratuitous nature by which we come to be enveloped within it.

Although Luther was ultimately excommunicated and much of Protestant theology was met with anathemas at the Council of Trent, the subsequent Catholic tradition recognized that Luther (and Protestantism generally) cannot simply be rejected. This is evident not only in the lifting of anathemas and the affirmation of *sola fide* in recent ecumenical dialogue but also in the willingness to acknowledge that something valuable was recovered in the sixteenth century. In a visit to Germany in 1980, for example, Pope John Paul II could even call Luther "a witness whose message of faith and justification should be listened to by us all."[24]

This is the single greatest contribution of Protestantism to the Christian church: its insight into the gracious heart of God revealed in the gospel, by which God offers to us as a free gift the righteousness we cannot attain through our own efforts. As Paul put it, "To the one who does not work but believes in him who justifies the ungodly, his faith is counted as righteousness" (Rom. 4:5). In its articulation of this happy truth, Protestantism has acted in the service of both the church and the One she worships.

PART 2

Protestantism
and Authority

CHAPTER 5

The Case for
Sola Scriptura

In my engagements with Christians from traditions outside of Protestantism, whatever issue is being addressed, the discussion almost always kicks back to questions of *authority*. By what standard do we evaluate our differences? What is the relationship between Scripture and tradition, and where does the ultimate authority of interpretation for both Scripture and tradition lie? It is hard to find any area of dispute that doesn't terminate in these more basic, methodological questions.

For this reason, we must press into the question of *ecclesial authority*. That is the task of this second section of the book. In the next two chapters, I make a positive case for the Protestant position on where ultimate authority over the church is located (*sola Scriptura*). Then in chapters 7 and 8, I survey some other conceptions of how authority works in the church.

But before arguing for *sola Scriptura*, we must define it. This is imperative because of what I call "the 80 percent rule": about 80 percent of the critiques of *sola Scriptura* misframe where it actually differs from its rivals.

What Is Sola Scriptura?

Stated responsibly, *sola Scriptura* is a modest doctrine. The core idea is that Scripture is the church's *only infallible rule*. A *rule* is a standard that governs the church's faith and practice. *Infallible* means being incapable of error. So *sola Scriptura* is essentially the claim that Scripture is the only authority standing over the church that is incapable of error.

Historically, the conviction that Scripture is infallible is a point on which Protestants have found general agreement with Christians in other traditions. The Protestant position on Scripture was opposed by the Eastern Orthodox tradition on the grounds that the church, "like the Divine Scriptures, is infallible."[1] But the infallibility of the Scriptures themselves was never in contention. Similarly, the Roman Catholic church affirms that Scripture is without error.[2] The dispute is over whether Scripture *alone* is infallible. In other words, the fault line of difference between *sola Scriptura* and alternative positions is this: Does the church possess any rule *other than Scripture* that is infallible? *Sola Scriptura* is simply the conviction that this question must be answered in the negative: Popes, councils, and all other post-apostolic organs of the church are fallible. As Anthony Lane puts it, "*Sola Scriptura* is the statement that the church can err."[3]

Unfortunately, debate about *sola Scriptura* frequently gets fixated on some other point. Here are two common examples. First, *sola Scriptura* is often caricatured as the idea that the Bible is the only authority. The error here is confusing the categories of infallibility and authority. These are quite distinct: Infallibility involves an incapacity for error; authority involves offering binding decisions. The former is a more metaphysical category; the latter, a more practical one. All that is infallible is authoritative, but not all that is authoritative is infallible. For example, the umpire at a baseball game has authority to make a definitive call whether a pitch is a ball or strike, but he is not infallible. He can be wrong. Another example is the U.S. Supreme Court, which has authority to interpret the Constitution, but can and does err in this responsibility. When you think about it, nearly all authorities we encounter in this world are fallible.

Sola Scriptura does not deny that creeds, catechisms, confessions, and councils function authoritatively. It just maintains that they are not infallible and therefore are placed under Scripture within a hierarchy of authorities. For example, one way of construing a Protestant conception of ecclesial authority is as follows:

1. Scripture is the *norma normans* (the norming norm).
2. Ecumenical councils are first-tier *norma normata* (norms that are normed).
3. Confessional and conciliar statements of particular ecclesial bodies are second-tier *norma normata*.
4. Doctrines espoused by individuals (including those regarded as Doctors of the church) that are not mere reiterations or entailments of matters that are *de fide* are *theologoumena*, or theological opinions.[4]

Sometimes critics of Protestantism say or imply that only infallible authority is *real* authority, but this is obviously wrong. On a moment's reflection, it is clear that fallible entities are capable of exerting a real, practically significant authority. For example, my ordination vows have real authority over me. I could lose my ministerial credentials if I opposed them. Our church's statement of faith has real authority over me. I could be barred from the Lord's Supper if I opposed it. Many other examples could be given. An obvious one is excommunication.

The recognition of real (though fallible) ecclesial authority is a consistent affirmation of historic Protestantism. Article 20 of the Anglican Thirty-Nine Articles affirms, "The Church hath power to decree Rites or Ceremonies, and authority in Controversies of Faith."[5] In the Reformed tradition, Francis Turretin distinguished the Scripture as a supreme and autocratic judge and the church as a subordinate and ministerial judge: "The question does not concern . . . whether any judgment belongs to the church and its officers in controversies of faith. . . . Rather, the question concerns only the supreme and infallible judgment by which everything must necessarily stand or fall."[6] So whatever other criticisms of *sola Scriptura* may arise, we will do well at the outset to leave off simplistic language about "Scripture as the only authority."

A second misunderstanding is that *sola Scriptura* entails that every point of doctrine has to be explicitly taught in the Bible. This is targeting a related doctrine, the sufficiency of Scripture, which has historically been seen as derivative of *sola Scriptura* (though critiques sometimes conflate the two).[7] The sufficiency of Scripture is construed a bit differently in various Protestant traditions, but in *none* of them does it mean that every doctrine falls ready-packaged from Scripture. In the Anglican tradition, article 6 in the Thirty-Nine Articles essentially stipulates that the Bible is sufficient *for salvation*.[8] That is a modest claim, when you think about it. For his part, Luther asserted that doctrines not substantiated by Scripture may be held as opinion but should not be required as dogma.[9]

The Reformed tradition generally offers the strongest artic-ulations of the sufficiency of Scripture, though even here they are carefully nuanced. For example, the Westminster Confession of Faith states, "The whole counsel of God concerning all things necessary for His own glory, man's salvation, faith and life, is either expressly set down in Scripture, or by good and necessary consequence may be deduced from Scripture."[10] Now, the whole point of the phrase "or by good and necessary consequence may be deduced" is to demonstrate that God's counsel concerning these stated topics will *not* always be expressly set down. It will come *either* explicitly or as a deduction. One or the other. Sadly, over and over, "the good and necessary consequence" clause is lopped off in criticism of Protestantism. For instance, critics often say, "*Sola Scriptura* isn't explicitly taught in the Bible; therefore, it is self-defeating." This kind of criticism only reveals that the doctrine hasn't been sympathetically understood.

So again, *sola Scriptura* means Scripture is the only infallible rule, not the only *authority* in the church, nor the *explicit* source for all doctrine. Put otherwise: Scripture is the only yardstick that cannot err, not the only norm to which you submit or the location in which you find all truth.

Conceptually, this basic idea shouldn't be hard to grasp, because it has a lot of similarity to how many religions work. The idea that there is one supreme text and then subsequent, ongoing, authoritative bodies that are subordinate to that supreme text—this is generally characteristic of how Muslims regard the Koran, how most Jews treat the Hebrew Bible, and how Hindus, Buddhists, and Sikhs treat their respective sacred texts. So the broad idea that a religion's founding texts have unparalleled authority shouldn't be difficult to grasp.

But why should we think Christianity works this way? Here I offer an empirical argument, consistent with the nature of *sola Scriptura* as a prolegomenon more than a doctrine proper.[11]

I propose that *sola Scriptura* is the cumulative entailment of two considerations: (1) Scripture's nature (what it *is*) and (2) Scripture's role among God's people (what it *does*).

Scripture's Unique Nature as the Inspired Word of God

Sola Scriptura is the conclusion to a thread of reasoning that begins with a simple question: What is Scripture? Simply put, Scripture claims to be the inspired Word of God. Now, in all Christian traditions, the phrase "the word of God" can be used in different ways. For example, Protestants have historically spoken of sermons or gospel proclamation as the "Word of God." But when we designate Scripture as the *inspired* Word of God, we are recognizing the unique ontological nature of Scripture.

In 2 Timothy 3:16, Paul calls Scripture *theopneustos*, often rendered "inspired by God" but literally meaning "breathed out by God" (ESV). As John Stott points out, this does not mean Scripture already exists and then is subsequently breathed into by God. Rather, Scripture itself *is* that which is breathed out by God:

> "Inspiration" is doubtless a convenient term to use, but "spiration" or even "expiration" would convey the meaning of the Greek adjective more accurately. Scripture . . . originated in God's mind and was communicated from God's mouth by God's breath or Spirit. It is therefore rightly termed "the Word of God," for God spoke it.[12]

We might call a sermon "the word of God" in a general sense, but we do not call it "God-breathed." This is the ontological distinction we seek to convey with the adjective "inspired." The words of Scripture are breathed out by God; the words of a sermon are not. Similarly, the apostle Peter teaches that, though Scripture comes through a human medium, its *origin* is not human but divine: "For no prophecy was ever produced by the will of man, but men spoke from God as they were carried along by the Holy Spirit" (2 Pet. 1:21). In his classic treatment of biblical inspiration and authority, B. B. Warfield comments on the verb used in the phrase "carried along by the Holy Spirit":

> The term here used is a very specific one. It is not to be confounded with guiding, or directing, or controlling, or even leading in the full sense of that word. It goes beyond all such terms, in assigning the effect produced specifically to the active agent. What is "borne" is taken up by the "bearer," and conveyed by the "bearer's" power, not its own, to the "bearer's" goal, not its own.[13]

Drawing from 2 Peter 1:21, one way to convey the notion of inspiration is to say that the words of Scripture are *from God*. Or, more colloquially, Scripture is God's words. It is divine speech. Indeed, this is how Scripture speaks of itself. For example, Romans 3:2 refers to the Old Testament *ta logia tou Theou*, meaning "the oracles of God" (ESV) or "the actual words of God" (NASB) or "very words of God" (NIV).[14] Similarly, Jesus will quote Old Testament Scripture as *God speaking* (for example, Matt. 19:4–5). It is on this basis—Scripture's nature as the words of God—that we speak of Scripture as infallible. Because the words of Scripture are the very words of God, they are incapable of error. As Jesus said in John 10:35, "Scripture cannot be broken."

When it comes to the nature of Scripture, Protestantism has much agreement with other Christian traditions. The Roman Catholic Church, for example, teaches that "Scripture is the speech of God as it is put down in writing under the breath of the Holy Spirit."[15] In Roman Catholic theology, Sacred Scripture and Sacred Tradition together constitute the Word of God, but in different ways—Sacred Tradition is not inspired by the Holy Spirit in the way Scripture is.[16] Similarly, while the magisterium is entrusted with the role of interpreting the deposit of faith contained in both Scripture and Tradition, the charism of infallibility extended to the church in that capacity is *distinguished* from divine revelation.[17] Thus, when a pope speaks *ex cathedra*, his words are not the words of God. When an ecumenical council delivers a verdict, its words are not the words of God. On the contrary, Roman Catholic theology maintains public divine revelation ceased with the deaths of the apostles: "We now await no further new public revelation before the glorious manifestation of our Lord Jesus Christ."[18] Similarly, though the Eastern Orthodox Church distinguishes her view of Scripture in many ways from a Protestant one, that Scripture is the inspired Word of God is not a point of difference.[19]

Thus, the vast majority of Christians today can agree that Scripture is ontologically unique in its nature. No other rule of faith we have is the inspired Word of God. Nothing else that we possess today constitutes the God-breathed, Spirit-carried, unbreakable oracles of God. *Sola Scriptura* is simply the position that, as the Bible is unique in nature, so it is correspondingly unique in authority.

The alternative positions, such as those of Roman Catholicism and Eastern Orthodoxy, separate infallibility from inspiration. Those positions have the burden to show why another rule of faith that is not the inspired Word of God should nonetheless be accepted as equal to Scripture with respect to infallibility. This consideration alone does not establish *sola Scriptura*, but it makes visible its coherence and underscores the need for alternative proposals to demonstrate the grounds for their elevation of additional rules of faith up into the realm of infallibility.

One can express this concern at a more metaphysical level: God is unique; therefore, his speech is unique. Why should we accept that which isn't the speech of God to have equal authority to that which *is* the speech of God? If you want to put something else into the "infallible rule" category alongside the very words of God, you will need a good reason.

Scripture's Unique Role among the People of God

The general importance of Scripture among the people of God can be seen by the frequent exhortations to meditate on it as a source of life and flourishing (Josh. 1:8, Pss. 1:2; 119) and by how its recovery leads to reform and renewal (for example, 2 Kings 22). But its more specific position of authority is evident in how *other* authorities, including legitimate authorities ordained by God, are consistently subordinated to it. An important example is Jesus placing Scripture over tradition in Matthew 15 and Mark 7.

When this passage is brought into debates, opponents of *sola Scriptura* will frequently argue it concerns only the "traditions of men," not divine traditions.[20] But here a dilemma emerges: How would anyone at the time have known that they are the traditions of men? Jesus himself affirmed that the Pharisees had a legitimate, God-given authority to teach God's people. Since they sit on the seat of Moses, Jesus commanded, "Do and observe whatever they tell you" (Matt. 23:3). The Pharisees themselves most emphatically did not regard their traditions as merely human! On the contrary, they affirmed an oral law from Moses handed down through successive lineage, and they claimed it was comparable in authority to the written law. This amounted to a similar kind of two-source theory to what we find in Roman Catholic Church today. D. A. Carson notes that Pharisees regarded their oral tradition as "having authority very nearly equal to the canon."[21] Similarly, F. F. Bruce observes, "As time went on the claim was made that this oral law, like the written law itself, was received by Moses on Sinai, and it was accorded with the same authority."[22] This is why the Pharisees accosted Jesus and his disciples for daring to disobey their traditions.

To defend their two-source view of revelation, the Pharisees could have made the same appeal to Jesus that is often put to Protestants today: "Jesus, where does the Old Testament explicitly say it has greater authority than our oral traditions?" But the answer to that is simple: The Bible need not anticipate every possible later error or alternative. It is enough to know that Scripture is the inspired Word of God and oral traditions are not. For this reason, it is only reasonable to measure oral traditions against the inspired Word of God—just as you might measure the word of a less trustworthy friend against that of a more trustworthy friend.

That is what Jesus does in this passage. He does not rebuke the Pharisees for offering the *wrong* traditions, as though the problem consisted simply in elevating human traditions over divine traditions. Rather, he corrects the Pharisees' traditions on the basis of the Word of God, with the term "the Word of God" referring to the teaching of Exodus 20:12 and 21:7. The handwashing traditions in view here are not *explicitly* contrary to Scripture, and the Pharisees would certainly not have granted that they contradicted Scripture. But Jesus infers that this is their practical result; further, he asserts, "many such things you do" (Mark 7:13). Thus, Jesus is not merely rejecting one particular

Pharisaical tradition but the Pharisees' inflated view of tradition as a whole. What is at stake is the entire theory by which the Pharisees falsely claimed divine authority for their traditions.

This error—the usurping of divine authority—is not unique to the Pharisees. It will be a perennial temptation for any group that has historical ties to a genuine work of God. Thus, it is good and appropriate to test claims of divine authority that are *uncertain* by those that are certain. In the New Testament, even apostolic preaching is measured against Scripture. This is why the Bereans are called noble in Acts 17:11: "These Jews were more noble than those in Thessalonica; they received the word with all eagerness, examining the Scriptures daily to see if these things were so." John Stott notes that the verb used for "examine" here "is used of judicial investigations, as of Herod examining Jesus, the Sanhedrin Peter and John (4:9), and Felix Paul (24:8)."[23] Here Luke praises the Bereans for examining the Scriptures to see if Paul and Silas's message is true. Further, in Galatians 1:8, Paul goes so far as to command that not only apostolic teaching but even *angelic* teaching must be tested according to the deposit of divine revelation given in the apostolic age.

This is the heart cry of *sola Scriptura*: Test that which isn't the inspired Word of God by that which *is* the inspired Word of God. This makes sense because God's speech is of greater authority than all other speech.

Alternative Proposals of Infallible Rules

These two considerations lead to the question: If the Bible is the inspired Word of God, and if the Bible functions with authority greater than other legitimate authorities in the church, what other rule exists for the church that would be comparable?

One possibility is oral apostolic traditions. However, there is a difference between oral teaching straight from the mouth of an apostle and the fallible transmission process by which it is bequeathed to subsequent generations. In his nineteenth-century defense of *sola Scriptura* against the Anglo-Catholics, William Goode pointed out that quickly after the apostles were gone, early church fathers appealed to apostolic tradition to establish contradictory views. For example, in a dispute concerning the date of Easter arising in the second century, both sides appealed to apostolic tradition to ground their view.[24] Eusebius records a letter from Polycrates, bishop of Ephesus, claiming that their position on the date of Easter was handed down to them from the apostles, and then records the response from Victor, bishop of Rome, who on the same basis sought to excommunicate churches holding to this position but was restrained by other bishops.[25]

Also as early as the second century, Irenaeus appealed to apostolic tradition to ground various claims, including his belief that Jesus died as a middle-aged man—a view hardly anyone affirms today.[26] Similarly, in the third century dispute concerning the rebaptism of those baptized by heretics, both sides appealed to apostolic tradition, claiming they were simply following the custom entrusted to the church by the apostles.[27] In response to this challenge, people often draw a distinction between local traditions and those apostolic traditions that are truly apostolic and divine. This is quite convenient, since each of the parties involved in these various disputes claimed their traditions were the ones that were apostolic and divine. Therefore, the person who makes such a *post hoc* maneuver has the burden to show that (and how) the erroneous tradition in each case can be plausibly shown to lack apostolicity.

The point is this: If transmission errors can happen on such relatively simple matters (some of which are sheer historical facts) within two or three generations of the apostles, how much more can they happen on complicated dogmas two millennia from the apostles? This does not mean patristic testimony to apostolic teaching is not valuable, but it certainly entails that it is not an *infallible rule* for the church.[28] The possibility of error in literary transmission, by contrast, is comparatively tiny and does not touch any dogmas of the faith.

The real alternatives to *sola Scriptura* are those that posit mechanisms of infallibility to the post-apostolic church—for example, *ex cathedra* statements from popes, certain of the deliverances of ecumenical councils, and/or teachings of the ordinary and universal magisterium. But the idea of infallibility as an ongoing feature of the post-apostolic church (through those or any other mechanism) has four problems that in cumulative weight are fatal.

First, it is without precedent in Old Testament. The Jewish people had no such ongoing organs of infallibility, so this would be an innovation within redemptive history if it came into being with the church. Second, it is without ground or instantiation in the New Testament. Although the New Testament is replete with information about the offices of the church, there is not even a hint of any post-apostolic office in the church that possesses infallibility (or any other kind of infallible rule that could arise for the church). However carefully the New Testament is scrutinized, not one word will be discovered about infallible authority being vested into an ongoing post-apostolic function in the church. Yet if the church did possess such a function, wouldn't this be *the single most important fact* for the New Testament to tell us?

Third, post-apostolic infallibility in the church is apparently also unknown to the early church. It's primarily a medieval development (more on that in chapter 7). Fourth, once the idea of ecclesial infallibility does arise, it seems to create more confusion than clarity. Supposedly infallible teachings don't have a good track record in church history. We have already seen changes to the doctrine of "no salvation outside the church" in both Eastern Orthodox and Roman Catholic traditions. Another example is Roman Catholic teaching concerning the death penalty. In their 2017 book on the topic, Edward Feser and Joseph M. Bessette documented the overwhelming support for the legitimacy of the death penalty in principle in Scripture, tradition, and church teaching, showing that this doctrine clearly qualifies as part of the infallible, irreformable teaching of the church.[29] One year later, under Pope Francis's leadership, the Catechism of the Catholic Church was changed to affirm that "the Church teaches, in the light of the Gospel, that 'the death penalty is inadmissible because it is an attack on the inviolability and dignity of the person', and she works with determination for its abolition worldwide."[30]

Those defending this revision often argue it is merely a disciplinary change, and thus not an absolute contradiction. It's difficult to imagine any medieval Christian accepting such an explanation, particularly since the rationale for the change is decidedly theological, grounded in both the dignity of the human person and the gospel itself. But the more basic point at the moment is that even if the change could technically avoid the charge of contradiction, this would not remove the practical concern about confusion. It's simply astonishing that a practice with universal support throughout Scripture and church history can now be called "an attack on the inviolability and dignity of the person." Why was this never taught before? What practical good is an allegedly infallible magisterium that can evidently be misunderstood for so long, by so many?

At the end of the day, there is simply no good biblical or historical reason to conclude that the post-apostolic church possesses ongoing capacities of infallibility. This does not mean the church died or fell away from God. It simply means the church can err and therefore must continually measure her doctrine and practice by the infallible words of Holy Scripture.

CHAPTER 6

Objections to *Sola Scriptura*

Having laid out a basic argument in favor of *sola Scriptura*, in this chapter we will probe this doctrine by considering some of the typical objections.

Objection 1: What about the Canon?

The church's role in canonization is often set against *sola Scriptura*. Such critiques, however, generally fail to touch the Protestant position. Protestants stand in broad agreement with other traditions that the church has been entrusted with the responsibility of discerning the canon. For example, Protestants find themselves in a broad agreement on this point with the Roman Catholic position, as articulated at Vatican I: "these books the church holds to be sacred and canonical not because she subsequently approved them by her authority . . . but because, being written under the inspiration of the holy Spirit, they have God as their author, and were as such committed to the church."[1]

The necessity of the church's witness unto the Word of God is a classical Protestant doctrine. (The seventeenth-century Dutch Reformed theologians were particularly adept at explicating this doctrine). For Protestants, the church's charge extends not only to recognizing the canon but also to protecting the Scriptures during times of persecution and to translating, teaching, and proclaiming them. Thus, Protestants have spoken of the church as not only a necessary witness to the Word of God, but also the custodian and herald of the Word of God.[2]

The necessity of the church, however, does not entail her infallibility. Protestants have often compared the church's role in the process of canonization to that of John the Baptist in pointing to Christ: It is a ministerial role of *witness* or *testimony*. That the church is entrusted with such a task in no way grants her infallible authority parallel to Scripture any more than John the Baptist possessed parallel authority to Christ. Rather, the one testifying is subordinate to that which receives the testimony. As Johannes Wollebius put it, "As it is foolish to tell us that the candle receives its light from the candlestick that supports it, so it is ridiculous to ascribe the Scripture's authority to the church."[3]

Infallibility is not necessary for canonization since the church's responsibility is not constituting Scripture but simply recognizing it. Such recognition is not *itself* the action of an infallible agent. As J. I. Packer more recently stated, "The Church no more gave us the New Testament canon than Sir Isaac Newton gave us the force of gravity. . . . Newton did not create gravity but recognized it."[4] Another metaphor for this action of the church used by the Anglican theologian William Whitaker is that of a goldsmith discerning true gold from other metals: "The goldsmith with his scales and touchstone can distinguish gold from copper and other metals; wherein he does not make gold . . . but only indicates what is gold. . . . In like manner the Church acknowledges the Scriptures and declares them to be divine."[5]

Ultimately, the trustworthiness of the canon is rooted in the guidance of the Holy Spirit, as well as the progressive nature of revelation itself. Thus, the Italian Reformer Peter Martyr Vermigli pointed out that in the work of discerning the Word of God, the church does not start from scratch, but measures each book against the previous revelation she has already received from God. As Richard Muller expounds Vermigli's view, the church "adjudges the canon only as she is taught so to do by the Spirit of Christ, her Teacher, and by the comparison of Scripture with Scripture—even as a counterfeit letter is proved by comparison with a genuine letter."[6] Muller points out that in explaining the church's role in this way, Vermigli and other early Protestants like William Tyndale were not innovating—they were simply repeating a view that had strong attestation in medieval scholastic debate, most recently by the fifteenth-century theologian Wessel Gansfort.[7] The idea of a hierarchy of authorities, with the Scripture at the top over other subordinate (but necessary) authorities, was by no means a novel approach in the sixteenth century.

To state the point plainly, setting *sola Scriptura* at odds with the process of canonization confuses the recognition of infallibility with the possession of infallibility. The simple fact is that it is not necessary to *be* infallible to *discern* that which *is* infallible. When Moses heard God at the burning bush, he didn't need a second voice whispering in his ear that this was indeed God. This is what Protestants intend when they speak of Scripture as self-authenticating. This simply means that the ultimate ground on which we receive the Scripture is inherent in it, rather than external to it. For there is no higher authority the Word of God could rest upon than the Spirit speaking through it. If you think you *do* have to possess infallibility to discern infallibility, you have a continual regress, because now you need infallibility to receive and interpret the infallible teachings of your church.

There is one way we can know with certainty that the church does not need infallibility to discern the canon: the facts of history. It just didn't happen that way. With respect to the New Testament canon, scholars debate the exact date of its finalization, but it is generally seen to have become fully settled in the fourth century. The process of canonization leading to that point was bottom up, not top down. It was a gradual, cumulative, widespread, and organic process by which the church discerned the Word of God through the enabling direction of the Holy Spirit. It was *not* the result of an infallible statement from the Pope of Rome or an ecumenical council. As Collins and Walls note, "The canon emerged independently about the same time in the East, the West, and northern Africa."[8] In this process, Athanasius's Thirty-Ninth Festal Letter in 367 was particularly significant, confirmed at the Synod of Hippo in 393 and the Council of Carthage in 397. It is disputed whether the same canon list was adopted at the Council of Rome in 382, but either way, this council was not regarded as settling the issue.[9] It was not an ecumenical council. It was not infallible.

The fourth-century New Testament canon was the result of a process that began within the New Testament itself, where various books are identified as Scripture (2 Pet. 3:16; 1 Tim. 5:18). Furthermore, as Michael Kruger points out, the New Testament authors frequently betray an awareness that they are writing with divine authority.[10] Hence throughout the second and third centuries, books like Matthew, Acts, and Romans were not in dispute and were quoted with the same authority as the Old Testament Scriptures.[11] The only dispute was around the fuzzy edges (for example, Revelation, 2 Peter, The Shepherd of Hermas). This does not render the final determination unimportant. It simply reinforces the central point here: Christians do not need an infallible act of the church to discern Scripture.

Similarly, the Old Testament canon was also not the result of an exercise of infallibility among the people of God. The Jewish people did not have an infallible teaching office, yet throughout their history, they were able to recognize and receive the Word of God given to them in what we call the Old Testament Scriptures. This is not to say, of course, that there were no disagreements about certain books (for example, Ecclesiastes and Esther) or alternative canons among various outlier groups (for example, the Samaritans, who were not considered Jews, held only to the Torah). Scholars debate when the canon of the Jewish people was closed, but it seems there was a "core" Old Testament canon in the mainstream Jewish tradition by the time of Jesus, sometimes referred to as the Law, the Prophets, and the Writings (or simply as the Law and the Prophets).[12] For example, the first-century Jewish historian Josephus referred to a Hebrew Bible of twenty-two books (corresponding to the thirty-nine books of the Protestant Old Testament), and appeared to conceive of the canon as closed.[13]

But what is significant for our purposes is simply to note that Jesus held the Jews of his day to the authority of Scripture despite the fact that there was not an infallible declaration of the canon among the Jewish people (Luke 16:16; 24:44; John 5:47, and more). This entails the possibility of receiving infallible revelation of God and recognizing it as such without an infallible decree from the church.

This argument from the canon against *sola Scriptura* is commonly made, but it falls apart under scrutiny. Even the Roman Catholic Church had a "fallible canon" for most of her history, since the canon was not infallibly defined until the Councils of Florence and Trent toward the end of the Middle Ages. Moreover, today the Roman Catholic Church also has a "fallible list of infallible teachings," since the number of *ex cathedra* statements and other infallible forms of teaching has never been infallibly defined and is disputed. Similarly, other churches have a "fallible list of infallible councils." This is not a problem for them; neither is canonization for *sola Scriptura*.

Objection 2: Doesn't the New Testament Teach Us to Obey "Traditions"?

Criticism of *sola Scriptura* often points to the positive role of tradition in the New Testament:

- "Now I commend you because you remember me in everything and maintain the traditions even as I delivered them to you" (1 Cor. 11:2).
- "So then, brothers, stand firm and hold to the traditions that you were taught by us, either by our spoken word or by our letter" (2 Thess. 2:15).

But these passages have nothing to do with *sola Scriptura*. Of course particular local churches would receive and obey apostolic traditions in the first century (as well as apostolic teaching in other forms). That would be true for *every* first-century apostolic church. This happened during the apostolic era, while Scripture was still being written. These traditions do not exist as an infallible rule for the church today—as I have noted, the transmission of oral teachings is fallible and led to immediate disputes in the early church.

Unfortunately, criticism of *sola Scriptura* sometimes completely overlooks the distinction between the apostolic age and the post-apostolic age. For example, Josiah Trenham, quoting 2 Thessalonians 2:15, asks, "Are we to suppose, as the *sola Scriptura* theory would have it, that you were only to obey the Apostolic teachings and injunctions that St. Paul wrote down and not those that you heard from his own mouth?"[14] But the notion that *sola Scriptura* would give license to first-century Christians to disobey the apostles' oral instruction is an extreme caricature. For starters, *sola Scriptura* in no way designates Scripture as the only *authority to be obeyed* (as opposed to only infallible rule). More basically, *sola Scriptura* is a framework for the church as such, not for Christians in the apostolic age sitting under the teaching of living apostles, during the era in which Scripture was still being written. When passages like 2 Thessalonians 2:15 are set at odds with *sola Scriptura*, this simply reflects that the doctrine has been misunderstood.

Setting *sola Scriptura* at odds with tradition typically involves an equivocation on the word *tradition*. Martin Chemnitz listed eight different definitions of the word *tradition* as it was used by the church fathers, the first seven of which are completely harmonious with *sola Scriptura*.[15] It is only the eighth kind of tradition, that which was affirmed at the Council of Trent, that *sola Scriptura* opposes. This kind of tradition Chemnitz defines as "traditions which pertain both to faith and morals and which cannot be proved with any testimony of Scripture but which the Synod of Trent nevertheless commands to be received and venerated with the same reverence and devotion as the Scripture itself."[16]

More simply, Heiko Oberman distinguished between two broad conceptions of tradition that developed throughout church history. "Tradition 1" sees tradition as indispensable but primarily in the role of *supplementing* Scripture, not as a separate source of divine revelation. In this view, Scripture must be interpreted in the context of the church and the rule of faith, but it is the sole source of divine revelation. "Tradition 2" sees tradition as a separate source of divine revelation, especially rooted in Christ's forty days of teaching his disciples between his resurrection and his ascension (Acts 1:3), not written down but allegedly preserved by the magisterium of the church.[17]

It took considerable time in church history for this second conception of tradition to emerge and then later become accepted. Historians disagree on when precisely the transition from "Tradition 1" to "Tradition 2" happened, but it is a controversial debate throughout the medieval era.[18] When early Christians like Irenaeus appealed to tradition, they were frequently referring to what was coincident with the content of Scripture, not a separate rule or source of revelation. It was not until the fourth century (in Basil's writings, for example) that there emerged a clear conception of unwritten tradition as a separate norm from Holy Scripture. But even there, the traditions more commonly referred to are liturgical practices, not universal obligatory dogmas that lack scriptural warrant. As J. N. D. Kelly notes,

All the instances of unwritten tradition lacking Scriptural support which the early theologians mention will be found, on examination, to refer to matters of observance and practice (e.g. triple immersion in baptism; turning East for prayer) rather than doctrine as such, although sometimes they are matters (e.g. infant baptism; prayers for the dead) in which doctrine is involved.[19]

Furthermore, even Basil shows concern for the necessity and priority of Scripture. For example, when arguing for the legitimacy of the phrase "with him" in the doxology, Basil appeals to tradition but then immediately adds, "but we are not content simply because this is the tradition of the Fathers. What is important is that the Fathers followed the meaning of Scripture."[20]

Despite the numerous different meanings of the word *tradition*, critics of *sola Scriptura* sometimes employ any positive instance of this term as though it were speaking of tradition in the sense defined at the council of Trent. But it is specifically *that* conception of tradition that *sola Scriptura* opposes—namely, that Scripture and tradition are to be received with equal reverence as they together constitute the deposit of the Word of God, and that the magisterium of the church can offer infallible interpretations of both.

Protestants reject this schema because tradition is *not* the inspired Word of God, and when it is made equal to Scripture and the magisterium is put in the role of interpretation, then it is really the magisterium that has ultimate authority. In this way, the church is ultimately untethered from accountability to the inspired Word of God, resulting in, as Keith Mathison puts it, "a Church which is a law unto itself."[21] Protestants have referred to this position with phrases like *sola ecclesia* and *solum magisterium* to reflect the concern that the practical effect of this position (if not the intention) is to place the church *above* Scripture (and tradition).[22]

Hence the scandal of obligatory dogmas that have no testimony in Scripture or early tradition (like the issues we will peruse next in this book, the bodily assumption of Mary and the veneration of icons). These are good examples of what is at stake with a Protestant conception of authority in the church. In sum, *sola Scriptura* is not a generic rejection of tradition; it's a rejection of *those* kinds of tradition.

Objection 3: *Sola Scriptura* Has No Precedent in Church History

Sola Scriptura is often portrayed as a late addition in church history. Yet while the term draws from a sixteenth-century context, the basic idea of the paramount position of Holy Scripture on grounds of its unique infallibility as the inspired Word of God was recognized by many within the pre-Reformation church. William Whitaker, in his 1588 *Disputation on Holy Scripture*, surveys about twenty church fathers, all of whom exhibit an awareness of the supreme and unparalleled authority of Scripture.[23] In my own research, I have focused on St. Augustine. Though people are often unwilling to accept it, Augustine taught with striking clarity that Scripture is the only infallible rule for the church.

There are too many passages in Augustine to this effect to cover them all, but it may be useful to canvass one example. In his treatment of baptism against the Donatists, Augustine opposes the position of Cyprian regarding rebaptism (evidently appealed to by the Donatists of his day). This leads him to a discussion of the authority of Scripture:

> But who can fail to be aware that the sacred canon of Scripture, both of the Old and New Testament, is confined within its own limits, and that it stands so absolutely in a superior position to all later letters of the bishops, that about it we can hold no manner of doubt or disputation whether what is confessedly contained in it is right and true; but that all the letters of bishops which have been written, or are being written, since the closing of the canon, are liable to be refuted if there be anything contained in them which strays from the truth, either by the discourse of some one who happens to be wiser in the matter than themselves, or by the weightier authority and more learned experience of other bishops, by the authority of Councils; and further, that the Councils themselves, which are held in the several districts and provinces, must yield, beyond all possibility of doubt, to

the authority of plenary Councils which are formed for the whole Christian world; and that even of the plenary Councils, the earlier are often corrected by those which follow them, when, by some actual experiment, things are brought to light which were before concealed, and that is known which previously lay hid?[24]

I have given a lengthier commentary (and my own translation) of this passage in videos. But the essential points can be enumerated briefly:

1. Scripture is qualitatively unique ("confined within its own limits");
2. the grounds for its uniqueness is infallibility ("we can hold no manner of doubt or disputation whether what is confessedly contained in it is right and true");
3. this unique infallibility is contrasted with an increasing chain of postbiblical authorities the church, including the highest expression of authority, namely, "plenary Councils which are formed for the whole Christian world."

What are "plenary councils?" In Augustine's time technical distinctions between different kinds of councils were not yet hardened, but the phrase here is certainly *inclusive* of what would later be classified as ecumenical councils—hence the qualifying phrase, "formed for the whole Christian world." *The Catholic Encyclopedia* notes, "the ecumenical councils or synods of the Universal Church are called plenary council by St. Augustine (C. illa, xi, Dist. 12), as they form a complete representation of the entire Church."[25] Elsewhere Augustine references Nicaea I specifically when prioritizing Scripture above councils.[26]

Thus, in the context of explicating the unique infallibility of Scripture, Augustine asserts that even ecumenical councils can be "corrected." Some try to paint this correction as mere doctrinal development, since it happens when "things are brought to light which were before concealed." But this is a category error: The fact that the particular form of correction comes through the unveiling of new information does *not* mean it is not the correction of genuine error (any more than when a jury discovers new evidence that overturns their verdict; the first verdict was not an error). Furthermore, such an explanation violates Augustine's language and meaning. The Latin word *emendo*, which is translated "corrected" above, does not mean "develop,"[27] and the whole point Augustine is making is that Scripture is confined to its own limits with respect to infallibility. To establish that point, he is ascending to successively greater authorities, in each case showing they are capable of error and being corrected. If Augustine switched from "correction" to "development" at the climactic point, then Scripture would *not* be confined to its own limits, and the originating point would be undermined. On top of all that, right before and after this passage, Augustine speaks of being "corrected" several times (for example, in the very next sentence), and it always entails changing from a genuine error.[28]

People sometimes react with bewilderment and disgust to the idea that Augustine affirmed the essential content of *sola Scriptura*. But honestly, I have yet to hear any good counterargument. Some argue that Augustine is merely referring to "robber councils" when he speaks of conciliar corrections, but Augustine gives no hint of that. He simply says, concerning plenary councils, "the earlier are often corrected by those which follow them." Others point out that Augustine held to a different Old Testament canon than Protestants, but that is irrelevant. The canon is about *which* books are Scripture; *sola Scriptura* is about the nature of their authority. It is possible to hold to both *sola Scriptura* and a larger canon.

Others point to Augustine's high view of the authority of tradition. But that is not contrary to *sola Scriptura*—it's perfectly consistent to accept a high view of tradition and the authority of the church while maintaining that only the Scripture is the infallible rule of the church. Furthermore, when Augustine speaks elsewhere of the importance of following universal traditions, his rationale is that they are likely to go back to apostolic teaching, not that the church *itself* has acted infallibly.[29] Still others point out that, just a bit later in the same work, Augustine thinks a plenary council can place a matter "beyond dispute."[30] But this confuses authority and infallibility—Augustine simply uses a verb meaning "solidified," "strengthened," or "consolidated" (which J. R. King renders "placed beyond dispute").[31] This language in no way entails that the council in question is infallible (if it did, Augustine would be contradicting himself in the space of two paragraphs).

The unavoidable fact is that Augustine appears to think Scripture is infallible, while all later functions of authority in the church are fallible. Even the Roman Catholic scholar Robert Eno, despite favoring the view that Augustine may have thought some councils could be infallible (though he is uncertain), admits that "Augustine then is completely committed to the principle that the testimony of Scripture is superior to any other," and that, for Augustine, "Councils are subordinated to Scripture."[32]

So it's wrong to charge Protestants with novelty for insisting on the unique position of Scripture over the church as an infallible rule. People sometimes ask, "But how would the earliest Christians have practiced *sola Scriptura*?" But remember, *sola Scriptura* is a conceptual framework for the church *as such*. It is not refuted by circumstantial variation in practice—for example, among Christians who lived prior to the closure of the canon, or who live in parts of the world today where the Bible has not yet been translated into their language. Similarly, there can be a Roman Catholic Christian or parish in a remote part of the world where the latest papal teaching has not yet arrived, or that has received erroneous information about the latest papal teaching. (There have even been times in history when individual Christians would not have known who the true pope was.) These circumstantial questions do not refute the overall framework in question.

Objection 4: *Sola Scriptura* Depends on Private Judgment, Leading to Anarchy

Sometimes people claim *sola Scriptura* places private judgment as the highest authority. But that is confused. Private judgment is not *itself* the authority. The most that could be said is that *sola Scriptura*, by placing Scripture as the ultimate authority, elevates private judgment too highly. This concern is partially met by our previous comments regarding the role of subordinate doctrinal standards. But it is also worth emphasizing here the necessity and dignity of private judgment. We all use private judgment for the most important and poignant decisions of life—including whether to be a Christian, which church to join, and whether to remain in that church.

Furthermore, while erroneous private judgment is a real danger, another danger is far worse: erroneous ecclesiastical judgments. It is one thing to be able to err; it is another to be *yoked* to error. This is what *sola Scriptura* seeks to guard against. Those of us who adhere to *sola Scriptura* simply seek to follow our conscience. Additional allegedly infallible rules prevent us from doing that because they mandate acceptance of what we regard as error. To submit to a system that requires assent to such beliefs would be dishonest and thus would violate our conscience.

To state this concern metaphorically: Democracy is clumsy, but it's better than tyranny. And for Protestants, it is nothing less than tyranny when churches require belief in indulgences, or the assumption of Mary, or the veneration of icons, or many other points of doctrine that we have no reason to believe are apostolic. That is why *sola Scriptura* is so important: It involves nothing less than setting the boundaries for what Christianity is. What are the necessary doctrines a Christian is required to accept? Without *sola Scriptura*, the parameters get widened to encircle all kinds of historical accretions.

People often seem to seek a sense of security by placing their trust in a church's claims of infallible authority. It is my sincere grief and worry that such people are ultimately *misplacing* their trust. *Sola Scriptura* is a summons to place our ultimate trust in God alone rather than in fallible, human claims. The wonderful promise of the gospel is that it is here, in simple faith in the Word of God, that we find the assurance and security our hearts so deeply long for (1 John 3:19–20; Heb. 11:1; 10:22; Rom. 8:16). I invite you to make the heart posture of Psalm 119 the bedrock of your life, as I have done with mine:

- "My soul longs for your salvation; I hope in your word" (v. 81)
- "You are my hiding place and my shield; I hope in your word" (v. 114).
- "I rise before dawn and cry for help; I hope in your words" (v. 147)

Make the inspired Word of God your ultimate hope and trust. It will never fail you, to all eternity.

CHAPTER 7

The Papacy

What are other possible conceptions of how authority should work in the church, and why do Protestants reject them? We cannot be exhaustive, and I have already somewhat addressed the general idea of post-apostolic infallibility. Now it is useful to give more concrete consideration to other proposals, particularly in their biblical and historical development. We begin with the largest and perhaps most infamous: the papacy.

Defining the Papacy

We must begin by defining the papacy. The reason for this is that once it emerges how slender and ambiguous the evidence for the papacy is in the Bible or early church history, appeal will often be made to doctrinal development. In other words, people will say, "The core idea of the papacy is there, but the details develop." (Sometimes people even argue that the historical instantiation of the office itself is a later development.) To prepare for these arguments, we need to know what the "core idea" is.

Minimally, the papacy is an office in the church characterized by succession, infallibility, and supremacy. *Succession* means the office originates with Peter and succeeds to the Roman bishops; *infallibility* means the pope is capable of speaking infallibly under certain conditions; and *supremacy* means the pope's leadership is not merely advisory, but rather constitutes an immediate, universal, and supreme power of jurisdiction over the whole church.

We will develop these a bit as we go. The important point to understand for now is that in describing these various characteristics of the papacy, Vatican I set limits concerning the amount of development that can be reasonably ascribed to the office. For example, *Pastor Aeternus*, the document at Vatican I defining papal authority and infallibility, stipulates that Scripture's teaching concerning the institution of the papacy "has always been understood by the Catholic Church."[1] It also taught that it "was known in every age" that Peter received the keys of the kingdom and that he lives in his successors in the Roman see;[2] and that it is demonstrated by "the constant custom of the Church" that the pope's supremacy extends to his teachings.[3]

Thus, while we can leave room for circumstantial variation in what the papacy looks like due to factors like cultural differences or persecution, it is nonetheless clear that Vatican I regarded the papacy as a perennial institution, broadly characteristic of the entirety of church history.

Is this true? Are supreme, infallible bishops of Rome a generally known fact of church history? The evidence—both biblical and historical—seems overwhelmingly against this claim.

The Papacy and the New Testament

The notion of papal succession is completely absent from the New Testament. However carefully you might scour from Matthew to Revelation with a magnifying glass, you will not catch the faintest hint of an ongoing office of any kind associated with Peter—let alone one that involves Roman bishops. The whole idea comes about well after the New Testament. It's difficult to even *argue* about papal succession from the New Testament because it's like trying to argue whether Pluto should be a planet or who shot J. F. K. based on the New Testament. There is just not any source material whatsoever.

This is why biblical arguments for the papacy typically focus on Peter, not the idea of an ongoing Petrine office. In so doing, they assume succession rather than trying to establish it. But this is problematic. Peter's office as an apostle was unique. The idea of a successive office stemming from Peter and imbued with his authority cannot merely be asserted. It needs to be demonstrated.

After all, the New Testament contains an enormous amount of detailed information about the offices of the church. Consider all you can learn from the pastoral epistles alone about the offices of presbyters and deacons. And then we have numerous passages that flesh out the offices of the church specifically with a view to its unity, like Ephesians 4:11–16 or 1 Corinthians 12:27–31. Why is there not a single verse anywhere that ever mentions, "By the way, there is actually a supreme and infallible office above all these others"? This would be rather important information! If Jesus and the apostles envisioned an ongoing office in the church characterized by supremacy and infallibility, it is not unreasonable to expect it to come up somewhere in their teaching or writings.

Consider what is at stake with the papacy. If the bishop of Rome can speak infallibly, then the boundaries of obligatory Christian beliefs are in part determined by his pronouncements. By locating in one person a supreme power of jurisdiction and the capacity for infallible pronouncement, the papacy has implications for every single aspect of how Christianity works. There could be nothing more important for us to figure out. Why would we be given such detailed information about lesser offices (for example, multiple qualification lists in 1 Tim. 3 and Titus 1) but not the slightest hint of this supreme office above them? This seems like a football coach giving detailed instructions to his lineman but neglecting to even send the quarterback out on the field.

Beyond the question of succession, Vatican I's claims about infallibility and supremacy are also difficult to square with the New Testament. Peter certainly had a unique leadership role among the apostles (though sometimes James and John were also singled out with Peter [Mark 5:37, 9:2, 13:3, 14:33]). Nonetheless, Peter's role falls significantly short of the kind of supremacy and unique infallibility envisioned at Vatican I for popes. Vatican 1 stipulated that "both clergy and faithful, of whatever rite and dignity, both singly and collectively, are bound to submit to this power by the duty of hierarchical subordination and true obedience."[4] This obedience concerns not only matters of faith and morals but also the discipline and government of the entire church.

But in the New Testament, the other apostles did not relate to Peter "by the duty of hierarchical subordination and true obedience." This was widely recognized in the early church, even after the Roman see had come to be associated with Peter's authority. In the third century, for example, Cyprian of Carthage wrote that "the rest of the apostles were also the same as was Peter, *endowed with a like partnership both of honour and power.*"[5] All the way in the seventh century, Isidore of Seville similarly claimed, "the other apostles also became equal sharers with Peter in honor and authority."[6] This view was not rare: I regard it as *close to a consensus* among the church fathers that the other apostles did not relate to Peter as one possessing greater authority over them and to whom they were subject.

The church fathers maintained this view because of the data of the New Testament. The simple fact is that Peter never claims supremacy or unique infallibility; no one else ascribes it to him; and the events of the New Testament nowhere depict him possessing such characteristics. There are *other* designations among the apostles—for example, in Galatians 2:9, James, Peter, and John are identified as "pillars." But nowhere is Peter singled out in terms of supremacy or infallibility—despite the fact that there are occasions where this would be expected. For example, when the first great doctrinal controversy arises in the early church, the apostles and elders in Jerusalem come together to resolve it in Acts 15. Peter is only one of several apostles who weighs in on the dispute, and he does not appear to speak definitively. Rather, the final and specific verdict is offered by James with the words, "therefore my judgment is . . ." (Acts 15:19). Preaching on this passage, John Chrysostom praised James for speaking more mildly than Peter, despite having greater authority: "James was invested with the chief rule. . . . Peter indeed spoke more strongly, but James here more mildly: for thus it behooves one in high authority, to leave what is unpleasant for others to say, while he himself appears in the milder part."[7]

The passage most frequently appealed to for Petrine supremacy is Matthew 16:18–19. However, the responsibilities of binding and loosing given to Peter here are reiterated to all the disciples just two chapters later (Matt. 18:18)—just as, generally throughout the New Testament, the authority to govern the church is entrusted to all the apostles conjointly (for example, John 20:23). Further, the context of Matthew 16 is Peter speaking on behalf of the other apostles in response to Jesus's question to them all: "Who do you [plural] say that I am?" (Matt. 16:15). This makes it legitimate to wonder: Must we see Peter as being given a unique, Vatican I supremacy here, placing him in a position of authority *above* the other apostles? Or might the responsibilities being given to Peter here ultimately be shared by the other apostles? In the early church, Augustine argued that Peter functioned in a *representative* role in this passage: "Did Peter receive the keys and Paul not receive them? Did Peter receive them, and John and James and the other apostles not receive them? . . . What was given to Peter was given to the whole church."[8] Augustine's position on this passage is not eccentric with respect to patristic thought. On the contrary, Ed Siecienski notes, "with few exceptions, patristic exegesis of Matthew 16 had nothing to do with the existence of an ongoing 'petrine' ministry in the church."[9]

If Peter is functioning representatively here, this will go a long way toward clarifying the famous "rock" imagery of the passage. Historically, there have been three proposals for the identity of the "rock" here after which Peter is named: Christ, Peter himself, or Peter's confession. However, as is widely recognized, the meaning can be polyvalent; these options are not necessarily mutually exclusive. In the early church, for example, all three options were widely held, with many church fathers combining them. In my view, the best interpretation is one that coordinates all three of these options: The rock is *Peter in his confessing Christ*. This view is well represented among many church fathers. Thus, Augustine's final view in his retractions was as follows:

> Peter, called after this rock, represented the person of the Church which is built upon this rock, and has received "the keys of the kingdom of heaven." For, "Thou art Peter" and not "Thou art the rock" was said to him. But "the rock was Christ," in confessing whom, as also the whole Church confesses, Simon was called Peter.[10]

Augustine's logic is that the rock is Christ, and since Peter confesses Christ, Peter is the rock in confessing Christ. Thus, Peter is the rock not as the first holder of an ecclesiastical office, but as representing the apostolic confession of Christ. This interpretation is supported by the fact that all throughout the New Testament, Christ is called the rock on which the church is built (Eph. 2:20; 1 Cor. 10:4; 1 Peter 2:8; drawing from Ps. 118), with the apostles as a group also at times participating in this imagery as well (Eph. 2:20; Gal. 2:9).

Some argue for Petrine supremacy from Jesus's restoration of Peter in Luke 22:31–34 and John 21:15–19. But there is nothing in Jesus's charge to Peter to "feed my sheep" and "strengthen your brothers" that remotely suggests supremacy or infallibility. He is just restoring Peter as an apostle, to normal apostolic functions, after Peter's denials of Christ. The effort to read Vatican I supremacy here is as *post hoc* and strained as arguing for Pauline supremacy from Paul's reference to his "concern for all the churches" in 2 Corinthians 11:28 (NASB). And again, patristic exegesis of these passages is nearly universal against the claim that Peter is envisioned as receiving greater authority than the other apostles. For example, David Bradshaw provides a helpful survey of various church fathers' exegesis of Peter's restoration in John 21. His conclusion is that the fathers he considers "do not find here the bestowal of any office or responsibility different from that of the other apostles."[11]

The Papacy and Early Church History

What about after the New Testament? As it turns out, the historical data is almost as problematic for papal claims as is the biblical. The papacy gives every appearance of being a slow historical accretion—a gradual accumulation and centralization of power within the Western church. In the first place, as we will explore in the next chapter, the early historical evidence indicates that not only was there not a bishop in Rome who functioned as the head of church, but there was not a single bishop at all. More basically, as church history progresses, though the Church of Rome (and consequently the bishop of Rome) comes into a kind of primacy, it falls significantly short of infallibility and supremacy throughout the patristic era and even into the medieval era. To put it simply, the first millennium of church history looks very different from the picture painted at Vatican I.

One way to see this concern is by considering opposition to Vatican I from within the Roman Catholic Church prior to and during the council. Johann Döllinger, a nineteenth-century Catholic theologian who was excommunicated for rejecting papal infallibility, maintained his opposition to the dogma mainly on historical grounds. In a letter recounting his concern he wrote, "We are still waiting the explanation how it is that, until 1830 years had passed, the Church did not formulate into an article of faith a doctrine which the Pope . . . calls the very foundation principle of Catholic faith and doctrine?"[12] Döllinger's excommunication was scandalous because prior to Vatican I he had been a leading Catholic historian. Yet he maintained that papal infallibility was plainly opposed to catholic precedent. For Döllinger, the notion that infallibility could be vested in one person in the terms of Vatican I was manifestly not how the church had functioned—especially in the patristic era and in the Christian East. Late in his life, responding to an appeal to save his soul from the everlasting consequences of exclusion from the church, he explained why he could not simply sacrifice his intellect on the question:

If I did so in a question which is for the historical eye perfectly clear and unambiguous, there would then be no longer for me any such thing as historical truth and certainty; I should then have to suppose that my whole life long I had been in a world of dizzy illusion, and that in historical matters I am altogether incapable of distinguishing truth from fable and falsehood.[13]

Döllinger was not the only Roman Catholic who regarded the ahistorical nature of the claims of Vatican I "perfectly clear and unambiguous." A minority of bishops at Vatican I had opposed *Pastor Aeternus* specifically on historical grounds. John W. O'Malley summarizes the opposition of these bishops as follows:

The most basic problem with Pastor Aeternus was its historical naivete. It took the present situation as the norm for interpreting the past and projected present practice and understanding onto it. Since it ignored differentiation between past and present, it lacked a sense of development from past to present, even though Newman's *Essay on the Development of Christian Doctrine* was by then twenty-five years old.[14]

That Vatican I amounted to a departure from historical precedent is also representative of the position of various Eastern churches, such as the Eastern Orthodox.[15]

Now, to be clear, the early Roman church *did* enjoy a kind of primacy. Rome was the capital of the Empire, it was the place of the martyrdom of Peter and Paul, and the early Roman church was a flagship church and bastion of orthodoxy for several centuries. So it's not hard to go back and find positive statements about the primacy, stature, and significance of Rome and her bishops. The problem is that *primacy* doesn't necessarily entail supremacy and infallibility, the specific qualities Vatican I asserted were characteristic of church history. Yet people stretch the data to make it seem like it does.

For example, Ignatius's assertion that the Church of Rome "presides in love" is often cited, despite the ambiguity of this language, the fact that Ignatius makes no mention of a bishop in Rome, and the fact that he used exalted language to describe other churches as well.[16] Or reference is made to Cyprian's teaching that the unity of the church is founded in the chair of Peter, but then no mention is made of the fact that Cyprian thought *every* bishop shared in this charter, such that no one bishop had authority over the rest.[17] We've already seen this in Cyprian's view of the relation of Peter to the other apostles; later, when Cyprian came into conflict with Pope Stephen over the question of rebaptism, he applied this principle to his own day: "Peter did not assert that he had rights of seniority and that therefore upstarts and latecomers ought to be obedient to him."[18]

When the target is clearly set at Vatican I-style infallibility and supremacy, it is clear the patristic and early medieval evidence doesn't hold up. Papal infallibility is generally seen as *explicitly* emerging only in the thirteenth century, and even then, it remains enormously controversial for several centuries (such that it was not adopted at the Council of Trent). The Roman Catholic scholar Brian Tierney, in a classic treatment of the subject, summarized his conclusion like this:

> There is no convincing evidence that papal infallibility formed any part of the theological or canonical tradition of the church before the thirteenth century; the doctrine was invented in the first place by a few dissident Franciscans because it suited their convenience to invent it; eventually, but only after much initial reluctance, it was accepted by the papacy because it suited the convenience of the popes to accept it.[19]

People often try to find examples of papal infallibility earlier in church history, but such efforts typically conflate infallibility *per se* with other qualities like papal indefectibility (i.e., not being subject to failure or flaw), papal immunity (i.e., not being subject to judgment from temporal authorities), or the general centrality, necessity, or importance of the bishop of Rome. But these are all distinct categories. For example, preservation from error in teaching is not the same as preservation from death or protection from the judgment of temporal authorities. There are also frequent conflations of personal versus ecclesial infallibility and/or infallibility in the preservation of tradition versus infallibility in the promulgation of dogma. But again, these are clearly distinct. The idea that *one man* can infallibly pronounce a dogma simply isn't present in the first millennium of church history.

Similarly, papal *supremacy* as defined by Vatican I is not representative of the first millennium of Christianity. This can be seen in many ways: One is how popes relate to ecumenical councils. *Lumen Gentium*, a dogmatic constitution promulgated at Vatican II, stipulates the role of the pope in relation to ecumenical councils: "It is prerogative of the Roman Pontiff to convoke these councils, to preside over them and to confirm them."[20] In contrast to this, *none* of the first seven ecumenical councils were convoked or presided over by a Roman bishop (rather, the emperor did so). In some cases, the Roman bishop was not even invited, nor were Roman legates present (for example, at Constantinople I). So people have to argue that the Roman bishop had that authority but simply didn't exercise it. But is this really plausible? What would be the point of the pope having such a prerogative only to never use it with respect to *any* of the early ecumenical councils, even in times of dire need?[21]

Furthermore, on various occasions, it is clear the bishops gathered in council considered themselves to have authority over and apart from the Roman bishop. This stands in contrast to the strand of teaching at Vatican II that the bishops' authority over the universal church "can be exercised only with the consent of the Roman Pontiff."[22] The conflict between Pope Vigilius and the bishops gathered at the Second Council of Constantinople in 553 (the fifth ecumenical council) illustrates this point dramatically. In the years leading up to the council, the Byzantine Emperor Justinian I had been seeking the condemnation of three persons and/or their writings (the "Three Chapters") in an effort to bring about reunion with the non-Chalcedonian Christians.[23] Pope Vigilius reversed his own position several times, but ultimately opposed the verdict of the council in a solemn declaration called the *First Constitutem*:

> Now that this had been determined by ourselves with all and every care and caution . . . , we enact and decree that no one with ecclesiastical dignity and rank is permitted to hold or write or produce or compose or teach anything about the oft-mentioned Three Chapters contrary to what we have declared and enacted in this present decree, or to raise any further inquiry subsequent to the present definition.[24]

According to Richard Price, Vigilius "could not have stated more unambiguously that his decree was final and left no room for discussion."[25] Yet the bishops at Constantinople II not only persisted in their course but also brought Vigilius under discipline, removing his name from the diptychs of the council (which would be read aloud during the liturgy) and functionally excommunicating him in his person (though not his office).

Having recounted Vigilius's refusal to appear at the council, they declared that "since therefore he has acted in this way, we have pronounced that his name is alien to Christians and is not to be read out in the sacred diptychs."[26] The bishops' reasoning was that their authority as gathered in council was greater than the pope's. Here is how Roman Catholic historian Klaus Schatz puts it in his history of papal primacy:

> [Constantinople II] not only condemned those three chapters but even excommunicated the pope. This was a unique case of an ecumenical council setting itself clearly against the pope and yet not suffering the fate of Ephesus II. Instead, over time it was accepted and even recognized as valid by the pope. The council got around the papal opposition by referring to Matthew 18:20: no individual could therefore forestall the decision of the universal Church.[27]

Vigilius eventually yielded, reversing his policy yet again and publishing the *Second Constitutem*, which solemnly condemned the Three Chapters. Price comments on Vigilius's two contradictory declarations: "It is unusual to have a debate in which two of the lengthiest contributions, arguing for diametrically opposed positions, are written by the same person. It is stranger still when both contributions claim to give the final and definitive ruling, closing the debate for all time."[28] Papal infallibility can perhaps be salvaged by arguing that Vigilius was under duress during this time, but it is difficult to see how papal supremacy can survive an episode like this. It seems clear that the other bishops, gathered in council, regarded themselves as having authority over and apart from the pope. This is their explicit argumentation and action—and at an ecumenical council, no less.

The Papacy Is Not the Solution to Division

This brief overview demonstrates some of the dire biblical and historical challenges to the claims of Vatican I with respect to the papacy. Yet many seem to find the papacy appealing for its practical value. Some argue, for example, that it offers the best pathway for procuring and preserving unity in the church. Only with a central authority that can speak infallibly, it is argued, do we have a decisive mechanism for resolving differences. And to be sure, there is real efficiency and power in having an office with such unparalleled authority.

But for the rest of the Christendom, including not only Protestants but also the Old Catholics and various non-Catholic Eastern traditions, the papacy is arguably the single greatest *barrier* to unity. A metaphor can help explain this. Suppose there are five brothers who quarrel. The eldest insists that everyone must meet at his house to resolve their differences. For him, this is how reconciliation is going to come about. However, because of the breach of trust that has occurred, the others are unwilling to meet there and request a neutral location. Whereas the eldest brother thinks his demand is the pathway to unity, from the perspective of his brothers, it is the greatest obstacle. His insistence on unity in *his* terms and in *his* way impedes the possibility of genuine unity.

This is the kind of concern that the gargantuan claims of the papacy generate throughout non-Roman Christendom. My making *itself* the locus of unity, the Roman Catholic system unfortunately hinders progress towards a true unity—which must be centered on Christ himself.

CHAPTER 8

Apostolic Succession

We have commended *sola Scriptura* as the overall Protestant framework for ecclesial authority, over and against alternatives such as the papacy. Yet more basic, practical questions about authority in the church remain. For example, are Protestant churches even *churches* in the first place? Do they have any authority for valid ministry and valid sacraments?

The non-Protestant traditions, stemming from their affirmation of apostolic succession, generally say *no* (with a few qualifications). It will be useful to briefly address such concerns before leaving this section of the book.

What Is Apostolic Succession?

The basic idea of apostolic succession is that there is an unbroken line of bishops extending from the present-day church back to the apostles. But in its fuller and more technical expressions, apostolic succession usually involves four tenets: (1) the office of bishop is distinct from the office of presbyter/elder *jure divino* (by divine right), with those in the former office specifically designated as the successors of the apostles; (2) bishops exercise regional jurisdiction in an overarching hierarchical unity; (3) valid episcopal succession subsists via the laying on of hands from one bishop to another; (4) apart from valid apostolic succession, there is normally no valid ordained ministry (holy orders) and thus no efficacious sacraments (with only baptism as a frequent exception).

The essential concept was well expressed by John Henry Newman while he was still in the Anglo-Catholic tradition. Addressing other clergy, he identified "apostolical descent" as the ground for ecclesial authority, asserting that "through the Bishop who ordained us, we received the Holy Ghost, the power to bind and to loose, to administer the Sacraments, and to preach."[1] He emphasized that the ceremony of ordination is not idle but actually confers these rights, such that "we must necessarily consider none to be *really* ordained who have not been *thus* ordained."[2] Seen in this light, the defining characteristic of apostolic succession proper is its exclusivism.

In general, apostolic succession is affirmed by all the major churches outside of Protestantism, though sometimes in different forms and with differing perceptions of the validity of each other's episcopal succession. For example, the Roman Catholic Church regards most other churches that affirm apostolic succession (say, the Eastern Orthodox and Oriental Orthodox Churches) to have valid ordinations and a valid Eucharist, but in 1896 Pope Leo XIII issued a papal bull entitled *Apostolicae Curae* declaring all Anglican ordinations null and void. The

Eastern Orthodox Church has tended to reject the validity of the ministry and sacraments in other churches, though there is not one universal view among Orthodox Christians—for example, there is historical precedent for even Anglican priests becoming Orthodox to only be "vested" rather than ordained afresh.[3]

By contrast, most Protestants reject apostolic succession. The exceptions would be among Anglicans, Moravians, neo-Hussites, and some Lutherans—though apostolic succession is not always interpreted as restrictively within these groups. For example, according to Stanley Archer, while the Anglican theologian Richard Hooker thought the historic episcopate "originated with the Apostles, enjoyed divine approval, and flourished throughout Christendom, he rejects the view inherent in the Catholic position that the office is divinely commanded or is a result of divine law."[4]

Those Protestants who oppose apostolic succession do not, of course, deny the general idea that the apostles' ministry succeeds to the post-apostolic Christian church. It is clear the apostles appointed various individuals to positions of leadership in the church with the intent that the ministry of the gospel would continue. As we will see, this is evident from the First Epistle of Clement 44, as well as from the New Testament. Rather, those who oppose apostolic succession in the technical sense object to the specific (and highly exclusivist) way of construing this succession involved in the four ideas listed above (as articulated, for example, by Newman). The deepest concern is not with the development of hierarchical government in the church as such. Rather, the concern is with the necessity of this specific *form* of organization, particularly the formal distinction between bishop and presbyter as of apostolic appointment and the resulting denial of valid ministry apart from this system.

Apostolic Succession in Scholarly Appraisal

Why do most Protestants reject apostolic succession in this sense? Essentially, because there is every reason to conclude that apostolic succession is *not* apostolic. Newman regarded his conception of apostolic succession as a "plain historical fact."[5] Yet this is rejected virtually everywhere in the scholarship. Back in the year 1868, the Anglican scholar J. B. Lightfoot (who was himself a bishop) opened his discussion of Philippians 1:1 with the acknowledgement, "It is a fact now generally recognized by theologians of all shades of opinion, that in the language of the New Testament the same office in the Church is called indifferently 'bishop' (*episkopos*) and 'elder' or 'presbyter' (*presbyteros*)."[6] This view—the original synonymy of the terms bishop and presbyter in the New Testament—has remained the mainstream scholarly position up to the present day. Usually, even those scholars who affirm apostolic succession acknowledge that the distinction between bishop and presbyter—and the notion that the bishop functions in succession to the apostles—itself lacks apostolic authority.

The Roman Catholic scholar Francis Sullivan, for example, opens his book on the topic as follows:

> The question whether the episcopate is of divine institution continues to divide the churches, even though Christian scholars from both sides agree that one does not find the threefold structure of ministry, with a bishop in each local church assisted by presbyters and deacons, in the New Testament. They agree, rather, that the historic episcopate was the result of a development in the post-New Testament period, from the local leadership of a college of presbyters,

who were sometimes called bishops (*episkopoi*), to the leadership of a single bishop. . . . Scholars differ on details, such as
how soon the church of Rome was led by a single bishop, but
hardly any doubt that the church of Rome was still led by a
group of presbyters for at least a part of the second century.[7]

Sullivan is by no means unusual in articulating this view.
Even those who defend episcopal church government typically
argue that it is a gradual development guided by the Holy Spirit,
not a structure extending back to the apostles. For example, the
Roman Catholic scholar Raymond Brown acknowledges that
"the presbyter-bishops described in the NT were not in any
traceable way the successors of the Twelve apostles." Thus, he
argues that "the affirmation that the episcopate was divinely
established or established by Christ himself can be defended in
the nuanced sense that the episcopate gradually emerged in a
Church that stemmed from Christ and that this emergence was
(in the eyes of faith) guided by the Holy Spirit."[8] Even the 1913
Catholic Encyclopedia, in its article on the office of bishop, identifies the following as "fully established" facts:

- "To some extent, in this early period, the words bishop
  and priest (*episkopos* and *presybteros*) are synonymous."
- "In each Community the authority may have originally
  belonged to college of presbyter-bishops."
- "In other communities, it is true, no mention is made of
  a monarchic episcopate until the middle of the second
  century."[9]

Moreover, even those few who deviate from the mainstream
scholarly view generally admit the office of bishop functioned
far differently than is understood by the notion of apostolic

succession. For example, in his recent book, Alistair Stewart argues bishops were distinct from presbyters from the beginning but that they were not successors of the apostles, they did not oversee presbyters, they had no regional jurisdiction (but only a congregational one), and we have no knowledge of how they were appointed or ordained.[10]

We mention the state of scholarship not to settle the issue but to provoke the question, Why do scholars so frequently take this view? The answer is: an abundance of consistent evidence.

Surveying the Early Evidence

Throughout the New Testament, there is a plethora of evidence that local churches had a plurality of leaders. Commonly these leaders are referred to with the term "elder" or "presbyter" (*presbyteros*). James instructed his readers to "call for the elders of the church" to pray for those who are sick (James 5:14). When Paul and Barnabas were in Derbe, Lystra, Iconium, and Antioch, they "appointed elders for them in every church" (Acts 14:23). The book of Acts also indicates there were "elders" at the church in Jerusalem (Acts 11:30; 15:2, 4; 21:18) and at the church in Ephesus (20:17). In Paul's first epistle to Timothy, he referred to "the elders who rule well" at the church at Ephesus (1 Tim. 5:17). In Paul's letter to Titus, he notes that he left Titus in Crete and instructed him to "appoint elders in every town" (Titus 1:5). In 1 Timothy 4:14, Timothy receives a spiritual gift when the council of elders lay hands on him. In 1 Peter 5:1–2, elders shepherd and oversee the flock. In many of these texts, elders appear to be regarded as the authoritative leaders of the church.

In other passages, these leaders are referred to with the term "bishop" or "overseer" (*episkopos*), as in Philippians 1:1, where the letter is addressed to "all the saints in Christ Jesus who are at

Philippi, with the overseers and deacons." Sometimes more general terminology (neither bishop nor presbyter) is used for this plurality of leadership, as in Hebrews 13:7 ("remember your leaders") and 1 Thessalonians 5:12 ("respect those who . . . are over you in the Lord"). In contrast to this, we *never* see a single bishop presiding over any church in the New Testament. Jesus's brother James has a leadership role in the church of Jerusalem, but he is never called a bishop. Paul's associates Titus and Timothy have a kind of itinerant ministry to various churches but are also never referred to as bishops.

Further, the terms *episkopos* (bishop) and *presbyteros* (elder) are clearly used interchangeably in the New Testament. Thus in 1 Peter 5:1–2, elders are described as "overseeing" (*episkopountes*) the church. In Acts 20, Paul addresses the Ephesian "elders" (v. 17) and subsequently calls them "overseers" (v. 28). Significantly, the list of qualifications for bishop in 1 Timothy 3 are unmistakably parallel to those for elder in Titus 1, and not only that, the two terms are used interchangeably in the latter passage:

> This is why I left you in Crete, so that you might put what remained into order, and appoint elders [*presbyterous*] in every town as I directed you—if anyone is above reproach, the husband of one wife, and his children are believers and not open to the charge of debauchery or insubordination. For an overseer [*episkopon*], as God's steward, must be above reproach.

The logic here is as follows: *appoint elders if they are above reproach . . . for a bishop must be above reproach.* This makes no sense unless the terms "bishop" and "elder" refer to one and the same office (for the greater office can include the lesser, but not vice versa). Thus, these two terms, as used by the apostles themselves, do not designate two distinct offices. Instead, the New Testament portrays two offices in the church: bishop/presbyter and deacon.

Looking at the extrabiblical first-century literature, we find the exact same picture. The early treatise the Didache instructs churches to appoint two offices: "Appoint for yourselves bishops and deacons worthy of the Lord."[11] Similarly, the First Epistle of Clement, dating to sometime in the late first century, teaches that the apostles appointed two offices in the church: "They appointed the first fruits [of their labours], having first proved them by the Spirit, to be bishops and deacons of those who should afterwards believe."[12] Clement interprets the constitution of these two offices—bishops and deacons—as the fulfillment of prophecy.[13] Later in his letter, Clement uses the terms *bishop* and *presbyter* interchangeably. For example, in chapter 44, Clement teaches that the apostles established the office of the episcopate and warns that it is no small sin to wrongfully depose those who hold this office (the occurrence of which in Corinth is the occasion of the letter). Yet he then immediately refers to godly holders of this office as "presbyters."[14] Later, in chapters 47 and 57, Clement again refers to the leaders of the church of Corinth—who were deposed but now must be submitted to—as presbyters.[15]

People frequently try to read later developments back into Clement's letter, but read on its own terms, it accords perfectly with the two-office view of the Didache and the New Testament. As Eamon Duffy, a Roman Catholic scholar, summarizes,

> Clement made no claim to write as bishop. His letter was sent in the name of the whole Roman community, he never identifies himself or writes in his own person. . . . The letter itself makes no distinction between presbyters and bishops,

about which it always speaks in the plural, suggesting that at Corinth as at Rome the church at this time was organized under a group of bishops or presbyters, rather than a single ruling bishop. A generation later, this was still so in Rome.[16]

Part of the reason Duffy (with most scholars) thinks the monoepiscopacy (i.e., rule by a single bishop) has not emerged in Rome even a generation after Clement is the testimony of the Shepherd of Hermas, which was written in Rome sometime in the early second century, and which references "the presbyters who preside over the church" and always speaks of the leadership of the church in the plural.[17] Also in the early second century, Polycarp's letter to the Philippians lists qualifications for two offices in the church: deacons and presbyters.[18] The reason scholars generally see the monoepiscopacy as a gradual development is because of these important early second-century texts viewed in combination with the *universal* first-century evidence for only two offices in the church.

The first testimony of the emergence of a clear distinction between the office of bishop and that of presbyter is found in the letters of Ignatius, who staunchly affirms the authority of bishops. However, Ignatius has no conception of apostolic succession: He nowhere speaks of bishops as successors of the apostles, but instead identifies the presbyters as "in the place of assembly of the apostles."[19] He also characterizes bishops as having a congregational rather than diocesan jurisdiction. As Herman Bavinck summarizes, "In the writings of Ignatius, the episcopal idea is still at the beginning of its development. The bishop, here, is not the bearer of tradition, nor a New Testament priest, nor an apostolic succession. . . . He is an office-bearer in a local church and has no authority outside of it."[20] Ignatius is best interpreted as the first witness to the emergence of the office of bishop as a distinct third office in the church in its earliest stage of development. Some have even argued the reason Ignatius so emphasizes the authority of bishops is precisely because the office is in an early, fragile stage.

Toward the end of the second century, in the writings of church leaders like Irenaeus and Tertullian, the seeds of what will eventually become apostolic succession proper begin to emerge. Yet even here, there are surprising wrinkles—for example, Irenaeus identifies the presbyters, also, as the successors of the apostles: "It is incumbent to obey the presbyters who are in the Church—those who, as I have shown, possess the succession from the apostles."[21] Irenaeus and Tertullian functioned in a highly polemical context, striving to protect orthodox teaching over and against Gnostic and other heretical groups that had arisen. For them, a recognition of succession of public office from the apostles was a means of protecting the succession of the true faith over and against Gnostic claims of private revelation.

It is significant that Tertullian, immediately after opposing heretics on the grounds that they lack apostolic succession, adds, "But should they even effect the contrivance, they will not advance a step. For their very doctrine, after comparison with that of the apostles, will declare, by its own diversity and contrariety, that it had for its author neither an apostle nor an apostolic man."[22] In other words, Tertullian reasons that even if the heretics had apostolic succession, it wouldn't matter, because their doctrine was not apostolic. This resonates with the later Protestant instinct to regard succession of office as penultimate and in service of the deeper and ultimate criterion for determining valid ministry: succession of doctrine.

It's not at all surprising that Christians like Tertullian and Irenaeus, living just a few generations from the apostles, would make an appeal like this—nor that they would assume the structure of government they inherited dated back to the apostles. But testimony from a century after the fact is obviously more liable to err than the evidence of the testimony from the time in question—particularly when the late second-century claims of lineal succession contradict each other (as is the case). For example, with respect to the church in Rome, Tertullian thinks Clement was the first bishop, ordained by Peter.[23] Irenaeus, by contrast, states the Roman episcopate began with Linus, who was appointed not by Peter specifically, but by Peter and Paul as apostles: "The blessed apostles, then, having founded and built up the Church, committed into the hands of Linus the office of the episcopate."[24]

Over the course of several centuries, the general idea of a succession of ministry from the apostles to bishops gradually tightened into the notion of a transmission of the spiritual grace necessary for valid ministry and sacraments from bishop to bishop through the laying on of hands. There are good reasons for thinking this larger transition was only accepted around the time of Augustine. In his classic study on the topic, Arthur Headlam describes apostolic succession (in the full-blown sense just defined) and then notes: "I have, I think, read everything from the Fathers which is quoted in favour of Apostolic Succession, and I do not know any passage which speaks of succession by ordination in this sense."[25] Former Archbishop of Canterbury Michael Ramsey notes that opponents of Headlam took the view that apostolic succession (in the sense of a succession of valid ministry) was *implicit* in the second and third centuries.[26]

Thus, in significant fourth-century church orders texts (manuals of disciplinary and liturgical rules for the church) one still finds the requirement that bishops be elected by the entire congregation. For example, canon 2 of the Canons of Hippolytus stipulates: "Let the bishop be ordained after he has been chosen by all the people."[27] Similarly, the Apostolic Constitutions stipulates that "a bishop to be ordained is to be . . . chosen by the whole people."[28] It then describes the people being gathered by the leaders of the church to be asked for their consent on the basis of the nominated bishop's character. After the nominated bishop is asked a series of questions, it states, "and if they agree the third time that he is worthy, let them all be demanded their vote; and when they all give it willingly, let them be heard."[29]

The Testimony of Jerome

Even after apostolic succession had been universally embraced, memory of its development in the early church persisted. Jerome, writing to a presbyter named Evangelus sometime in the late fourth or early fifth century, appealed to many of the same passages I have marshalled here to advance his claim that "the apostle clearly teaches that presbyters are the same as bishops."[30] Jerome saw the development of the monoepiscopacy as a later decision among the presbyters, designed to fight against schism: "When subsequently one presbyter was chosen to preside over the rest, this was done to remedy schism and to prevent each individual from rending the church of Christ by drawing it to himself."[31] Now, Jerome regards this transition as beginning to take place very early on. Nonetheless, the important point is that he does not regard it as by apostolic command. Elsewhere he writes,

> It is therefore the very same priest, who is a bishop, and before there existed men who are slanderers by instinct, and [before] factions in the religion . . . the churches were governed by a

common council of the priests. But after each one began to think that those whom he had baptized were his own and not Christ's, it was decreed for the whole world that one of the priests should be elected to preside over the others.[32]

Jerome then appeals to several biblical passages designed to address "if someone thinks that this is our opinion, but not that of the Scriptures—that bishop and priest are one."[33] These include Philippians 1:1; Acts 20:28; Hebrews 13:7; and 1 Peter 5:1–2. Following his comments on these passages, he concludes,

To the men of old the same men who were the priests were also the bishops; but gradually, as the seed beds of dissensions were eradicated, all solicitude was conferred on one man. Therefore, just as the priests know that by the custom of the church they are subject to the one who previously appointed over them, so the bishops know that they, more by custom than by the truth of the Lord's arrangement, are greater than the priests.[34]

There is much that could be explored in this passage, but what is important for now is simply that Jerome regards the distinction between bishops and presbyters (priests) as originating among the presbyters themselves, in response to a particular historical circumstance—not at the direction of the apostles, as a permanent feature of the Christian church. This is why he calls it a "custom," as distinct from a commandment of the Lord. It is also significant that he sees this transition as gradual. Of course, one could simply argue that Jerome is wrong (though one would then have to posit where he would get such a theory, particularly since Jerome is one of the most erudite historians and scholars in the early church). But it is significant that Jerome's proposal accords with the *unanimous* testimony of the evidence from the time in question. This makes it extremely difficult to avoid the conclusion that apostolic succession, as Jerome teaches, is "custom" rather than *jure divino.*

Interpreting the Development of Apostolic Succession

Nothing conspiratorial need be envisioned to make sense of the development of apostolic succession in the early church. Almost every institution goes through rapid institutionalization after its founder or founders are gone. It is the most natural thing in the world that the early church, facing the triple pressures of heresy, schism, and persecution during the tempestuous second century, and in the absence of the apostles, would evolve a more centralized, hierarchical organization. And indeed, further such developments continue (for example, the emergence and evolution of the office of archbishop in the fourth, fifth, and sixth centuries).

The recognition that apostolic succession is not of divine constitution but rather represents a gradual development in the early church need not necessarily entail that there is anything particularly *wrong* with episcopal church government as such. On prudential grounds, one could make a case for elevating one presbyter into a unique role above others or even calling such a presbyter a different term. But *requiring* such a structure—as well as limiting valid ministry to those churches adhering to it—unnecessarily injures and divides the church.

Only within Protestantism can one be free from such a requirement.

One last observation: Sometimes people wonder how apostolic succession can be wrong if it's present in *all* the non-Protestant traditions? A metaphor can help us answer this worry.

Suppose in the year 2030, the state of California splits up into three distinct states: Southern California, Central California, and Northern California. Subsequently, in the year 2100, a sociologist conducts a study of the culture, politics, and language of the three states. He is amazed by all the commonalities between them and cannot explain how this could have come about.

The proper response to the sociologist is, *Duh!* Shared culture is exactly what we would expect, given the shared history. A rupture of institutional or formal alignment does not preclude common belief and common culture. In the same way, having common beliefs among the non-Protestant traditions is totally unsurprising, since they have a shared history in which the beliefs came about. What is more surprising is why these traditions retain a necessary commitment to such beliefs when (1) they have such poor evidence backing them and (2) they serve to separate each tradition, not just from Protestantism, but to some extent from each other.

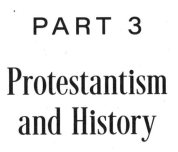

PART 3

Protestantism
and History

CHAPTER 9

Protestantism as Retrieval

There is perhaps no more popular anti-Protestant slogan than the famous quip by John Henry Newman: "To be deep in history is to cease to be Protestant."[1]

The statement comes near the beginning of his famous *Essay on the Development of Doctrine.* In context, Newman is interacting with the seventeenth-century Anglican theologian William Chillingworth, who had argued that church history lacks coherence or unity, and therefore only Scripture can provide a solid foundation for Christian belief. As Chillingworth had put it,

> I see plainly and with my own eyes, that there are popes against popes, councils against councils, some fathers against others, the same fathers against themselves, a consent of fathers of one age against a consent of fathers of another age, the church of one age against the church of another age. . . .

In a word, there is no sufficient certainty but of Scripture only for any considering man to build upon.[2]

Interestingly, Newman responded by conceding that there is a degree of ambiguity in the testimony of church history and then casting his theory of doctrinal development in response to this challenge: "This is a fair argument, if it can be maintained, and it brings me at once to the subject of this Essay."[3] Nonetheless, before embarking on that larger task, he offers "one remark to Chillingworth and his friends." This remark is essentially that while church history may be ambiguous at points, it is *unambiguous* in standing against Protestantism. As he puts it,

> And this one thing at least is certain; whatever history teaches, whatever it omits, whatever it exaggerates or extenuates, whatever it says and unsays, at least the Christianity of history is not Protestantism. If ever there were a safe truth, it is this.[4]

Newman further states that Protestantism has always recognized this, citing the neglect of church history among Anglicans in his own day as an example. Then comes, without any further elaboration or explanation, his famous assertion: "To be deep in history is to cease to be Protestant."

Evidently Newman thought this point was so obvious that it did not even need to be argued. It concludes his brief digression responding to Chillingworth, though a bit later he adds, "That Protestantism, then, is not the Christianity of history, it is easy to determine,"[5] and elsewhere, "This utter incongruity between Protestantism and historical Christianity is a plain fact."[6]

Those who triumphantly deploy this passage against Protestants today often underappreciate how fiercely controversial it was within the Catholic Church when it was first written—at a time when Newman was himself still Protestant and suspected by many to have an outlook that remained too Anglican.[7] There are other ambiguities in Newman's position that are often overlooked in its popular usage as well (e.g., his usage of the word "Protestant" in this sentence is ambiguous, since he has just been referring to England's "popular religion," and later in the essay he distinguishes Protestantism and Anglicanism somewhat).[8] But here let us pass over these to tackle the main issue: Is church history fundamentally opposed to Protestantism, as Newman claims?

An initial point of awkwardness with the "deep in history" line is all the counterexamples. Take, for instance, the massive contributions of Protestant scholarship to the field of church history. What student of church history does not benefit from Philip Schaff's pioneering work in patristics or J. N. D. Kelly's popular text *Early Christian Doctrines*?[9] It was a Protestant (James Ussher) who identified the authentic letters of Ignatius; it was a Protestant (J. B. Lightfoot) who produced the first definitive critical edition of the writings of the apostolic fathers. On and on we could go with examples like these. We stand on the shoulders of their labors. By any reasonable criterion, they seem to be exceptions to Newman's quip. They were deep in history. They remained Protestant.

But perhaps Newman was speaking of a more general tendency. So, leaving individual scholars aside, what about general Protestant beliefs and practices? Are they obviously undermined by church history, as Newman claims?

It is worth engaging this perspective a bit because this is one of the most common critiques of Protestantism. Although Newman himself became Roman Catholic, critiques from other traditions often share this basic perception that church history and Protestant Christianity are utterly alien to one another. And granted, there is much in contemporary, popular-level Protestant practice to make this characterization comprehensible.

At the same time, Newman's criticism is more difficult to pin on official expressions of historic Protestant theology. In fact, it is the exact opposite of how the original Protestants understood their efforts. To be "deep in history" was the whole rationale for Protestantism. It will be useful to simply describe the Protestant claim in this regard before evaluating it.

Calvin on Renewing the "Ancient Form of the Church"

Long before Newman, the Reformers faced the charge of *novelty* from their opponents in the Counter-Reformation. Essentially, many claimed Protestants were introducing new doctrines, unknown to prior church history. In response, the Reformers did not appeal to Scripture alone, ceding church history to their opponents. Rather, they argued *from* history, casting the Protestant effort as a retrieval of patristic practice and thereby a return to catholicity—that is, the doctrine and practice that is most representative of the fullness of the church.

The Protestant outlook was that alongside all the good God was doing in the history of the church, various aberrations, declensions, innovations, accretions, and errors crept in along the way. The point of Protestantism was to remove the errors. Their goal was to return to ancient Christianity, to a version *prior* to the intrusion of various accretions.

For example, the early Protestants argued *on catholic and historical grounds* against the idea that there are seven sacraments, that the bishop of Rome has universal and immediate jurisdiction over the church, that Mary was bodily assumed to heaven, that kissing and bowing down to icons is necessary, that transubstantiation is the mechanism of real presence in the Eucharist, that the treasury of merit benefits Christians, that indulgences or masses for deceased Christians could grant them reduced time in purgatory, that the Scripture need not be translated into the vernacular languages of the laity, that the Lord's Supper need not be taken in both kinds, and so forth. We will review some of these arguments in the following chapters; first we want to explicate the *nature* of the Protestant claim.

In his prefatory letter to King Francis at the start of the *Institutes*, John Calvin protested how selectively the church fathers were deployed against the Protestants, claiming that "if the contest were to be determined by patristic authority, the tide of victory . . . would turn to our side."[10] Calvin then worked through twelve examples of specific points of dispute, highlighting church fathers who opposed Roman Catholic teaching concerning ministerial celibacy, the use of images in worship, the doctrine of transubstantiation, the administration of the Mass to the laity, fasting regulations, the authority of councils in relation to Scripture, and on many other points.[11]

For Calvin, the church fathers were not neatly and unanimously in line with either the Protestants *or* the Catholics. He did not claim patristic support on every point of dispute. Indeed, he pointed out that the church fathers were not even consistent with each other, since they "often disagreed among themselves, and sometimes even contradicted themselves."[12] Calvin maintained that their writings contained many good and excellent teachings, but also argued that they were not infallible and thus made errors. So for Calvin, the church fathers were a subordinate testimony to holy Scripture. Nonetheless, Calvin respected and valued the patristic witness and maintained that, on the whole, it undermined the Catholic position.

In his reply to Cardinal Jacopo Sadoleto a few years later,

Calvin cast Protestantism as, at its core, an effort to renew ancient Christianity:

> You know, Sadolet . . . not only that our agreement with antiquity is far closer than yours, but that all we have attempted has been to renew that ancient form of the Church, which, at first sullied and distorted by illiterate men of indifferent character, was afterwards flagitiously mangled and almost destroyed by the Roman Pontiff and his faction.[13]

By "antiquity" and "ancient," Calvin appears to have been thinking broadly of the third to fifth centuries. (Later he qualifies the time period he is thinking of as "the age of Chrysostom and Basil, among the Greeks, and of Cyprian, Ambrose, and Augustine, among the Latins."[14])

Much of his response to Sadoleto consisted in working through various examples of how the Church of Rome in his day had totally abandoned the early church's doctrine, discipline, sacraments, and ceremonies, such that only the "ruins" of this ancient church remained in his own day: "Where, pray, exist among you any vestiges of that true and holy discipline, which the ancient bishops exercised in the Church? Have you not scorned all their institutions? Have you not trampled all the Canons under foot?"[15] Calvin maintained that on these and many other points, being deep in history only strengthened the Protestant concerns: "The ancient Church is clearly on our side, and opposes you, not less than we ourselves do."[16]

Lutheran and Anglican Testimonies

This historical argumentation was not unique to Calvin or the Reformed tradition more generally. Though the Anabaptist tradition generally took less interest in church history, Calvin's approach is representative of the magisterial Reformation on the whole. The Augsburg Confession, the primary Lutheran confession and one of the most important Protestant confessions, opens its preface to Emperor Charles V by expressing a desire for unity among Christians. Stemming from this, it describes Lutheranism as, quite simply, a rejection of novelty for the sake of retaining catholicity: "In doctrine and ceremonials among us there is nothing received contrary to Scripture or to the Catholic Church, inasmuch as it is manifest that we have diligently taken heed that no new and godless doctrines should creep into our Churches."[17]

What kinds of novelties and abuses were the Lutherans attempting to reform? They argued that there were too many to recount them all, but as one representative example they identified the degeneration of monasteries into widespread and pervasive legalism. By the late medieval era it had become sadly prevalent to seek forgiveness of sins and justification from God in mendicant orders, in pilgrimages and indulgences, and in avoiding marriage and civil office. The Lutherans built a historical case against such practices by contrasting the nature of monastic obligations in Augustine's day with the vows and other observances that were afterwards added on, little by little, as accretions.[18]

To give another example, the Lutherans objected on historical grounds to the violence and tyranny that resulted from a confusion of ecclesiastical and civil power in the church:

> There have been great controversies touching the power of bishops; in which many have incommodiously mingled together the ecclesiastical power, and the power of the sword. And out of this confusion there have sprung very great wars

and tumults; while that the pontiffs, trusting in the power of the keys, have not only appointed new kinds of service, and burdened men's consciences by reserving of cases, and by violent excommunications; but have also endeavored to transfer worldly kingdoms from one to another, and to despoil emperors of their power and authority.[19]

We have already discussed medieval papal claims over civil authorities; for now it is sufficient to note that when the Lutherans objected to this theology, they did so on historical grounds. They saw it as a departure not merely from Scripture, but from how the early church wielded authority and related to civil power.

Within the Anglican tradition, John Jewel's *Apology of the Church of England* represented this same kind of historical and catholic argumentation for Protestantism. Over and over, he appealed to the "Catholic fathers," the "primitive church," and "the examples of many ages" as a criterion for dissent from Rome, in addition to Holy Scripture.[20] "The ancient bishops," he maintained, "and the primitive Church do make on our side."[21]

A flavor of Jewel's historical posture can be gathered from his treatment of the Eucharist. Jewel opposed transubstantiation with quotations from Gelasius, Ambrose, Theodoret, Augustine, Cyrpian, Chrysostom, Origen, and others.[22] He then clarified that, in affirming that bread and wine remain in substance, he had no intention of thereby denying the real presence of Christ in the Eucharist: "and in speaking thus we mean not to abase the Lord's Supper, that it is but a cold ceremony only, and nothing to be wrought therein (as many falsely slander us we teach). For we affirm, that Christ doth truly and presently give His own self in His Sacraments."[23] For Jewel and most of the early Protestants, the concern was not that Christ is *not* present in the Eucharist, but that bread and wine *are* present. In other words, all they denied was that, in the communication of Christ to the believing recipient of the Eucharist, the bread and wine ceased to be bread and wine in substance.

But even more basically, apart from the question of how Christ is present in the bread and wine, the Protestants were concerned with all manner of abusive and negligent practices in the administration of the Eucharist in the late medieval Western church. Jewel, for example, railed against the wanton buying and selling of masses, the parading about and venerating of the consecrated host (and the pomp associated with it), the extremely infrequent partaking of the elements by the laity, and the withholding of the wine from the laity and giving of the bread only.[24] Such practices, Jewel maintained, amounted to clear departure from patristic precedent and resulted in a starvation of the laity from a regular and full experience of feasting on Christ. Jewel also opposed the notion that the merits of Christ's death are applied in the mass through the action of the priest, irrespective of the faith or understanding of the recipient.[25]

Over and over these concerns are established not just by Scripture but also by appeals to Augustine, Origen, Theodoret, and more. The general character of Jewel's Eucharistic theology— both in its concern for the laity and its appeal to history—can be gleaned from this passage, as an example:

> When the people cometh to the Holy Communion, the Sacrament ought to be given them in both kinds: for so both Christ hath commanded, and the Apostles in every place have ordained, and all the ancient fathers and Catholic bishops have followed the same. And whoso doth contrary to this, he (as Gelasius saith) committeth sacrilege. And therefore we say, that our adversaries at this day, who having violently

thrust out, and quite forbidden the Holy Communion, do, without the word of God, without the authority of any ancient council, without any Catholic father, without any example of the primitive Church, yea, and without reason also, defend and maintain their private masses, and the mangling of the Sacraments, and do this not only against the plain express commandment and bidding of Christ, but also against all antiquity, do wickedly therein, and are very Church robbers.[26]

Note here Jewel's appeal not only to the apostolic practice but also to the church fathers, councils, and indeed, "all antiquity."[27]

Summarizing the Protestant View of History

For centuries, this kind of historical argumentation was part of the classical way of doing "Protestant apologetics." This was the whole appeal of magisterial Protestantism: patristic moorings plus catholicity. Some Protestants devoted their entire theological careers to exploring patristic and medieval texts, developing ever more nuanced accounts of the slow development of the church's faith and practice throughout history. The Lutherans were particularly sophisticated in this effort. It was in relation to such attempts that the words *patristics* and *patrology* arose in their technical meanings from within the Lutheran tradition in the seventeenth century.[28] It is unfortunate that this historical approach is less common among Protestants today, and part of the implicit goal of this book is to retrieve this more catholic and historical way of envisioning Protestantism.

At this point a few clarifications are in order. First, as I have already indicated, the early Protestants were not arguing that on *every* point, the patristic testimony favored Protestantism.

This is not so. Various matters of doctrine or ceremony came in early in church history that, yet, the Protestants saw as error. An easy example is praying for the dead (yet it is also worth saying that many Protestants have no objection to this practice *as such*). The patristic era had, for all the glorious work God did during that time, its own eccentricities and oddities. For Protestants, the early church does not represent an exact blueprint to be followed in all details—though we benefit greatly from learning from the early Christians. Still, Protestants argued that on the *primary* matters of the Christian religion, the early church supported their cause while also undermining the overly ambitious historical claims of their opponents in the Church of Rome (and, we would say today, of several of the Eastern traditions as well).

Second, the Protestants were not arguing that, by the late medieval era, the church had died and needed resurrection. This is a common caricature. Consistently the Reformers affirmed the opposite—that God had faithfully preserved his church, even in the darkest times. Calvin, for example, denied the charge that Protestants believed the true church had fallen away: "Surely the church of Christ has lived and will live so long as Christ reigns at the right hand of his Father. It is sustained by his hand; defended by his protection; and is kept safe through his power. . . . Against this church we have no quarrel."[29] All Calvin maintained is that the true church is not discerned by outward magnificence and is not identified with the Roman Catholic hierarchy.[30] Luther held the same view, as we have already seen. The Reformers disagreed on many points, but on this point, they were all united. The church never died. Jesus had faithfully preserved her for every nanosecond of church history. We may call this Protestant doctrine "the preservation of the church."[31]

Thus, the Protestants understood themselves to be reforming an imperfect thing, not resurrecting a dead thing or creating a new thing. On this basis they resisted terms like *new* or *novelty* to describe their historical position. The Reformed theologian Francis Turretin put it like this: "It is one thing to purge an ancient doctrine of its corruption and recall men to it; another to devise a new doctrine not as yet delivered and propose it for belief. The former, not the latter, was done by the Reformers."[32] Elsewhere Turretin furthered this contention by distinguishing between different senses of the word *new*. The reform effort was new, claimed Turretin, but not the religion *being* reformed. Turretin complained that the charge of novelty against the Protestants confused these two categories: "The newness of the Reformation is urged as showing the newness of the religion." But according to Turretin, the former does not entail the latter. As he argued,

> Reformation is nothing else than the purging of the errors and corruptions brought by the papacy into the doctrine of faith and practice delivered by Christ. The Reformation is indeed new (i.e., recently made, as supposing the preceding state of the church to have been corrupt), but not on this account by this Reformation was a new religion or church instituted which had not existed before; rather that which existed already was made better by the ancient rule (to wit, the word of God).[33]

Ultimately, Turretin reversed the charge of novelty against the Catholics. Listing as examples the veneration of images, the supreme authority of the pope in both temporal and spiritual matters, transubstantiation, purgatory, and communion in only one kind, he argued that "it could easily be shown both that they were unknown to the apostolic and primitive church and were introduced afterwards at various times and so are novel and more recent."[34] Turretin sketched out a timeframe for the development of each of these doctrines, highlighting when they fully blossomed in the medieval period.

Now, let us suppose for the sake of argument that all the Protestants were wrong. Calvin, Jewel, Gerhard, Turretin, and the rest misread the fathers. In that circumstance, what would be necessary is a careful investigation of the historical evidence to demonstrate how the Protestants erred in their historical claim. What obviously will not suffice is jubilant quotations of Newman, as though simply repeating "to be deep in history is to cease to be Protestant" settled the matter. Instead, we must patiently work through the historical data.

That is essentially what we will do in the next two chapters. But before getting into the specifics, we must qualify the Protestant claim in three ways: first, by acknowledging how much of contemporary Protestantism has indeed fallen away from the original Protestant vision; second, by specifying what it means to be "deep in history" from a Protestant viewpoint; and finally, by clarifying that the Protestant historical argument is not focused on the outward form or appearance of the church but more on her essential faith and doctrine.

The Drift of Many Contemporary Protestant Churches

Many critics of Protestantism will immediately dismiss the interpretation of the Reformation as a historical retrieval and a removal of accretions because of the general sense of historical shallowness in many contemporary Protestant churches. This brings up a point that represents a theme of this book: We must distinguish between particular contemporary expressions of Protestantism versus Protestantism *as such*. Too often a criticism of the former is construed as a necessary rejection of the latter.

Part of the reason more caution is needed in describing Protestantism is that in many contemporary contexts (like the United States), Protestantism is the dominant form of religion, and the prevailing form of Protestantism tends to be more "free-spirited" and individualistic. Many contemporary Protestant churches have drifted from historic Protestant expressions of worship, from historic Protestant understanding and administration of the sacraments, and even from historic Protestant views of church membership, the nature of preaching, and how faith and works go together in salvation. Thus, the average experience at a contemporary Protestant church in such a context may not be characterized by historical depth. (This is one reason why Protestants can be tremendously enriched by dialogue with the non-Protestant traditions. It will challenge us in our modern deviations.)

When I press this distinction between contemporary expressions of Protestantism versus Protestantism as such in dialogue with Catholic and Orthodox interlocuters, I often meet resistance. Many people have seen so much historical, liturgical, and sacramental shallowness within Protestantism that they believe such features are essential to the movement. I would appeal for greater charity and carefulness. By analogy, think of a country in the world that is majority Catholic or majority Orthodox. Is it not the case that street-level practices and beliefs in such a context will often fail to give you an accurate and full-orbed representation of the official teaching of the church in question? Any reasonable appraisal of a tradition must distinguish between street-level expression and official representation. It is unfair to judge the whole from the parts or the official from the happenstance.[35]

So yes, Protestant churches often suffer from "historical drift" and need reform. But crucially, so do many non-Protestant churches. In the next few chapters I will argue that many of the essential, necessary features of Roman Catholic and Eastern Orthodox theology and worship represent historical innovation and error. The difference, then, between the various sectors of Christendom is not whether we need reform. The difference is this: Protestants are *able* to reform themselves because built into the Protestant system at the outset is a mechanism of self-reform (*semper reformanda*, always reforming). By contrast, the practices that need reform in Roman Catholic and Eastern Orthodox contexts result from what is held to be infallible teaching and are thus irreformable.

When in dialogue with non-Protestant friends, I often press this definition of Protestantism as the removal of accretions in pursuit of catholicity. Sometimes the response is, "But Protestantism has accretions, too!" This I happily concede. Accretions are inevitable. In an imperfect world, the intrusion of errors will be a constant possibility and frequent occurrence.

The difference is that Protestant accretions are not enshrined within allegedly infallible teaching.

What Does It Mean to Be "Deep in History"?

Another complicating factor in assessing the historical placement of Protestantism is that each side has different intuitions and presuppositions for how to conceptualize historical depth. We will talk past one another unless we probe what the word *deep* means in the phrase "deep in history."

One way of envisioning historical depth is by focusing on what is most visible, most prominent, and/or most widely represented throughout church history. On this view, to be "deep in history" has a more diachronic thrust: It is more oriented toward the trajectory and overall result of church history. Thus, historical depth will focus more on what *eventually* becomes mainstream, widely accepted, or officially selected along the way of history. I will call this understanding of being deep in history "majority depth."

This is the kind of historical depth that is assumed in many historical criticisms of Protestantism. For example, I sometimes encounter the appeal, "How can you possibly maintain that Protestants are deep in history when they reject the seventh ecumenical council?" Now, not all Protestants *do* reject the seventh ecumenical council. But the relevant point right now is that the seventh ecumenical council took place in 787, which is farther from the apostles than we are from the Reformation. My argument in chapter 11 will be that this council represents the triumph of a position that was virtually unknown for the first several centuries of church history, almost unimaginably contentious for the next several, and ultimately resisted in various regions of the West for several further centuries after that. Whether this historical interpretation is correct, it is already clear that to assess whether Nicaea II is "deep in history," we must work through different ways of measuring what constitutes historical depth.

To be clear, Protestants do not regard "majority depth" as insignificant or unimportant. On the contrary, it is a behemoth, a force to be reckoned with. But they do maintain that what is finally decisive is the original teaching of the apostles, and that there are practices and beliefs that occasionally become mainstream despite departing from apostolic teaching. On this view, what is *deepest* is what is *oldest* and thereby most plausibly rooted in the first-century apostolic deposit. This view is also interested in what remains most constitutive of basically all Christians throughout church history (what C. S. Lewis called "mere Christianity"). We can call this "ancient depth."

So we have two different kinds of depth: majority depth and ancient depth. The Protestant position is that the majority must be measured by the ancient, not vice versa. In adopting this position, the early Protestants appealed to a principle widely articulated among the church fathers: namely, that in the absence of biblical attestation, earlier traditions were more reliable than later traditions because they more plausibly represented faithfulness to apostolic teaching. For example, in his *Examination of the Council of Trent*, the Lutheran theologian Martin Chemnitz used this passage in Cyprian, noting Augustine's approval of it as well:

> If we return to the head and origin of the divine tradition, human error will cease. For if the channel of water, which before flowed copiously and purely, either fails or brings muddy water, then certainly one goes to the source in order to find out whether there is something wrong in the veins or in the source, or whether something got in midway.[36]

This metaphor captures the Protestant approach to historical depth: When you have muddy water in a stream, you have to go back to see where it came in. The pure water will be found *before* the muddy water started. When you hear Protestants speak of being "deep in history," picture the *deeper* (earlier) parts of the channel of water. "Deep" means early.

The ultimate reasons for prioritizing ancient depth over majority depth result from the arguments of part 2 of the book (for example, the unique authority and nature of Scripture). But here we can canvass two further considerations from a historical point of view that underpin the Protestant mentality.

The first consideration is something Newman was forced to reckon with: What eventually becomes mainstream or a majority view in church history is an unstable guide. One striking example is Augustine's affirmation of the damnation of unbaptized babies. While there were qualifications to this notion, such as the idea of limbo, Augustine's general position remains overwhelmingly dominant, such that I am not aware of *any* Western theologians who affirmed that deceased unbaptized babies receive the beatific vision (full salvation) in the West between Augustine and the Reformation.

A 2007 Roman Catholic study, resulting from a commission from Pope John Paul II on this matter, surveys Latin fathers who affirmed Augustine's view (Jerome, Fulgentius, Avitus of Vienne, and Gregory the Great), as well as medieval theologians such as Anselm and Hugh of St. Victor; the only exception in the late medieval period (following Peter Lombard) is the mitigation of this punishment to mere deprivation of the beatific vision.[37] Again, I cannot find a single person during this time period who affirmed that deceased unbaptized infants are fully saved. This was common in the East as well (though I do not know the historical record there well enough to say whether there were exceptions).[38] For example, the seventeenth-century Patriarch of Jerusalem Dositheus, claimed, "and, therefore, [Baptism] is necessary even for infants, since they also are subject to original sin (τῇ ἀρχεγόνῳ ἁμαρτία), and without Baptism are not able to obtain remission." If majority depth is our criterion, I can imagine little possibility to overturn this view. Happily, many in both the East and the West no longer hold this view today.

There are many other examples of the slipperiness of "majority depth" we could work through. Gregory of Nyssa's condemnation of slavery is, sadly, in the overwhelming minority among premodern Christians. There were many criticisms of slavery in the premodern world, but usually they concerned the abuse of the institution, not the institution as such. Gregory argued that slavery is inherently and essentially wrong; most others, from St. Augustine to Thomas Aquinas, held slavery to a less-than-ideal but permissible social arrangement. [39]

Similarly, few Christians today would maintain the common perception among premodern Christians that women are inferior to men in various regards. Thomas Aquinas spoke of women as "defective and misbegotten," resulting from a kind of defect in male seed. (Regrettably, the passage is not more forgivable in context.)[40] Augustine likewise held many other views most of us would find sexist today, such as the claim that, if it were not for the purpose of procreation, another man would have been a far more suitable companion to Adam in the Garden of Eden: "how much more agreeably, after all, for conviviality and conversation, would two male friends live together on equal terms than man and wife?"[41] The influence of Augustine and Aquinas was such that it led to a widespread perception in premodern theology that men and women did not constitute the image of God equally (e.g., a common theme is that men constitute the image of God by themselves, while women only did so in coordination to men). As one who regards Augustine and Aquinas in the highest regard and who regularly seeks to defend them from critique, I have to acknowledge that they held problematic views in some areas, many of which became mainstream in the church.

I understand that these are not points of magisterial teaching for Catholic or Orthodox Christians. The point is simply to show that mainstream depth is a slippery guide. After all, Newman's quip was not referencing merely magisterial teaching, but history generally. The point here is simple: Errors can become mainstream. Anyone who studies church history knows how easily this can happen.

Imagine someone saying to you, "To be deep in history is to cease to affirm the salvation of unbaptized babies who die."

How would you respond? As you think through an answer, you are likely on the road to understanding why Protestants want to clarify the meaning of the word *deep*.

Another reason to be uneasy with "majority depth" as our criterion is the history of the people of Israel. If anything emerges from the story of the Old Testament, it is surely this: God's people continually fall away and need to return to the Lord. The people of God have *never* enjoyed unbroken spiritual steadiness from one century to the next. On the contrary, the entire history of the Jewish people prior to Christ can be summarized as a recurrent pattern of idolatry and reform. Think of the book of Judges, for example. Or take the downward spiral of the book of Kings. So prevalent were idolatrous accretions that even during the reform efforts of good kings like Josiah and Hezekiah, many of the idolatrous high places remained in use.

Again and again throughout redemptive history, the majority goes awry. The followers of Ahab could have appealed to majority depth against Elijah or Micaiah, who stood alone with the truth against a huge majority of false prophets and corrupt leaders. In the New Testament as well, the apostles could have been condemned by this same criterion by the Pharisees, who claimed to be the legitimate successors of Moses. As Jewel puts it:

> So likewise the false prophets of all ages, which stood up against the prophets of God, which resisted Esaias, Jeremy, Christ, and the Apostles, at no time craked of anything so much as they did of the name of the Church. And for no other cause did they so fiercely vex them, and call them runaways and apostates, than for that they forsook their fellowship, and kept not the ordinances of the elders. Wherefore, if we would follow the judgments of those men only who then governed

the Church, and would respect nothing else, neither God nor His word, it must needs be confessed, that the Apostles were rightly and by just law condemned of them to death.[42]

Christians in the non-Protestant traditions will often argue that God has promised to watch over his church in ways that distinguish her from Israel. For example, Christ promised that "the gates of hell shall not prevail" against the church in Matthew 16:18. But this is a promise that the church will never die or fail to accomplish her purpose, not that she will never sin or err. The verb "prevail" can be translated "overpower" or "overcome";[43] to be "prevailed against" by the "gates of hell" refers essentially to death.[44] If a wrestling coach promised one of his wrestlers that "your opponent will not prevail against you," this means his wrestler will ultimately win, not that he will avoid making any mistakes during the match.

Furthermore, this is a promise to the church as such, not to one particular teaching office or hierarchy within her. Therefore, that Christ will never abandon his church to hell no more substantiates claims of ecclesial infallibility than God's Old Testament promises to Israel validated the Pharisees' teachings and claims. God has promised many things to his people, but he has nowhere promised that they will not fall into sin and error. This is why Protestants, in the face of some frankly *brutal* historical realities, consider majority depth to be a frequently superficial criterion.

So again, imagine someone saying to you, "To be deep in history is to cease to follow Elijah and instead trust the Israelite monarchy God established." As you think through how to respond, you will likely gain some sympathy for why Protestants want to clarify the meaning of the word *deep*.

The Outward Form of the Church

Someone might say, "Okay, even if we grant that the Catholic and Orthodox traditions have some accretions, what do you say about all the ways Protestantism looks different from the early church?"

Part of the answer to this is that, again, people are often looking at street-level practice rather than official theology. But another factor is that we must distinguish between what is accidental versus essential in the church. There are lots of ways the early church looks different from *every* church today concerning her outward forms and expression. For example, it was hugely significant for the early church's government, administration, and even doctrine that she germinated in the context of the Roman Empire. The Roman Emperor was understood as the co-ruler with God, the guardian of the peace of the church, and so forth. A Roman Emperor convoked and presided over all the ecumenical councils, and many emperors made other important contributions. It is hard to even begin to fathom how different the church might have looked had Constantine never converted to Christianity.[45]

Yet after the Roman Empire ended, the church continued. That imperial structure was not essential to the church. The Roman Empire is an example that something can be enormously influential to the church's development but still accidental to her identity.

This is one reason why Protestant Christians generally have a more flexible view of how the true church passes from one place and time to another. The church can and does take many different outward forms and expressions and yet remain the true church because what makes her the church is the presence of Christ in word and sacrament. Thus, Protestants are *not* claiming the early church looked like Protestant churches in all aspects of their outward form and appearance. On matters that are central to the church's life and doctrine, however, I maintain that Protestantism represents a genuine return to the general, earlier, catholic precedent.

And, in the other direction, Protestants absolutely reject the claim that the non-Protestant churches have preserved the faith untainted. No contemporary church looks just like the early church. Only the most superficial acquaintance with church history can deny this. Speaking of Roman Catholicism, for example, C. S. Lewis put it like this: "The Roman Church where it differs from this universal tradition and specifically from apostolic Christianity I reject. . . . The whole set-up of modern Romanism seems to me to be as much a provincial or local variation from the ancient tradition as any particular Protestant sect is."[46] Thus, when Protestants are told by other Christians that their church looks different from the early church, Lewis's reply probably provides the best brief retort: *So does yours.*

Looking Ahead

This has been a modest chapter. We have not yet done the kind of in-depth work that would constitute a decisive historical argument for Protestantism. That comes next. We have simply tried to prepare the way by accurately describing Protestant's overall historical claim, as articulated by its founders.

Now we turn to assess some of these historical claims. In advance, I will say that the historical evidence usually does not support simple and triumphalist answers. Apologists on all sides love to say, "*All* the church fathers said _____." Sometimes the historical evidence is neat and uniform like this, but usually it is not. Rarely will we find history convenient. Often all sides will be challenged. Honestly, to be truly in history is, before anything else, to cease making simplistic appeals to history.

Nonetheless, on a few points, the historical picture is quite decisive. And when it is so, we don't want to understate our case, either. So I will preface the next two chapters by risking a bold summary: To any sane historical evaluation, it is *overwhelmingly* probable that neither the assumption of Mary nor the veneration of images were known to the apostles—or any Christian within several centuries of their lifetimes.

CHAPTER 10

Case Study: Mary's Assumption

These final two chapters will be, necessarily, a bit more involved. Having described Protestantism's historical posture as reforming the ancient church through the removal of accretions, we now turn to evaluate whether this effort has any merit. *Are the doctrines and practices rejected by the Reformers accretions?*

Obviously, we cannot cover every possible doctrine. So the best way to proceed is to canvass representative examples or case studies.

There are many issues we could choose. I have done lengthy videos on topics like purgatory, for example, and praying to the saints. Here I begin with the bodily assumption of Mary. Several factors combine to make this dogma a particularly apt starting point.

First, as the most recent Roman Catholic dogma, it represents a point at which the Protestant-Catholic divide is widening.

While ecumenical dialogue has made progress in other areas, with respect to Mariology we are arguably further apart today than we were in the sixteenth century—particularly since the immaculate conception of Mary was defined in 1854 and her bodily assumption was defined in 1950. Meanwhile, calls for a fifth Marian dogma in some Roman Catholic circles raise questions of future trajectory. One website associated with this movement notes that "well over 8 million priests, religious and lay faithful and over 800 Cardinals and Bishops from more than 180 countries have sent petitions to recent popes in favor of the solemn definition: the Mother of Jesus is Spiritual Mother of all humanity in her three maternal roles as Co-redemptrix, Mediatrix of all graces and Advocate."[1] Whatever happens, Mariology is undeniably a live, critical area of ecumenical concern.

Second, Mary's bodily assumption into heaven is not just a Protestant versus Roman Catholic issue, since it is included in the liturgy of Eastern Churches like Eastern Orthodoxy and Oriental Orthodoxy. These traditions have minor differences with the Roman Catholic position. For example, in the East, Mary's Dormition (or falling asleep) is generally affirmed prior to her assumption (whereas the Roman Catholic dogma leaves open whether Mary died or not). Nonetheless, these various traditions are united in their affirmation of Mary's ultimate bodily entry into heaven. Thus, the assumption of Mary marks a fault line of division between the vast majority of Protestantism versus the vast majority of non-Protestant Christendom. With only a few exceptions, it's a "Protestantism vs. everyone else" issue. (Nonetheless, for clarity and scope, our focus in this chapter will be on the Roman Catholic dogma, specifically.)

Third and most significant, the importance placed upon Mary in the non-Protestant traditions make it an unavoidable barrier. For example, immediately after the definition of the bodily assumption of Mary in Pope Pius XII's 1950 Encyclical *Munificentissimus Deus*, the following consequence is attached: "if anyone, which God forbid, should dare willfully to deny or to call into doubt that which we have defined, let him know that he has fallen away completely from the divine and Catholic Faith."[2] Just afterwards another warning is added:

> It is forbidden to any man to change this, our declaration, pronouncement, and definition or, by rash attempt, to oppose and counter it. If any man should presume to make such an attempt, let him know that he will incur the wrath of Almighty God and of the Blessed Apostles Peter and Paul.[3]

This language can be qualified in various ways (e.g., what precisely constitutes a "willful" rejection? What kind of opposition is made by "rash attempt"?). But the general point remains that the bodily assumption of Mary is held to be an infallible dogma, and thus an irreformable and obligatory part of Christian revelation.

For this reason, critical analysis of this dogma from a historical vantage point is entirely fitting for the purposes of this book. When a church claims a particular teaching to be infallible and obligatory, and yet it is actually neither catholic, ancient, biblical, nor apostolic—indeed, when it is completely unknown to the early church fathers—this is obviously relevant to claims about being "deep in history."

The Embarrassment of the Roman Catholic Dogma

The definition of Mary's assumption in 1950 was controversial. For many, it confirmed fears of how papal infallibility would be exercised, since it pronounced an infallible dogma without biblical or historical support. In his book chronicling the history of the popes, the Roman Catholic historian Eamon Duffy notes, "the definition embarrassed many Roman Catholic theologians, since it was unsupported in scripture and was unknown in the early Church."[4] In response to this challenge, there have been waves of scholarly efforts to find information about Mary's ultimate fate. Yet many Roman Catholic scholars concede that such efforts have produced no historical or biblical foundation for the assumption of Mary. In his book on Mary, Duffy puts it more plainly: "there is, clearly, no historical evidence whatever for it (unless one counts the negative evidence of the lack of post-mortem relics of the Virgin)."[5]

Why does Duffy say the assumption is unsupported in Scripture or the early church? Since some of the relevant texts do not have critical editions and a few remain untranslated, it will be helpful to start by summarizing some of the excellent scholarship that is working in this field. Here is Stephen Shoemaker's summary of the historical data from his widely respected recent study:

> There is no evidence of any tradition concerning Mary's Dormition and Assumption from before the fifth century. The only exception to this is Epiphanius' unsuccessful attempt to uncover a tradition of the end of Mary's life towards the end of the fourth century, and his failure confirms the otherwise deafening silence. The fifth century itself also has very little to offer, until the very end, when the first fragments of a Dormition narrative appear, as well as limited indications from a few independent sources that confirm a sudden interest at this time in the end of Mary's life.[6]

Later in the book Shoemaker identifies "the period between 450 and 500 CE as the time when the ancient Dormition traditions first come into historical view from a somewhat uncertain past."[7] Elsewhere Shoemaker discusses a few of the texts that come into view within this time frame that likely date earlier—most notably, the Book of Mary's Repose (*Liber Requiei*), which probably dates to somewhere around the third century.[8] But as we will see, this is a Gnostic text with thoroughly heterodox theology. It is highly significant that the earliest known attestation to Mary's assumption in church history comes in a heterodox context (more on that, as well as on Epiphanius, in just a bit).

So we can speak broadly of a *late fifth-century* entrance into orthodox Christianity of belief in the bodily assumption. This general timeframe is consistent with that offered by other scholars working in this area, particularly Roman Catholic scholars. Brian Daley, another leading scholar in this area, argues that "the origins and original intent of the story of Mary's death and entry into glory . . . seems to have taken shape in Antioch, Palestine, and Egypt during the century or so after the Council of Chalcedon."[9] According to Daley, these traditions probably originated among non-Chalcedonian groups around this time (i.e., late fifth century, in the wake of the Council of Chalcedon in 451), possibly within monastic communities in Syria and around Jerusalem.[10]

This more recent scholarship is also in accord with how older Roman Catholic scholars have assessed the emergence of belief in Mary's assumption in the church. Here is how the Roman Catholic scholar Ludwig Ott put it in his older work, often considered the definitive work summarizing Roman Catholic dogma: "the idea of the bodily assumption of Mary is first expressed in certain transitus-narratives of the fifth and sixth centuries. . . . The first Church author to speak of the bodily assumption of Mary, in association with an apocryphal transitus B.M.V., is St. Gregory of Tours."[11] In another significant older text, Roman Catholic scholar Walter Burghardt writes, "The investigation of patristic documents might well lead the historian to the conclusion: In the first seven or eight centuries no trustworthy historical tradition on Mary's corporeal Assumption is extant, especially in the West."[12]

These scholars cannot be accused of anti-Catholic bias. All but Shoemaker are themselves Roman Catholic, and one of the themes of Shoemaker's book is to lament how dogmatic interest has influenced the historical study of Mary's life; he concludes the entire book critiquing another scholar's conclusion for its anti-Catholic prejudice.[13] Nor are these scholars eccentric in their outlook. We could stack up many more quotes just like these.

So the obvious question that emerges is this: How do we account for these hundreds of years of silence between Mary's death and the emergence of a tradition within the church of her assumption? It's an entirely natural question. When Brian Daley asserts that "the fifth century was a time of meteoric rise for the figure of Mary,"[14] we cannot help but wonder, where did the meteor come from?

There are various responses to this challenge. One is to reject the general scholarly picture recounted here and attempt to locate earlier written attestation of Mary's assumption. For example, some attempt to detect the bodily assumption of Mary in Revelation 12 (we will address that later in the chapter). Others have tried to argue that a set of Syriac fragments provide earlier attestation for Mary's assumption, but Brian Daley notes that even older French Roman Catholic scholars like Martin Jugie and Antoine Wenger (who are often seen as seeking to defend the Roman Catholic dogma on historical grounds) accept a fifth-century dating for these Syriac fragments.[15]

Others point to references to Mary's assumption in Gnostic legends circulating around the third century. We will return to this later as well; for now, it is worth noting such efforts are resisted by the best Roman Catholic theologians working in this area. For example, according to the brilliant Matthew Levering, "there certainly were early traditions such as the *Liber Requiei*, but their historical and theological unreliability make them unworthy of constituting a basis for a historical reconstruction of the event of Mary's assumption, and in fact such a historical reconstruction based on the legends would be a mistake."[16] Levering notes that other significant Roman Catholic theologians, such as John Henry Newman, likewise avoid efforts at historical reconstruction from these legends.[17] Levering instead argues that Mary's assumption could have been unknown to the apostles but taught by the Holy Spirit "in the Church beginning in the late fifth century as part of unfolding and developing the deposit of faith."[18]

Another possible response is to claim that the bodily assumption was indeed known to the apostles and maintained within the early church by *oral* tradition. We may have no literary evidence of the bodily assumption in early Christianity, but that does not prove no one believed in it. Absence of evidence is not evidence of absence. To argue otherwise, we are told, is an "argument from silence."

To consider whether these responses are tenable, we must trace the specifics of how belief in Mary's assumption evolved into being within the early church.

Epiphanius and Other Early Testimonies

The first problem with the "argument from silence" response is simply that we are *not* dealing with silence. Epiphanius, bishop of Salamis in the late fourth century (just prior to the fifth-century "meteoric rise" of assumption narratives in the church), conducted a thorough investigation of what happened to Mary at the end of her life. Epiphanius was opposing certain idolatrous practices among heretical groups that involved offering bread sacrifices in the name of Mary.[19] This leads him to address the question of Mary's ultimate end in this world, which was evidently becoming a topic of speculation around this time.

Epiphanius lived near Palestine and had contacts there (where most of the later traditions purport Mary died), so if there was an oral tradition circulating about Mary's assumption to heaven, it is unreasonable to suppose that he could have missed it. According to Burghardt, Epiphanius "knows the Holy City and its traditions as few others of his time."[20] The very fact that he had to carefully investigate the matter already suggests there was not a generally known view of the matter. But even more telling is the uncertainty of his findings:

> The holy virgin may have died and been buried—her falling asleep was with honor, her death in purity, her crown in virginity. Or she may have been put to death—as the scripture says, "And a sword shall pierce through her soul"—her fame is among the martyrs and her holy body, by which light rose on the world, [rests] amid blessings. Or she may have remained alive, for God is not incapable of doing whatever he wills. No one knows her end. But we must not honor the saints to excess; we must honor their Master.[21]

Here Epiphanius identifies three possible outcomes for Mary's ultimate fate: natural death and burial, martyrdom, or remaining alive. But he ultimately leaves it open which of these is correct, concluding that the answer is not known by anyone. Elsewhere, he insists that we cannot know Mary's ultimate fate because Scripture is silent concerning it.[22]

Roman Catholic apologists often claim that this is not at odds with the assumption, since Mary could have died (whether by natural causes or martyrdom) and then been resurrected and assumed to heaven. (It is true that the dogma leaves open whether or not Mary died prior to the assumption.[23]) Thus, for example, Tim Staples writes, "the fact that Epiphanius says Mary may have 'died and been buried' says nothing of the Assumption. We say in the creed that Christ was 'crucified, died, and was buried'—this does not mean he was not resurrected.'"[24]

But the Apostles Creed immediately adds, "on the third day he rose again." Epiphanius, by contrast, says nothing about a bodily assumption to heaven. That has to be read into the text. Instead, Epiphanius considers the possibility of death (either from natural causes or as a martyr) as an *alternative* to her remaining alive. Further, he ultimately indicates uncertainty about which possibility is correct. In other words, Epiphanius does not say, "No one knows Mary's end *prior to her assumption*." Rather, his uncertainty is without qualification: "No one knows her end."

It is not as though an assumption to heaven would be irrelevant to the matter under Epiphanius's investigation. Supposing Mary had been buried, for example—an assumption would then involve her not remaining buried, but being resurrected from the grave. If, on the other hand, she had simply remained alive, an assumption to heaven would explain *how* she remained alive—namely, translation to heaven. Is it really plausible that Epiphanius knew about an oral tradition of Mary's assumption to heaven and simply found it *not worth mentioning* in the context of a discussion of the end of her life? Awareness of such a tradition would have presented to him the answer to the very question he was investigating.

Thus, Epiphanius's testimony about the results of his investigation indicates that in the late fourth century there appears to have been no generally known oral tradition concerning the end of Mary's life—especially considering that the *Panarion* was read widely throughout the church during Epiphanius's own lifetime, and yet his findings appear to have provoked no controversy or countertestimony. Andrew Jacobs notes that the *Panarion* "circulated throughout the Christian world even during Epiphanius's lifetime and became the foundation text of subsequent premodern Christian heresiography."[25] If Epiphanius's testimony in the late fourth century contradicted a known oral tradition, why didn't someone point this out? As the Roman Catholic scholar Walter Burghardt puts it, "Epiphanius's approach suggests strongly the absence of fixed tradition on Mary's final lot."[26]

Some argue that Epiphanius affirms Mary's assumption in the chapter immediately after the initial passage we quoted. Opposing the Kollyridians' idolatrous excess of devotion to the Virgin Mary, he writes:

> For what this sect has to say is complete nonsense and, as it were, an old wives' tale. Which scripture has spoken of it? Which prophet permitted the worship of a man, let alone a woman? The vessel is choice but a woman, and by nature no different [from others]. Like the bodies of the saints, however, she has been held in honor for her character and understanding. And if I should say anything more in her praise, [she is] like Elijah, who was virgin from his mother's womb, always remained so, and was taken up and has not seen death. She is like John who leaned on the Lord's breast, "the disciple whom Jesus loved." She is like St. Thecla; and Mary is still more honored than she, because of the providence vouchsafed her.[27]

But here Epiphanius is simply comparing Mary to Elijah, John, and Thecla on account of their being honored for character and understanding. The reference to Elijah's bodily assumption is illustrative of these qualities; it does not apply to Mary any more than the comparable facts mentioned about Thecla or John. In other words, we can no more insist that Mary was "taken up" like Elijah than that she "leaned on the Lord's breast" like John. In each case, the relative clause is simply illustrating the superlative godliness of each figure. Such a reading makes sense since an assumption is not the common thread between the three figures (Thecla, for example, was not assumed); instead, the common thread is honor and godliness.

As a comparable example, consider this sentence: "George W. Bush was a president who served with honor, just like his father, who presided over the final years of the Cold War; and Ronald Reagan, who oversaw a resilient economy; and Jimmy Carter, who fought for disease prevention and human rights abroad." Here the point of comparison is the fact of serving with honor; the relative clauses then illustrate how each particularly has done so. No one could insist from such a sentence that George W. Bush must have presided over the final years of the Cold War (particularly when they don't interpret the subsequent two relative clauses this way).

If Epiphanius *had* intended in this sentence to convey that Mary was assumed to heaven, he has surely chosen the most oblique and cryptic imaginable way to do it. Remember, Epiphanius has just told us *in the immediately preceding chapter* that no one knows Mary's end. So why should we accept that here, immediately after, he would offer a kind of veiled affirmation of Mary's assumption to heaven, smuggled into this relative clause describing Elijah? Such an effort seems to reflect the contemporary dogmatic need, not a fair-minded interest in Epiphanius's meaning.

Later, into the seventh century, Isidore of Seville evidences that even at this time, amazingly, there is still uncertainty and rumor concerning Mary's ultimate fate:

> Some say that Mary departed this life by passing through the coarse torments of martyrdom, since the just man Simeon, holding Christ in his arms, was prophesying when he said to his Mother, "A sword shall pierce your heart" (Luke 2:35). But it is not certain whether he was speaking of a material sword or if he meant the word of God, which is stronger and more cutting than any two-edged sword. In any case, no particular historical narrative tells us that Mary was killed by the stroke of a sword, since one reads nothing about it, and nothing about her death either. However, some say that her tomb is to be found in the valley of Josaphat.[28]

Evidently, in Isidore's day, some two and a half centuries after Epiphanius, there was still circulating the theory that Mary was a martyr (this belief may have arisen in the fourth century, when it was opposed by Ambrose). In opposing the certainty of this view, Isidore shares a similar uncertainty about Mary's ultimate fate with Epiphanius, though seeming to assume she died and was buried.[29]

Again, the point is not that Mary's death is necessarily at odds with the assumption. Rather, the point is that Isidore, like Epiphanius, does not seem to evidence any awareness of an oral tradition concerning Mary's ultimate fate. Like Epiphanius, Isidore does not simply say that it is unknown whether Mary died *prior an assumption*. Rather, he states uncertainty about her ultimate fate without qualification. Isidore's testimony is also significant in demonstrating how slowly the tradition of a bodily assumption spread throughout the church.

When we scour the early church for references to the end of

Mary, it seems to confirm the picture gleaned from Epiphanius and Isidore. To the extent that Mary's end *is* discussed among earlier patristic sources, the general idea seems to be she simply died and was buried. There are numerous references to her death, but never with any awareness of it being succeeded by an assumption to heaven. The earliest reference to Mary's death comes in Tertullian, who simply notes that Mary remained a virgin until her death.[30] Burghardt works through this passage and other various references to Mary's death in the patristic era, concluding that the church's assumption seems to be that she simply died.[31]

Further, some of these references to Mary's death speak as though her bodily existence is now over. For example, around the turn of the fifth century, Severian of Gabala references Mary's happy state in heaven at being called blessed, and then adds, "in point of fact, while she was yet living in the flesh she was called blessed; for she heard felicitation *while still in flesh*."[32] Roman Catholic scholar Walter Burghardt comments on this passage, "in its obvious implications it suggests a moment when Mary ceased living in the flesh, when spirit was severed from flesh, when Mary died."[33] Burghardt also cites a passage in Pseudo-Antoninus Placentinus in which Mary is referred to as being "taken up out of the body";[34] and later he cites passages in Adomnán (seventh-century abbot of Iona Abbey) and Bede (seventh-eighth–century English monk and writer) referencing Mary's body as taken from the tomb but *awaiting* a future resurrection while her soul alone is taken up to heaven.[35]

Augustine references Mary's death in numerous passages,[36] which he interprets as a consequence of original sin: "for to speak more briefly, Mary who was of Adam died for sin, Adam died for sin, and the Flesh of the Lord which was of Mary died to put away sin."[37] As J. N. D. Kelly notes, Augustine maintained that Mary was sinless but "did not hold (as has sometimes been alleged) that she was born exempt from all taint of original sin (the later doctrine of the immaculate conception)."[38] For example, Augustine stipulates that Mary's flesh, though holy, was nonetheless "derived from the propagation of sin."[39] Shoemaker likewise notes that Augustine "attributes Mary's death to original sin."[40] This is contrary to the rationale often given for Mary's assumption, namely, its fittingness in relation to her preservation from original sin.

Even more strikingly, in patristic literature there are many lists of those believed to be translated to heaven, but Mary is never among those listed. When Tertullian is expounding the perfection of the resurrection body, he lists Enoch and Elijah as his examples of those translated to heaven;[41] elsewhere, in opposing the denial of various heretics that death is the debt of sin, he lists Enoch and Elijah again as exceptions, identifying them as the two witnesses of Revelation 11:3.[42] Mary is absent in these as well as other passages that specify which human beings have been assumed to heaven.[43] When Irenaeus wants to list examples of those translated to heaven in order to prove that God can resurrect our bodies, he lists Elijah and Enoch—no mention of Mary.[44] When Methodius wants to defend the resurrection of the body, he distinguishes between those who rose to die again (such as those performed by Elijah and Elisha, or the raising of Lazarus) and those who were taken up into immortality, such as Elijah and Enoch—again, no mention of Mary.[45]

When Origen lists exceptions to the general pattern of death, he mentions Enoch and Elijah—no mention of Mary.[46] When the *Apostolic Constitutions*—a fourth-century compilation of texts dealing with various church orders—appeals to examples of the power of God in raising the dead, he mentions both those translated to heaven (Enoch and Elijah) and those raised in this life (the widow's son raised by Elijah, and the Shunammite's son

raised by Elisha)—again, no mention of Mary.[47] When John
Chrysostom wants to prove that bodily existence does not make
virtue impossible, he appeals to those who did great deeds while
in the flesh, and then those translated to heaven, mentioning
Enoch and Elijah as examples—no mention of Mary.[48] Later he
notes "many ask whither Enoch was translated, and why he was
translated, and why he did not die, neither he nor Elijah."[49] He
proceeds to admonish the question, apparently seeing these two
as the examples that occasion it.

In listing those who are not greater than John despite being
bodily assumed to heaven, Cyril of Jerusalem provides Enoch
and Elijah as examples—no mention of Mary.[50] Later he defends
Jesus's ascension by referencing Enoch and Elijah's translation to
heaven, as well as Paul's travel to heaven, and even the story of
Habakkuk's translation from Israel to Babylon in the Bel and the
Dragon narrative—but still no mention of Mary's assumption.[51]
When Jerome wants to exposit the nature of the resurrection
body, he appeals to Enoch and Elijah as examples—still no
Mary.[52] Ambrose, as well, lists Enoch and Elijah as among those
"caught up" to be alive with Christ, along with Paul and some
apostles—still no Mary.[53] Augustine references Faustus's belief
that Elijah, Moses, and Enoch were bodily assumed to heaven in
the context of his refutation of Manichaean views about Jesus;[54]
elsewhere he references Caelestius's question about the location
of Enoch and Elijah, rebuking it for its lack of modesty.[55] Still
no mention of Mary.

Thus, the church fathers are hardly silent on the idea of
bodily assumption to heaven. Over and over and over Enoch
and Elijah are discussed as the examples of this, with occasional
reference to Paul's experience in 2 Corinthians 12 as well. Once
or twice Moses's entrance to heaven is mentioned, and Eusebius
even records the possible assumption to heaven of an old bishop

named Chaeremon.[56] Of course Jesus's ascension to heaven is frequently discussed as well. Yet *nowhere*, in the entire massive stretch of time represented by these church fathers, do we find in the church the slightest hint of a bodily assumption of Mary.

In my mind I can just hear some readers screaming: "Argument from silence!" But arguments from silence have plausibility value to the extent that you expect the sources in questions not to be silent on the matter at hand. Perhaps some of these texts could be explained in that the author simply chose not to include Mary as an example, or was speaking strictly of those assumed to heaven without an intervening death, or simply wasn't aware of the oral tradition. But *all of them*? If Mary was as important in the early church as she is in Roman Catholic theology, is it really plausible that so many church fathers would discuss bodily assumptions to heaven and simply fail to mention that it happened to the most important creature?

To consider the legitimate role some arguments from silence can have with respect to plausibility, consider the following scenario: You hear on the radio that a shooting has occurred at a local school (but the radio doesn't specify which one). Worried, you drive onto the nearby campus where your child attends and walk around campus, asking if anyone has heard of a shooting happening there. If the entire school has a thousand students, and you interviewed twenty-five students, and none had heard of such a thing, that would make it less plausible that a shooting happened there. You would likely be relieved. Now, if you go on to interview fifty more people from different locations on campus over the next hour, including several teachers and staff, and *none* of them had heard of a shooting happening, your confidence and relief would then increase further. Of course, the fact that none of them heard of it doesn't logically demand that it didn't happen there. It's possible, however unlikely, that the shooting was somehow kept very quiet, and you had rotten luck in that the people you chose to interview didn't know about it. But the point is clear: Silence affects plausibility to the degree that you expect the sources *not* to be silent.

In this way, the complete and unmitigated silence of the early and mid-patristic witness on Mary's assumption *in the context of lists of those believed to be bodily assumed to heaven* undermines the plausibility of the idea of a commonly known oral tradition about Mary's assumption. If such a belief was apostolic and known in the early church, it is scandalous that it would never be referenced by Tertullian, Irenaeus, Methodius, Origen, the Apostolic Constitutions, John Chrysostom, Cyril of Jerusalem, Ambrose, Jerome, and Augustine, etc., when their whole goal is to provide examples of who was bodily assumed to heaven. Meanwhile, we have all the references to Mary's death early on, none of which seem to indicate anything out of the ordinary about her end, and some of which seem to assume it involved a separation from her body. Then, on top of all that, we have the testimony of Epiphanius (and others like Isidore) concerning the ultimate uncertainty of her end despite careful investigation into the matter.

As damning as all this is, there are even stronger reasons to be skeptical of the plausibility of an oral tradition of Mary's assumption in the early church.

Apology, Diversity, and Heterodoxy in Early Dormition Narratives

Let's suppose you want to fall back on the "argument from silence" charge. Yes, you say, it may be unlikely, but it's not impossible, that Mary was assumed despite the fact that there is no mention of it among Christians for centuries after the fact—even when they are listing bodily assumptions, discussing Mary's death, or investigating her end. Fine. There is an additional problem: When we do finally find references to Mary's assumption, they seem to be at odds in several ways with the idea of an earlier tradition going back to the apostles. In the first place, many of the early texts mentioning the assumption appear to exhibit *an awareness* of its late arrival. Shoemaker, for example, draws attention to the "apologies for the late appearance of the Dormition traditions" in several texts, including Pseudo-Melito's Transitus narrative and John of Thessalonica's homily on the dormition of Mary, concluding that

> the primary value of these candid admissions lies in their confirmation of modern scholarship's inability to identify any significant traditions concerning the end of Mary's life from before the fifth century. The Christian writers of late antiquity themselves warn us that we should not expect to find very much on this subject from earlier Christian centuries.[57]

If there was an oral tradition of the bodily assumption, why wouldn't its earliest proponents point that out, rather than apologize for the late arrival of the tradition?

Moreover, when attestation of the story of Mary's assumption does emerge within the church in the fifth century, it does so simultaneously with a number of alternative accounts of Mary's end (which it only gradually eclipses). These various traditions reflect an astounding diversity. Even the city in which Mary dies is often different—it is usually Jerusalem, but a few of the traditions place it in Ephesus; and some accounts also include Mary travelling to Bethlehem and performing miracles there. Nearly all the traditions include some kind of conflict with the Jewish leadership, culminating in Christ's reception of Mary's soul. But on virtually everything else they differ.[58]

One of the points the traditions differ on is whether Mary's body and soul are both received into heaven, or only her soul. Significantly, in many of the earliest traditions, there is a narration of Mary's dormition without any mention of a bodily resurrection or bodily assumption. For example, the dormition homily of Jacob of Serug, probably dating to 489, references the Seraphim escorting Mary's soul into heaven, but says nothing about her body.[59] An assumption of soul only, not the body, is also described in the narrative in Pseudo-Dionysius.[60] Another common idea attested in several early narratives is that Mary's body is neither buried nor assumed to heaven but kept guarded in a special place until the final resurrection. For example, the Coptic Gospel of Bartholomew, which scholars generally date to the fifth or sixth century, depicts Christ promising to take Mary's soul to heaven, and then adding: "I will place your body under the tree of life, where a cherub with a sword of fire will watch over it, until the day of my kingdom."[61] Similarly, in *On the Dormition of the Holy Mother of God* by pseudo-John the Evangelist, Christ promises Mary "from this time forth your revered body will be transposed to paradise, but your holy soul will be in the heavens."[62] Obviously, the transfer and preservation of Mary's body to a special location, separate from her soul, is not the same as the bodily assumption of her body into heaven in reunion with her soul.

To reiterate: Many of the earliest traditions do not support a *bodily* assumption of Mary into heaven, but some kind of alternative account of her end that is inconsistent with that belief. Here is how Shoemaker puts it, describing the emergence of dormition traditions in the late fifth century:

> At this time we encounter not a single, unified tradition,
> but instead we find several, diverse narratives, including

the earliest exemplars of three major literary traditions, as well as a handful of independent or atypical narratives. One particular point on which there is simultaneously both significant unity and diversity among these earliest narratives is Mary's ultimate fate. Although all the narratives conclude with Mary's transfer to the garden of Paradise, some versions describe Mary's bodily resurrection in Paradise, while other narratives report only the transfer of Mary's lifeless body to Paradise, where it remains separate from her soul.[63]

Among traditions that *do* mention a bodily assumption, there is remarkable diversity in how it is narrated. Some describe Mary's death and burial and then an interval of time between Mary's resurrection and assumption. Thus, in some stories the apostles are reunited with Mary toward the end of her life, bury her body after she dies, and then wait for Christ's return outside her tomb. After several days Christ returns and takes them all to heaven (at which point Mary's body is reunited to her soul).[64] Other various Coptic texts describe the apostles gathering around Mary's tomb for 206 days after her death before witnessing her resurrection and assumption.[65] In one later set of traditions, one of the apostles arrives late and does not witness Mary's death and burial. The other apostles reopen Mary's tomb and discover that her body is unable to be found (in most accounts they instead find what become relics).[66] In many other traditions, Christ receives Mary's soul directly into heaven without an interval of death at all. As we have already noted, in some of these her body is not assumed to heaven but rather taken to paradise to await reunion with her soul at the final resurrection; in others, Mary's body is resurrected and restored to her body immediately.[67]

These various traditions appear to have coexisted for quite some time before a unified narrative emerges. Here is how Daley summarizes the timeline: "It is not until the end of the sixth century that the narrative of Mary's death and entry into glory seems to have become fixed in its general outline and accepted by all the major churches of the eastern Mediterranean world."[68]

This raises the obvious question: *If there was an apostolic tradition of Mary's assumption, why does written evidence of it just happen to emerge around the same time as these alternative ideas about her fate* (for example, the idea that her body was taken to a special place to await resurrection, or that she was simply buried and her soul went to heaven)? And why does it take so long for it to win out over its competitors? Still further, why are there so many discrepancies, and for so long, in the traditions that affirm a bodily assumption?

Many scholarly efforts have been made to see the bodily assumption as the earliest traditions, and the alternative traditions as deviations from this prior belief. Even if you could try to explain how such a staggeringly diverse set of deviations could have arisen so quickly, the problem is that the timing doesn't fit. Here is how Shoemaker puts it:

> There is simply no historical evidence for any sort of typological or theological evolution: each type of narrative and all manner of opinions regarding Mary's ultimate fate are evident simultaneously when these narratives first appear at the end of the fifth century. Thus, the literary history of these traditions affords no evidence of any narrative type or theological position antedating the others; rather, they attest to synchronic coexistence of a variety of traditions.[69]

At this point some may want to point out that some recent scholars argue that at least one text—*Liber Requiei Mariae* (which we will refer to by its English title, *The Book of Mary's*

Repose)—likely provides an earlier attestation of Mary's assumption (Shoemaker, for example, as we noted above, dates this text to around the third century). But this is a Gnostic legend, bearing little resemblance to orthodox Christianity. For example, it advances an angel Christology; at one point Mary calls Christ "the Great Cherub of Light, who dwelt in my womb";[70] at another point the Christ-angel claims, "I am the third that was created, and I am not the Son."[71] The actual narrative features all kinds of bizarre and shocking details, including Joseph rebuking Mary for failing to preserve her virginity ("Why didn't you guard your virginity?"[72]) and wondering whether he himself impregnated her while intoxicated ("But I have thought in my heart, perhaps I had intercourse with you while drunk"[73]). Further, the narrative contains many distinctly Gnostic features, such as an apparently Gnostic creation myth.[74]

The narrative's interest in Mary seems not to lie with her virginity or goodness, but in her role as the possessor of esoteric, secret knowledge about cosmic mysteries, entrusted to her by the Christ-angel. Indeed, Mary is depicted as being afraid of dying because of her sin. Before her departure, Mary says to her bystanders: "And because of this I fear: because I did not believe in my God for even one day. Behold, I will tell you about my sin."[75] She then narrates an episode of her disbelief during her flight to Egypt with Joseph and several of his children. Her actual dormition follows the pattern of many of the other so-called Palm traditions; Mary is reunited with the apostles; Christ returns to receive her soul; her body is buried; there is a plot to steal/burn it by the Jewish leadership; the plot is foiled miraculously; and then finally Christ returns to take her body to heaven to be reunited with her soul.[76] There are all kinds of other strange parables and fantastic events, such as the apostles and Mary touring hell.[77]

The fact that the earliest attestation of the bodily assumption comes in a Gnostic text has led many scholars to conclude the assumption is a heterodox intrusion into mainstream Christianity. R. P. C. Hanson represents a typical claim along these lines, arguing that the assumption "can be shown to be a doctrine which manifestly had its origin among Gnostic heretics."[78] It is difficult to be certain, but if this is true, it would also help account for the fierceness of Epiphanius's invectives against the Kollyridians, a heretical group associated with the *Six Books Dormition Apocryphon* (another early set of texts) whom Epiphanius condemned as engaging in Marian idolatry.[79]

All of this combines to make the notion of an oral tradition of Mary's assumption within the early church, tracing back to the apostles, credible only if one exerts a kind of Herculean effort. Why should anyone accept Mary's assumption as apostolic when it (1) is completely absent in the church for several centuries, even when one would expect it to come up (for example, in Epiphanius's search, in lists of those bodily assumed, etc.), (2) seems to originate in heterodox contexts, like *The Book of Mary's Repose*, (3) is recognized as tardy when it does finally arise, and (4) comes into view simultaneously with seemingly countless alternative accounts of Mary's end? The bodily assumption of Mary gives every impression of being a postapostolic accretion that only gradually wormed its way into the piety and imagination of the church.

The manner in which belief in Mary's assumption developed in the early church also raises challenges against the idea that the Holy Spirit gradually taught it after the fact. We can justifiably wonder why the Holy Spirit would teach about a specific historical event so many centuries after its alleged occurrence, and only after it was circulated first in heterodox contexts, and alongside so many competing alternative beliefs that arose simultaneously.

It seems difficult to locate any reason to conclude that the source of such a process is really the Holy Spirit.

One final point. Sometimes it is argued that the trustworthiness of assumption of Mary is indicated by the fact that, despite all these problems, it quickly became universally accepted. In truth, however, this process was not quick at all. For example, the Roman Catholic scholar Michael O'Carroll notes uncertainty about the bodily assumption in the seventh and eighth centuries among figures like Adamnán of Iona and Bede, and observes that Paschasius Radbertus in the ninth century "declared that nothing was certain about the end of the Virgin's life, save that she left the body."[80] In his own sermons, Radbertus describes Mary's end as an assumption "of the soul only."[81] According to O'Carroll, Radbertus's influence "arrested development of thought on the Assumption for two-and-a-half centuries."[82] Radbertus's influence is partially explained by his usage of a letter falsely attributed to Jerome, expressing uncertainty about Mary's assumption.[83] According to O'Carroll, the influence of Pseudo-Jerome can be seen in the tenth/eleventh century in Aelfric of Eynsham's rejection of the bodily assumption,[84] and all the way into the twelfth century in the professed ignorance about the bodily assumption in figures such as Isaac of Stella,[85] Peter of Celle,[86] and Aelred of Rievaulx.[87] Beyond these examples, Walter Burghardt also notes the rejection of the bodily assumption among some in Spain in the eighth century, and hesitation about it elsewhere;[88] and Brian Daley draws attention to a wave of skepticism concerning her bodily assumption around the tenth century, in both the East and West.[89]

So the idea that the bodily assumption was universally accepted by the church when it did arise is simply false. Over a millennium after Mary lived, it was still not a settled matter in the church.

What about Revelation 12?

As we have mentioned, some seek to read the bodily assumption into John's vision in Revelation 12 of "a woman clothed with the sun, with the moon under her feet, and on her head a crown of twelve stars." There are two problems: This woman is *neither* Mary nor assumed to heaven.

First, the description of the woman is drawing from Old Testament imagery used to describe God's people, particularly the faithful under persecution. A woman in the travail of labor pains in Revelation 12:2 is a common image throughout the Old Testament for God's people (Jeremiah 4:31, Isaiah 26:17, 66:7, Micah 4:10), and the specific imagery of the sun, moon, and twelve stars in Revelation 12:1 recall Genesis 37:9, where Joseph's brothers (who became the twelve tribes of Israel) are described as "the sun, the moon, and eleven stars."[90] The sweeping away of stars in Revelation 12:4 draws from Daniel 8:10, where it depicts persecution of God's people. The woman's flight into the wilderness in Revelation 12:6 for 1,260 days is the *exact* same amount of time as the persecution described in Revelation 11:1–3, probably corresponding to the persecution for "time, and times, and half a time" in Revelation 12:14, the same time frame as the persecution described in Daniel 7:25 and 12:7–12.

In essence, this passage is describing a persecution of the church, not an assumption of Mary. That is why interpreting the woman as Mary has *no* precedent in the church until around the time people begin to wonder about Mary's ultimate fate. As Shoemaker observes, "Although this exegesis would subsequently become quite popular and has endured even to this day, there is no evidence of its existence before Epiphanius. On the contrary the early church unanimously identified this apocalyptic woman with the church."[91] Even after the rise of belief in the assumption of Mary, many did not even think to detect such a notion in Revelation 12. All the way into the eighth century, for example, Andrew of Crete admitted in his dormition homily that "none of the sacred writers, as far as we know, wrote about the immaculate, supernatural passing of the Mother of God, or left us any account of it at all."[92]

Further, even if Revelation 12 was about Mary, it says nothing about a bodily assumption. The woman is *already* in heaven (verse 1) prior to the birth of the Messiah (verse 5). Her flight from the dragon (verse 14), her stay in the wilderness for 1,260 days (verse 6), the persecution of her other children (verse 17)—all of this happens subsequent to John's initial vision of her in heaven. The idea that Mary was bodily assumed to heaven *at the end* of her life, after these events, is completely alien to the passage. Some attempt to see the bodily assumption in Revelation 12 by drawing from typology with Mary and the ark of the covenant, which is referenced in Revelation 11:19.[93] But in addition to the problem of dischronology just mentioned, this usage of typology is highly tendentious: Even if we granted the typology fully, why should it yield a *bodily assumption* of Mary? Further, Revelation 12:1 does not identify the woman with the ark of the previous verse; rather, her introduction is described as a "great sign" appearing in heaven. The chapter division here is sensible, since the appearance of the ark in Revelation 11:19, together with the lightning, thunder, earthquake, etc. conclude the judgments depicted with the seven trumpets of Revelation 8–11.

From all this it is difficult to conclude that the bodily assumption would be found in Revelation 12 unless it is first inserted there. The way I like to make the point is this: If you took a hundred people who had never heard of Mary's assumption and told them to study Revelation 12 in its New Testament context, would any of them get it from the text? I doubt it. What about a thousand? What about ten thousand? Honestly, I still doubt it in each case.

Summing It All Up

So to sum up, what do we conclude from all this? Recall Newman's claim: "The Christianity of history is not Protestantism. If ever there were a safe truth, it is this."[94] Yet when it comes to the assumption of Mary, what is the actual Christianity of history?

Pius XII claimed that those who oppose the bodily assumption will face the wrath of God as well as Peter and Paul. Yet there is no reason to think that Peter or Paul, or anyone else within many generations of their influence, had ever imagined such a thing as a bodily assumption of Mary.

The reality is this: The major non-Protestant churches have embraced a historical innovation, whereas the Protestant resistance reflects the ancient ("deep") faith of the Christian church.

CHAPTER 11

Case Study: Icon Veneration

We are exploring examples of what Protestants regard as accretions. We have considered Mary's assumption, one of the most significant areas of disagreement within Christendom in more recent centuries. Now we turn to the issue that generated perhaps the greatest conflict in the early medieval church: the veneration of icons. The result of this conflict (often called the iconoclast controversy) was an affirmation of the practice of icon veneration at the seventh ecumenical council in 787, Nicaea II. At the end of the council, the bishops present articulated a series of anathemas against those who opposed their verdict:

> To those who apply to the sacred images the sayings in divine scripture against idols anathema!

> To those who do not kiss the holy and venerable images anathema!
>
> To those who call the sacred images idols anathema!
>
> To those who say that Christians had recourse to the images as gods anathema! To those who knowingly communicate with those who insult and dishonour the sacred images anathema![1]

The list of anathemas proceeds at length and with color, but these suffice to give a flavor of what the bishops at Nicaea II believed was at stake in icon veneration.

What is an "anathema," precisely? Some try to downplay the significance of an anathema, as though it were a mere warning, or an excommunication from the church (but not from heaven). But historically, an anathema was generally understood as entailing damnation to hell, drawing from Paul's use of the term to reference someone being "accursed" (Rom. 9:3, Gal. 1:8–9, 1 Cor. 16:22).

This was certainly the understanding of the bishops at Nicaea II. For example, Tarasios, the patriarch of Constantinople who presided over Nicaea II, delivered a speech three years prior upon his nomination as patriarch in which he asserted, "An anathema is a terrible thing: it drives [its victims] far from God and expels them from the kingdom of heaven, carrying them off into the outer darkness."[2] Lamenting the current state of division in the church, he insisted upon an ecumenical council to bring unity to the church. Among his stated reasons is concern for his own soul: "lest I be subjected to an anathema and found condemned on the day of our Lord."[3] After the council, Tarasios and the bishops of Nicaea II sent a letter to the emperor Constantine and his mother Irene, summarizing the conclusions of the council. In the letter, they link the iconoclasts with the heresies condemned by the first six ecumenical councils, characterizing them as conducting an "insane war against piety," and specifying the result of their condemnation by the council: "an anathema is nothing other than separation from God."[4]

In another letter from the council to the clergy of Constantinople, they warn about the "unbearable wrath" reserved for those who, like the iconoclasts, oppose the church, again drawing a comparison between their opponents and older heretics: "by abolishing the traditions of the church they scorned the word of the Lord, and therefore God has scored them, and numbered the riotous assembly of their company with Arius, Eunomius, Macedonius, Apollinarius, Nestorius, Eutyches and Dioscorus, Sergios and Honorius and all their heresy."[5] They proceed to compare the iconoclasts to the Jews who opposed Christ, describing them as making "satanic statements," possessing "a spirit of bogus Christianity," and as "scattered by the flail of divine judgment."[6]

So don't be duped when you hear modern revisionist interpretations of anathema. "Nothing other than separation from God" is as bad as it sounds.

We mention the anathemas of Nicaea II here at the outset because both the Roman Catholic and the Eastern Orthodox Churches are committed to this council as infallible in its essential theology (exactly which parts are infallible are disputed). For this reason, icon veneration is, like the bodily assumption of Mary, a watershed issue in ecumenical debate. We will focus specifically on the Eastern Orthodox view of icon veneration here (just as we focused a bit more on the Roman Catholic view of Mary's assumption in the last chapter), though it must be understood that although icons are not emphasized as prominently in the Roman Catholic Church, the legitimacy of icon veneration as outlined at Nicaea II is affirmed.[7]

In this chapter we will uncover the shocking truth that the position anathematized as damnable heresy at an ecumenical council was, essentially, the universal position of the early church. Not only does the veneration of icons manifestly not date back to the first century, the only question is whether it originated in the sixth or seventh century. The bulk of this chapter will be a historical overview, tracing in three phases how icon veneration came into being. This will be followed by a consideration of the biblical background that informs the Protestant interpretation of this historical development. But first we must briefly consider what icon veneration is, because much confusion stems from a failure to distinguish venerating icons from other uses of religious art.

What Is Icon Veneration?

Icons are works of art—most commonly paintings depicting a person, such as Christ, an angel, Mary, or another saint. But they are not *merely* art. Icons have a mediatorial role in liturgical practice (e.g., prayer). The Antiochian Orthodox Christian Archdiocese of North America defines an icon as follows: "In the Orthodox Church an icon is a sacred image, a window into heaven. An image of another reality, of a person, time and place that is more real than here and now. More than art, icons have an important spiritual role."[8]

In the Eastern Orthodox tradition, the theology of icons is grounded in the incarnation of Christ, who is the *image* of the Father. Since God has taken on human flesh, revelation takes the forms of both word and image. Thus, icons play an essential role in the church, standing alongside Scripture as how God reveals himself to us: "the icon is placed on a level with the Holy Scripture and with the Cross, as one of the forms of revelation and knowledge of God, in which Divine and human will and action become blended."[9] This is why, in Orthodox thinking, the denial of icons is a denial of the truth of the Incarnation.

Icons also constitute a point of contact for the human response to divine revelation. As God became human, salvation now consists in the opposite, that the human might become god (deification)—not by nature, but by grace. This divine glory is reflected in the transfiguration of Christ.[10] Icons function as a point of access to this realm of divine light and glory; they transmit to us the transfigured state of the saints. "The icon is not a representation of the Deity, but an indication of the participation of a given person in Divine life."[11] In this manner, icons become a means of striving after deification ourselves: "the icon is both the way and the means; it is prayer itself."[12]

Just what does this mean, precisely? It is sometimes described as praying not *to* the icon, but *through* the icon. As we will consider more later, the behavior directed toward the icon is understood to be transmitted to what the icon represents. This behavior includes prostration, deep kneeling, kissing, and the lighting of candles. What is important to understand now is that it was this theology—not general use of religious art, but specifically the veneration of icons in connection to a theory of figural representation between the icon and its prototype—that provoked the iconoclast controversy in the eighth and ninth centuries.

In the context of this dispute, the term *iconophile* (or *iconodule*) referred to those who affirmed the veneration of icons, while the term *iconoclast* was used for those who opposed the practice. The iconoclasts themselves preferred the term *iconomachy*, meaning "struggle about icons." Most did not oppose all religious art, but they argued that the specific theology of venerating icons affirmed among the iconophiles was idolatrous. The iconophiles, in contrast, distinguished between *worship*, due to God alone, and *veneration*, which could appropriately be directed toward creatures without the sin of idolatry.

This brief overview is simply to elucidate two distinctions that can clarify the target of criticism in this chapter. First, icons are not the same as religious art generally. Second, the act of *venerating* icons must be distinguished from aesthetic, didactic, and/or commemorative use of religious images (and possibly, even milder forms of veneration). We must keep these distinctions in mind as we proceed, because what was anathematized at Nicaea II was opposition to this specific theology of icon veneration.

Historical Development of Icon Veneration in Three Phases

It will be useful to provide a brief summary of the general state of scholarship on this question before we work through some of the patristic material ourselves. Richard Price's widely respected recent translation and commentary on Nicaea II opens by outlining recent scholarly discussion as to whether the rise of icon veneration should be dated to late in the seventh century or slightly earlier. He then comments:

> The fathers of Nicaea II would have found this whole debate bizarre: their concern was not to argue that the veneration of images went back to the beginning rather than end of the seventh century, but that it had the support of the great church fathers of the fourth and fifth centuries and went back through them to the apostles themselves.[13]

Price, himself a Roman Catholic priest, finds iconoclasm an isolated view today; but he is honest about what the historical evidence suggests:

The iconoclast claim that reverence towards images did not go back to the golden age of the fathers, still less to the apostles, would be judged by impartial historians today to be simply correct. The iconophile view of the history of Christian thought and devotion was virtually a denial of history.[14]

Price's position is entirely representative of the general scholarly consensus concerning the origins and development of the cult of icons in the church. Mike Humphreys, for example, notes the "long scholarly tradition dating the rise of the icon from relative obscurity to ubiquity to (the 6th and 7th centuries), at least in the Eastern Mediterranean."[15] Within this general timeframe, there are two basic schools of thought. In the "traditional view" most associated with the renowned historian of Byzantine art Ernst Kitzinger, icon veneration arose within the Byzantine Empire beginning in the second half of the sixth century, in the period after the reign of Justinian I (527–565):

The late sixth and seventh centuries saw the rise of a new kind of piety expressing itself in a vastly increased use of images in worship and in devotional practices. . . . The ground had been prepared in the preceding centuries by the use of commemorative portraits on the one hand, and by ceremonial representations with their majestic central figures of the Deity on the other. Now these central figures were put before the worshiper in stark isolation as a statue of a god or goddess had been in a Greek temple.[16]

Important to note here is the gradual development of prior uses of images up to the specific practice of *venerating* icons in a manner that parallels pagan use of cultic images. In an influential 1973 article, Peter Brown followed this general timeline, noting that "the rise of the cult of icons, therefore, in the sixth and seventh centuries, and not the origins of Iconoclasm—this is the central problem of the Iconoclast controversy."[17] A late sixth-century date for the emergence of icon veneration has remained popular among others in the field.[18]

More recent scholarship, sometimes called the "revisionist view," is well represented by the authoritative work of Leslie Brubaker and John Haldon, who argue that Kitzinger's framework relies on iconophile interpolations onto the texts. As a result, they date the emergence of icon veneration much later, around 680 AD: "There is little support for a 'cult of sacred images' in pre-iconoclast Byzantium. The textual and material evidence agree that sacred portraits existed, but there is no indication that these images received special veneration in any consistent fashion before the late seventh century."[19]

Again, the claim is not that images generally began at that time. There is no doubt that portrait images of Christ, the Virgin Mary, and other saints date back earlier, the first few probably emerging in the fourth century. According to Paul Finney, "the absence of portraits depicting Jesus or Mary or the disciples is a conspicuous feature of all third-century Christian figural traditions."[20] So icons themselves were not new; still less religious art generally. But Brubaker and Haldon argue that images of Christ and the saints *functioning as a channel to the person depicted* and serving for the purpose of veneration arise, with only a few possible exceptions, only in the final quarter of the seventh century. They conclude:

> The iconoclasts of 754 were right when they condemned image veneration as an innovation that ran counter to the venerable traditions of the church: holy portraits were not new, but their magnified role was an ongoing contemporary development and their veneration was a recent phenomenon.[21]

Part of what makes it difficult to arbitrate this dispute is the problem of sources: Almost all our information comes from committed iconophiles, who essentially rewrote the history of the controversy.[22] As a result, it is often difficult to disentangle genuine historical evidence from the propaganda, interpolations, and doctored texts the iconophiles used to smear their opponents. It is not necessary for our purposes, however, to resolve whether the cult of icons emerged in the sixth or seventh century. The general point will be sufficient for our purposes that the practice of venerating icons does not date back to the apostles, or anywhere remotely close to them.

Why does the scholarship go this direction? Let us consider the historical evidence itself. We will work through three historical phases.

Phase 1: The Ante-Nicene Period

Cultic usage of images and physical objects (especially statues) is one of the most common features of human history, as widely attested as religion itself. Within the Graeco-Roman world, in particular, religious usage of images depicting the divine was extremely common, particularly with the understanding that the image was a means of embodying or mediating the divine person it depicted. As Mike Humphreys observes,

> It was part of the religious common sense of the classical world that images of the gods could and should be made, some of which could and should be the focus of various cultic practices. For presumably many viewers, the cult statue was more than a simple representation, a reminder, a useful focusing tool for worship. Rather, it embodied or mediated the divine, making it in a way really present and therefore engaged with the ritual being performed with it. In short, the kind of

idolatry condemned in the Old Testament was ubiquitous in
the Roman world, and the Jewish and Christian rejection of
it really did mark them off from the religious mainstream.[23]

It is commonplace to observe that early Christianity,
responding to this environment, was *aniconic* (opposed to the use
of images). However, what this precisely means is disputed. In
his influential study on early Christian art, Paul Finney quotes
the observation of Cyril Mango: "The Iconoclasts were closer to
the historical truth than their opponents in affirming that the
early Christians had been opposed to figurative arts."[24] Finney
then notes that "Mango's assessment of this issue represents a
kind of modern critical consensus."[25]

However, as Finney notes, this summary requires clarifica-
tion. The ante-Nicene Christians were not usually iconoclast in
the sense of opposing all religious art whatever. It is true that a
few early Christians (like Tertullian or Clement of Alexandria)
were more rigorously aniconic. But from at least the third
century we also find paintings on tombs in the catacombs, symbolic engravings on lamps, carvings on furniture, (eventually)
sarcaphogi, and so forth.[26] The primary concern of the early
Christians was the *cultic uses of images* that were so ubiquitous in
the surrounding pagan culture. Their wholesale rejection of such
practices formed a distinctive point of contrast between early
Christian worship and pagan religious practice.

Early apologists like Justin Martyr and Athenagoras, for
example, ridiculed the pagan practice of making images to be
invoked and revered, claiming that such figures are lifeless and
it is only demons who act through them. The true God, they
insisted, was invisible and distinct from matter altogether as
the Creator and Sustainer of all things.[27] Their pagan critics,
in return, derided the early Christians for their lack of images

in worship. For example, in the fictional dialogue written by the North African apologist Marcus Minucius Felix (d. c. 250) entitled *Octavius*, Christians were criticized for lacking images in worship: "Why do they endeavour with such pains to conceal and to cloak whatever they worship? . . . Why have they no altars, no temples, no acknowledged images?"[28] This would be an odd question to ask if the early Christians actually *did* use images in the context of worship. In response to this charge, Octavius (the Christian convert in the dialogue) explained the nature of Christian worship by appealing to the invisibility of God: "The God whom we worship we neither show nor see. Verily for this reason we believe Him to be God."[29]

When the pagan critic Celsus attacked Christians for their lack of images, Origen retorted that Christians, "being taught in the school of Jesus Christ, have rejected all images and statues."[30] To explain this practice, Origen appealed to the second commandment, commenting that "it is in consideration of these and many other such commands, that [Christians] not only avoid temples, altars, and images, but are ready to suffer death when it is necessary, rather than debase by any such impiety the conception which they have of the Most High God."[31] Elsewhere Origen notes Celsus's critique that Christian rejection of altars, statues, and temples is seen as "the badge or distinctive mark of a secret and forbidden society."[32] In response, Origen argues that Christians have their own *kinds* of statues, altars, and temples, using these terms as metaphors for prayer, Christian virtues, and the Christian body.[33]

Origen's teacher, Clement of Alexandria, was arguably even more aniconic, arguing that the law of Moses teaches abstinence from "sensible images," contrasting this with the true worship of God.[34] Clement seemed to embrace a Platonic preference for the invisible realm, explaining Moses's commandment against graven images on the grounds that "familiarity with the sight disparages the reverence of what is divine."[35] Because images were of the material realm, "works of art cannot then be sacred and divine."[36]

In opposing the cultic use of images, the early Christian often appealed to a contrast between earthly (visible) things and heavenly (invisible) things, asserting that God is too pure to be depicted by that which can be seen. This is a theme in Lactantius, for example, who followed earlier Christians in asserting that cultic images are lifeless and yet presided over by demons, and that to worship the true God, we must lift our eyes up from the things of this earth. He concluded:

> Wherefore it is undoubted that there is no religion wherever there is an image. For if religion consists of divine things, and there is nothing divine except in heavenly things; it follows that images are without religion, because there can be nothing heavenly in that which is made from the earth. . . . There is no religion in images, but a mimicry of religion. That which is true is therefore to be preferred to all things which are false; earthly things are to be trampled upon, that we may obtain heavenly things.[37]

Can anyone seriously imagine Lactantius speaking like this if the theology of Nicaea II had been alive in his day?

Tertullian wrote an entire treatise on idolatry, in which he observes that idolatry did not exist in ancient times under the same name, since temples and shrines were devoid of images. He continues:

> But when the devil introduced into the world artificers of statues and of images, and of every kind of likenesses, that former rude business of human disaster attained from idols both a

name and a development. Thenceforth every art which in any way produces an idol instantly becomes a fount of idolatry.[38]

Tertullian cites a barrage of Old Testament passages to oppose both the making and worshiping of images patterned after objects in the world. To make them is as bad as to worship them: "The images of those things are idols; the consecration of the images is idolatry. Whatever guilt idolatry incurs, must necessarily be imputed to every artificer of every idol."[39] Tertullian proceeds to insist that the prohibition against images in the second commandment is binding on Christians. If the incarnation had introduced a change in how the second commandment applies, as John of Damascus would later argue, neither Tertullian nor any Christian in his day evidenced the slightest awareness of that fact.

In their criticism of cultic images, some of the early Christians almost sound as if they are anticipating the distinctions that would later be made at Nicaea II to justify them. In his attack on pagan use of images in the early fourth century, the apologist Arnobius deals with the objection that it is not the images that are worshiped, but what they represent: "What then? Without these, do the gods not know that they are worshipped? . . . What greater wrong, disgrace, hardship, can be inflicted than to acknowledge one god, and *yet* make supplication to something else—to hope for help from a deity, and pray to an image without feeling?"[40] He proceeds to scorn the practice of relating to a deity through a physical object, comparing it to seeking a human opinion by asking "asses and pigs" what should be done.[41] Again, it is difficult to fathom Arnobius arguing like this if he had been aware of the idea that "what is given to the image passes to the prototype," which (as we will discuss) was a linchpin in later iconophile theology.

The rejection of images in churches is evident in the canons of some local councils as well, such as canon thirty-six of Synod of Elvira in the early fourth century: "Pictures are not to be placed in churches, so that they do not become objects of worship and adoration."[42] Robin Jensen observes that it is uncertain whether the term *picturas* here refers to frontal portraits that could be used as objects of homage or prayer or all kinds of figurative art.[43] But if it does not include both, it certainly includes at least the former.

It is sometimes said that what the early Christians were opposing was simply the cult images among *pagans*, and thus did not apply to the appropriate use of images in worship among Christians. But this simply doesn't square with the evidence. The practice of honoring images is *itself* regarded as pagan; whenever it is referenced in the early church, it is condemned as such.[44] The consistent contrast was not between pagan use of images versus Christian use of images, but pagan use of images versus Christian *rejection* of images.

If Christians had their own cultic use of images in worship, they could have simply said that. They were perfectly capable of articulating, had they wished to do so, a distinction between bad (pagan) cultic use of images and good (Christian) cultic use of images. Instead, they said that Christians are "those who have rejected all images and statues" (Origen) and have "no acknowledged images" (*Octavius*) and that "there is no religion wherever there is an image" (Lactantius), and so forth. It is impossible to fathom that such statements could be made if in fact the early Christians were bowing down to images and praying through them to their prototype.

It must be emphasized that there is no resistance to these criticisms of cultic images within the church in this period. These various statements we have surveyed generated no controversy.

The rejection of cultic use of images is the unanimous, resounding testimony of the ante-Nicene church.

Phase 2: Between Nicaea I and Nicaea II

In 313, the Edict of Milan provided Christianity legal status in the Roman Empire. Then in 380, under Theodosius I, Christianity officially became the state religion. The fourth century was thus a time of seismic changes for the church as she adjusted to what James Breckenridge calls "the mountainous wave of new converts from idolatrous paganism following the Edict of Toleration."[45] At this time art and statuary dramatically increased in churches, and we see the first pictures of Christ and Mary and other saints. As Robin Jensen notes, "Iconic portraits of apostles, saints, and Christ mostly appeared only toward the end of the 4th century."[46] Although portraiture art was still rare and not yet used for veneration or prayer, now there was at least the possibility of new temptations that had been completely unthinkable in the ante-Nicene period.

We can gather a sense of the developing tensions of the fourth century from a letter written by the church historian Eusebius to Constantia, the Emperor Constantine's sister. Apparently, Constantia had requested an image of Christ. Eusebius harshly rebuked her for this request, stating that any attempt to depict Christ either in his glorified state or in his human state prior to his glorification is both impossible and unlawful, akin to pagan idolatry. He wonders at how Constantia can even make the request:

> Can it be that you have forgotten that passage in which God lays down the law that no likeness should be made either of what is in heaven or what is in the earth beneath? Have you ever heard anything of the kind either yourself in church or from

another person? Are not such things banished and excluded from churches all over the world, and is it not common knowledge that such practices are not permitted to us alone?[47]

It is evident that Eusebius regards avoiding images of Christ to be common knowledge among Christians, since (according to him) it is the universal Christian practice in obedience to the second commandment. He proceeds to recount another episode in which he had to confiscate an image purported to be of Paul and Christ: "I took it away from her and kept it in my house, as I thought it improper that such things ever be exhibited to others, lest we appear, like idol worshippers, to carry our God around in an image."[48] Elsewhere Eusebius also makes reference to Christians paying homage to statues, commenting that he is not surprised since they are acting out an old habit they retained from their former pagan world.[49]

It is hard to overstate the significance of this letter to Constantia. Eusebius is the father of church history. His knowledge of the early church is second to none. If venerating icons was really an apostolic practice, as the bishops of Nicaea II later claim, is it really fathomable that Eusebius could speak of it "common knowledge" that images are "banished and excluded from churches all over the world?"

Later in the fourth century, Epiphanius, the bishop of Salamis, relates the following incident in a letter to John, bishop of Jerusalem:

I came to a villa called Anablatha and, as I was passing, saw a lamp burning there. Asking what place it was, and learning it to be a church, I went in to pray, and found there a curtain hanging on the doors of the said church, dyed and embroidered. It bore an image either of Christ or of one of the saints;

I do not rightly remember whose the image was. Seeing this, and being loth that an image of a man should be hung up in Christ's church contrary to the teaching of the Scriptures, I tore it asunder and advised the custodians of the place to use it as a winding sheet for some poor person.[50]

He proceeds to explain that he has sent a new curtain to replace the one he destroyed, and then makes a request to John:

I beg that you will order the presbyter of the place to take the curtain which I have sent from the hands of the Reader, and that you will afterwards give directions that curtains of the other sort—opposed as they are to our religion—shall not be hung up in any church of Christ. A man of your uprightness should be careful to remove an occasion of offense unworthy alike of the Church of Christ and of those Christians who are committed to your charge.[51]

What is especially striking about this incident is that when Epiphanius asserts that these kinds of images are contrary to Scripture and unworthy of the church, he does not evidence any awareness that this position would need to be argued for. The kinds of counterarguments that would later be developed by the iconophiles apparently do not cross his mind, nor does he anticipate any possible resistance on this general position from John (despite the fact that they have a strained relationship). On the contrary, Epiphanius appears to assume that his action of removing the curtain containing these images is simply what any church leader should do. There are other places in his writings where Epiphanius affirms an even more rigorous iconoclast position, though I do not include them here because their authenticity is uncertain.[52]

We have already pointed out that what the early Christians rejected was not simply the pagan use of images, but cultic use of images *as such*. This can be further seen by the manner in which Christians continued to attack pagan idols even after churches began to have more physical objects in the post-Constantinian era. Augustine, for example, will criticize pagan use of images on the grounds that "by considering these works themselves as deities, and worshipping them as such, they serve the creature more than the Creator."[53] But then Augustine anticipates someone laying the same charge could be laid against the churches for the instruments used in churches to celebrate the sacraments:

> But, it will be said, we also have very many instruments and vessels made of materials or metal of this description for the purpose of celebrating the Sacraments, which being consecrated by these ministrations are called holy, in honour of Him Who is thus worshipped for our salvation: and what indeed are these very instruments or vessels, but the work of men's hands?

To counter this charge, Augustine rejects the whole conception of figural representation, in which prayer given to the image passes to its prototype:

> But have they mouth, and yet speak not? have they eyes, and see not? *Do we pray unto them, because through them we pray unto God?* This is the chief cause of this insane profanity, that the figure resembling the living person, which induces men to worship it, hath more influence in the minds of these miserable persons, than the evident fact that it is not living, so that it ought to be despised by the living.[54]

As we will see, the notion of transmission through the image to the prototype is the entire foundation of the theology of Nicaea II; yet Augustine finds not merely the pagan exercise of this but also the idea itself to be "insane profanity."

Iconoclast efforts continue to arise in the fifth and sixth centuries, as Christians worried about when the role of images was crossing the line into idolatry. For example, Philoxenus of Mabbug (d. 523), bishop of Hierapolis, felt the need to oppose both images of angels as well as images of Christ, destroying the former and hiding the latter (he also opposed images of the Holy Spirit as a dove).[55] However, it is important to emphasize again that the primary concern with images concerned their *cultic* use. For many Christians during these centuries, the usage of art for didactic or aesthetic purposes was perfectly acceptable. A particularly instructive flashpoint in this regard comes in the year 600 in Gregory I's letter to Serenus of Marseilles, who has been destroying icons:

It has come to our ears that your Fraternity, seeing certain adorers of images, broke and threw down these same images in Churches. And we commend you indeed for your zeal against anything made with hands being an object of adoration; but we signify to you that you ought not to have broken these images. For pictorial representation is made use of in Churches for this reason; that such as are ignorant of letters may at least read by looking at the walls what they cannot read in books. Your Fraternity therefore should have both preserved the images and prohibited the people from adoration of them, to the end that both those who are ignorant of letters might have wherewith to gather a knowledge of the history, and that the people might by no means sin by adoration of a pictorial representation.[56]

Here, Gregory opposes the destruction of images on the grounds that they serve a didactic purpose, especially for the illiterate, while at the same time making clear he regards the adoration of images (or "anything made with human hands") to constitute sin. Thus, the contrast for Gregory is not between worship and veneration, but between adoration and *teaching*. On this basis Serenus is reproved for his destruction of images—but at the same time is instructed to prohibit the people from adoring them and commended for his zeal in this regard. In a subsequent letter to Serenus, Gregory maintains the same position.[57]

Jensen helpfully summarizes how this episode enhances our understanding of the evolution of the church's use of images:

> The exchange between Gregory and Serenus shows that the Christian problem with holy images is more complicated than simply a matter of general disapproval of pictorial art. It also gives a more nuanced view of the gradual but inexorable inclusion of iconography in Christian worship spaces. Narrative images were never an evident problem and so were accepted from the beginning. The emergence of saints' portraits in the 4th and early 5th century posed new problems, insofar as these eventually came to be regarded as objects of veneration and a widely accepted component of Christian devotional practice.[58]

As we have mentioned, the veneration of icons—and the theology of icons as mediatorial—is generally seen to emerge sometime in the sixth or seventh century. The process by which this practice came into being is not entirely clear, but may have involved the veneration of relics as an intermediate step.[59] Brubaker and Haldon summarize the development as follows:

Holy portraits did not carry the same range of meanings in late antiquity as they did in the Byzantine Middle Ages, and their significance changed profoundly over the course of the sixth, seventh, and eighth centuries. By the year 800, the "icon" could serve as an intermediary between the viewer and the holy person represented; this was not the case around the year 400, nor even around the year 600. . . . It was only in the seventh century that all of the features we now associate with holy portraits fell into place, and only in the eighth and ninth that they were codified.[60]

Yet it is important to understand that this process was not neat and tidy. Even into the seventh century and later, many prominent churches remained aniconic. Price notes that during the reign of Constantine V (741–775), for example, "there were some prominent aniconic churches that lacked even decorate frescoes or mosaics, including Hagia Sophia in Constantinople. . . . Likewise, the aniconic churches of Cappadocia are likely to be even later than the ninth-century 'triumph of orthodoxy.'"[61]

Phase 3: Nicaea II and Its Context

The criteria for what constitutes an "ecumenical council" are notoriously challenging, and for our purposes here we do not need to resolve the question. It is enough to note that when we speak of Nicaea II as an ecumenical council, we do not mean that it represented the happy consensus of the church at that time. On the contrary, Nicaea II was one particular episode within a vicious, back-and-forth, highly political power struggle that dominated the Eastern church for generations. As we will show, Nicaea II then had to survive further waves of opposition in the East during the ninth century, and it was opposed for several centuries among Western churches.

The iconoclastic controversy between the iconophiles and the iconoclasts was, in the words of Georges Florovsky, "violent, bitter, and desperate."[62] It would frequently appear that one side had triumphed only for an incoming emperor to reverse policies. The grisliness of the contest is hard to grasp. One emperor would be an iconoclast, torturing iconophile priests; the next would be an iconophile, mutilating iconoclast monks. It is a story of tongues cut out, noses sawed off, eyes gouged out, skulls turned to drinking bowls, castration, torture, and family members betraying one another unto death.[63]

The individual responsible for convoking Nicaea II, Empress Irene, had her son Constantine VI's eyes gouged out before sending him to prison, where he died.[64] It is widely acknowledged that Irene's motivations for summoning Nicaea II were political. Humphreys notes that "Irene chose her path for cold political reasons"—specifically, to strengthen alliances and allow herself "to play the role of champion of Orthodoxy."[65] Further, the council's proceedings and outcome were strictly determined by imperial pressure—as Richard Price observes, "the council was strictly controlled, with the bishops acting the part that had been assigned to them."[66]

Before Irene's actions, iconoclasm appeared to have gotten the upper hand during the long reigns of the iconoclast emperors Leo III and Constantine V. The Council of Hieria, attended by some 338 bishops in 754, condemned the iconophile position on christological grounds, arguing that images of Christ tend to either separate his human and divine natures (leading to Nestorianism) or confuse them (leading to monophysitism).[67] Hieria had claimed ecumenical status. The bishops at Nicaea II would dispute this on the grounds that it lacked representation from the five major patriarchates of the early church (Rome, Constantinople, Jerusalem, Antioch, and Alexandria). However,

Nicaea II also lacked this, since the supposed oriental legates were not actually representing the Eastern patriarchs.[68] Noting this fact, Richard Price observes that "the oriental patriarchs did not know the decrees of Nicaea II and presumably did not recognize it as the seventh council. And indeed, for centuries afterwards Nicaea II was not added to the list of ecumenical councils in Syria-Palestine."[69] Despite this, Nicaea II eventually prevailed in obtaining ecumenical status.

The reaction among the Carolingian theologians in the West sheds light on Nicaea II. Around 790, Theodulf of Orleans produced his *Opus Caroli*, hundreds of pages of scathing critique of the practice of venerating icons. In 794, Charlemagne convoked the Council of Frankfurt, which was also strongly critical of Nicaea II and refused to call it an ecumenical council. But the council adopted a more moderate position than Hieria. The essential Western position was that figural art is acceptable for decorative or commemorative purposes, but it should not be worshipped or bowed to; and it ought to be neither destroyed nor mandated.[70] This final point, what Thomas Noble calls their "principled indifference," was a particular point of emphasis in Frankish theology. What was so reprehensible about Nicaea II, to the Western mind, was its insistence on the *necessity* of venerating icons, at the risk of anathema. As Theodulf put it, "It is one thing to have (images) for fear of oblivion and another to have them for love of ornament; one thing for will, another for need."[71]

It is sometimes stated that the Frankish tradition simply did not understand the issues at play in Byzantine theology, perhaps on account of lacking adequate translations of the Acts of Nicaea II. This is generally wrong. Thomas Noble has demonstrated that "the Carolingians themselves exhibited for some fifty or sixty years an essential familiarity with all the basic elements

in discussions about sacred art."[72] In reality, the Western tradition was working through its own distinctive theology of icons,
which overlapped with the concerns of Nicaea II but was not
reducible to being a mere reaction against it. In this process, the
Carolingian theologians were able to point out some real weaknesses in the theology of Nicaea II. In the first place, they noted
the abundance of forged, spurious, and apocryphal documents
upon which Nicaea II depended. Some of these were obvious
at the time, such as the letters supposedly from Jesus to King
Abgar of Edessa.[73] Other forgeries have been only more recently
discovered.[74]

Another concern raised at the Council of Frankfurt was the
strained employment of Scripture at Nicaea II. The acts of the
second session of Nicaea II, in Pope Hadrian's letter, which the
bishops approved, contain appeals like the following:

> When making his great announcement of the coming of our
> redeemer and the incarnation of the very Son of God, he
> recommends the worship of his face according to the dispen-
> sation of his manhood by saying: "I shall seek, O Lord, your
> face." And Later: "All the wealthy of the people will suppli-
> cate your face." And again: "The light of your face is stamped
> upon us, O Lord."[75]

Western theologians mocked the attempt to use these Psalms
as a support for icon veneration. Martin Chemnitz would later
echo these sentiments: "Surely, if some satirist had wanted to
attack the teaching of the papalists about images wittily, and to
set it forth to be ridiculed, he could not have adduced Scripture
more ridiculously."[76]

Western theologians also criticized Nicaea II for twisting
certain statements from earlier church fathers to make them

sound like they supported icon veneration. Perhaps the most famous example is the statement from Basil that "the honor shown to the image is transmitted to its prototype," which became foundational to the theology of Nicaea II. In context, Basil's statement was not about icons in worship; it was a theological argument concerning the Trinity drawn from an analogy of the emperor and his image.[77] The term "image" was frequently equivocated upon in this manner at Nicaea II.

But the more pervasive issue was simply the lack of any patristic support for icon veneration whatsoever. Referring to the period between Nicaea I (325) and Chalcedon (451) as the "golden age," Price summarizes the problem:

> The real problem for the iconophile cause lay . . . in the poverty of support for their cause even in the golden age of the fathers. . . . In a context of a debate that treated the fathers of the golden as the prime authority, it was a serious weakness in the iconophile cause that no single passage from any of these fathers gave an explicit stamp of approval to such veneration.[78]

Similarly, Mike Humphreys notes the attempt at Nicaea II to develop a florilegium (essentially a list of patristic citations) to prove the antiquity of icon veneration, and then observes, "What strikes a neutral reader of Nicaea's florilegium is the relative paucity of its evidence. The compilers could not find any church fathers explicitly supporting icons."[79] He then notes that neither side could find any explicit treatment of the subject because it simply wasn't an issue in the early church, and thus the iconophiles had to rely on "more recent and less authoritative figures like Leontios, hagiography, and statements from church fathers that were not originally about icons but could be used in such a way."[80]

The more moderate Western position—that icons should be neither destroyed nor venerated—was maintained at a council in Paris in 825, responding to the second wave of iconoclasm in the East. It was again articulated in 840 in Jonas of Orleans's *De cultu imaginum*, written in response to iconoclast actions of Claudius, bishop of Turin. Debate about icons continued in the West throughout the ninth century. It was not until 880, more than a century after Nicaea II, that Rome affirmed the ecumenical status of Nicaea II. Slowly, and not without controversy, the practice of venerating icons spread throughout Western churches during the eleventh through thirteenth centuries, only becoming part of canon law around 1140.[81]

The Protestant Interpretation
of Icon Veneration

How do we interpret the late arrival of icon veneration in church history? Some seek to present it as a "doctrinal development." But doctrinal development is too often harnessed as a catch-all solution for any contradiction, making the belief system in question essentially unfalsifiable. John Henry Newman himself offered strict criteria for distinguishing a valid doctrinal development from a corruption, stipulating that developments "which do but contradict and reverse the course of doctrine which has been developed before them, and out of which they spring, are certainly corrupt; for a corruption is a development in that very stage in which it ceases to illustrate, and begins to disturb, the acquisitions gained in its previous history."[82] In light of the early church's clear opposition to icon veneration, the word "disturb" is a mild one for the relation of Nicaea II to prior history.

Furthermore, the bishops at Nicaea II themselves ruled out any conception of a gradual development of icon veneration. On the contrary, they claimed that kissing icons was the "faith of the apostles" and the "ancient legislation of the catholic church."[83] Prostration and bowing before images, as well as lighting candles and incense as an offering in their honor, is "the pious custom of the men of old."[84] In maintaining this custom, the bishops insisted that "we follow Paul who spoke in Christ and the whole divine company of the apostles."[85] The whole appeal of their opposition to the iconoclasts is premised upon strict and wholesale preservation of tradition: "We anathematize those who either add anything or remove anything from the church. We anathematize the intrusive innovations of the accusers of Christians. We accept the sacred images."[86]

But if icon veneration cannot be seen as a valid development, how should its emergence and eventual acceptance in the church be regarded? With a few exceptions, the general Protestant interpretation of this historical unfolding is that it represents the creeping intrusion of idolatry into the church. Throughout the Old Testament, idolatry is presented as a continual, ensnaring temptation of the people of God. Nothing is warned against more frequently and urgently. It is clear that idolatry is not the kind of sin that one simply needs to be informed of on one occasion; rather, it appears to be a subtle, constantly encroaching danger. And indeed, the people of God continuously lapse into the idolatrous practices of the surrounding nations. From the golden calf episode at Mt. Sinai to the lurid imagery of spiritual prostitution in the later prophets, this is an ever-present theme in the story of Israel.

A conscience informed by this background will already be wondering, before reading a single page of church history: *Will the people of God fall into idolatry in the new-covenant era, as they did in the old?*

One expression of idolatry that is expressly forbidden in

Scripture involves bowing down to images. This is the concern of the second commandment (Ex. 20:4–6) and is reiterated in many other passages (for example, Lev. 26:1). The basis for this concern is the invisibility of the true God, as distinct from false gods (Deut. 4:15–18).

Hence, one quality that distinguishes the good kings of Judah like Hezekiah or Josiah is their iconoclasm—though even during their reigns cultic objects are usually not *fully* removed. A representative example is Josiah's activity in 2 Kings 23:15: "the altar at Bethel, the high place erected by Jeroboam the son of Nebat, who made Israel to sin, that altar with the high place he pulled down and burned, reducing it to dust. He also burned the Asherah." This is portrayed positively in the text; many more such examples could be adduced. As Humphreys puts it, "The Hebrew Bible is stridently, repeatedly, unavoidably anti-idolatry, and pro-idol destruction."[87]

Now, of course, defenders of icon veneration resist the charge of idolatry by distinguishing veneration, which may be appropriately directed to images, and worship, which is reserved for God alone. But such a distinction with reference to cultic practices like bowing to images is completely alien to both Scripture and the consciousness of the early church. The *act* of bowing down to images and praying through it is itself forbidden. Nowhere do we read: "Thou shalt not bow down to images—unless, of course, you are merely *venerating* them. Then it is fine!" There is not a single example of bowing down to images for *any* purpose that is portrayed positively in Scripture or the early church. The distinction between worship and veneration in this context is an innovation, later employed to justify a practice that had already come into being.

Imagine a husband and wife who live in a culture where kissing is a culturally accepted form of greeting. The wife, jealous for her husband's affections, instructs him, "Don't kiss other women!" Later he is discovered to be frequently kissing other women. When confronted, he replies, "But it is a kiss of friendship, not a kiss of romance." The wife could justifiably feel that this distinction is simply a way of getting around her request. After all, the request was simply about kissing, and no such distinction was on the table at the time. Neither is the distinction between worship and veneration visible in the context of God's commandments about images.

This is not to say that the distinction between worship and veneration is invalid in any context. When a knight bows down to a king, for example, this can be an homage, not idolatry. Bowing before people has many different meanings throughout different cultures and occurs in many places in the Bible. But this is disanalogous to an ongoing liturgical act of veneration directed to nonliving objects. Here is how this distinction was put at the Council of Frankfurt:

> It is one thing to adore a man, that is, to greet him with the duty of a salutation and with the obeisance of politeness and reverence; it is another to adore a picture. For that we should show brotherhood, love, and reverence toward our neighbors we are taught by examples of Scripture, but we are expressly forbidden to adore or to greet images. (Ex. 20:4–5)[88]

In actual practice, it is impossible to tell the difference between a person who is bowing before a nonliving object in veneration, and a person who is doing so in idolatrous worship. Imagine a man lying prostrate before a statue of Mary, praying for forgiveness. Or imagine a woman lighting candles and kneeling before an icon of her favorite saint, offering respect and seeking blessing and guidance through his intercessions.

Would any Christian in the first five hundred years of church history, observing such activities, *not* conclude it was idolatry? In the heart of the person engaging in such activity, is it not easy for feelings of loyalty and hope and affection and trust to arise that should be reserved for God? Given the dire mentality of Scripture regarding idolatry, why are such practices not regarded with greater concern?

What about the Ark or the Bronze Serpent?

In the context of this discussion, appeal is frequently made to the temple iconography, such as the cherubim on the ark of the covenant. But the ark didn't receive ongoing devotional practices of veneration. Nowhere do we find the Israelites bowing down before the ark, kissing the cherubim, lighting candles before it, or praying through it as a window to heaven. On the contrary, the ark of the covenant was built according to the express commandment of God for specific, public purposes among his people (Ex. 25:10–21).

The ark held the tablets of the law and other objects that had a special signatory role for the Israelites; for example, Aaron's staff was put there, "to be kept as a sign for the rebels" (Num. 17:10). Over its lid, the mercy seat, blood was sprinkled during the Day of Atonement ritual (Lev. 16:15); this typified Christ's atoning death (Heb. 10:19–21). It also represented the place of God's special presence among his people and was where God spoke to Moses (Ex. 25:22). There is simply no comparison between iconography expressly commanded by God for public purposes of symbolism, instruction, commemoration, etc., and iconography that is *nowhere* commanded by God (but left to the discretion of the one constructing and using it) and used for private devotional purposes of an entirely different character (bowing to it, praying through it, etc.).

Sometimes people try to use the bronze serpent held up by Moses in Numbers 21 as support for icon veneration. But again, this was a unique event for a specific purpose; and again, it was not bowed down to, prayed through as a window to heaven, etc. In fact, this example backfires on iconophile argumentation, since afterwards, when it did become an object of ongoing devotion, Hezekiah is praised for destroying: "He broke in pieces the bronze serpent that Moses had made, for until those days the people of Israel had made offerings to it (it was called Nehushtan)" (2 Kings 18:4).

There is simply no biblical basis for icon veneration. Rather, it gives every appearance of being an intrusion of idolatry into the life of God's people, as so often happens throughout redemptive history. Perhaps because it lacks any biblical foundation, icon veneration is often framed as an implication of the goodness of creation, as well as of incarnation. This has the rhetorical advantage of making the iconoclast concern sound like Gnosticism or an aversion to physicality.[89] But it is a misdirection: Both sides fully agree on the goodness of creation and the nature of the incarnation. From neither of these principles does it logically follow that it is permissible to bow down to nonliving objects in an act of religious devotion.

Conclusion

Is to be deep in history to cease to be Protestant? When it comes to the venerating of icons, to be deep in history is, emphatically to the contrary, to cease to be Roman Catholic or Eastern Orthodox. For the witness of the early church is unanimously and thunderingly opposed to the practice, in consistency with the witness of Scripture. Yet the seventh ecumenical council, which both the Roman Catholic and Eastern Orthodox traditions regard as infallible, casts anathemas widely and liberally at all who abstain from the practice (or "knowingly communicate" with those who do!).

This is not a case of doctrinal development, but doctrinal U-turn: The seventh ecumenical council *reversed* the view of the early church on the veneration of icons.

Unfortunately, traditions that consider Nicaea II to represent infallible teaching cannot reform its teaching. It is, by definition, irreformable. The Protestant tradition, by contrast, offers us a pathway of meaningful return to the practice and theology of the early church, as well as to that of later contexts like the Council of Frankfurt. It also allows us to obey the second commandment. Further, it obligates no anathemas. Therefore, it is the Protestant position on icon veneration that is not only deep in history, but biblical and catholic.

Conclusion

To Those Considering Ecclesial Changes

Throughout this book, I have articulated a vision of Protestantism in the spirit of Philip Schaff as a renewal effort within the one true church. I have argued that Protestantism represents the best available pathway to catholicity—not because it does not set boundaries to what the church is, but because those boundaries are not determined *institutionally*. By defining the church as wherever Christ is present in word and sacrament, Protestantism enables us to recognize true Christians and true churches within multiple institutional expressions of the church. This is not only the more generous position to adopt toward other Christians today, it is also the one that is most faithful to the New Testament's witness for how we discern Christ's presence and activity in his church (Matt. 7:15–20; 12:22–33; Mark 9:38–41; 1 Cor. 12:3).

I have also commended Protestantism as a return to the authority of Scripture. Protestantism does not reject tradition or other authoritative norms in the church. It simply subordinates them under the superior authority of Scripture. Nothing else the church possesses as a rule rivals the very inspired words of God given to us in the text of Holy Scripture. This alone is an infallible rule because God alone is infallible, and nothing else we have as a rule consists of the very speech of God. Other mechanisms of allegedly ongoing infallibility in the church (such as the papacy) lack biblical and historical support. The New Testament clearly stipulates the offices of the church, and the idea of a supreme, infallible head of the church identifiable with the Roman bishop isn't one of those offices. We have no reason to think the apostles ever imagined such a thing. Nor is such an office recognizable in early church history, for even after a single bishop in Rome emerges, he does not wield supremacy or personal infallibility for a very long time. Nor is there biblical or early historical support for any other alleged infallible rule outside of Scripture.

Finally, I have argued for Protestantism as a removal of historical accretions. Protestantism is not the creation of a new church, but simply the ancient faith in the posture of dynamic change and reform. That the true church never died is the consistent perspective of the magisterial Protestants—so often so that it has a label: the preservation of the church. The early Protestants sought nothing other than to pare off novel deviations from catholicity and to return to those mainstream practices and beliefs that can be plausibly related back to apostolic teaching. At the heart of what the Protestants sought to recover was the Pauline teaching that "one is justified by faith apart from works of the law" (Rom. 3:28).

What does all this ultimately yield? Simply put, if you are going to be a Christian of some kind or another, it makes the most sense to be a Protestant. This is the position that enables you to embrace the fullness of the church while simultaneously holding fast to the New Testament's witness to the apostolic deposit. This is the position, in other words, that enables you to fulfill both the obligations of love and unity, on the one hand, and the obligations of conscience and truth, on the other. Protestantism is the most catholic *and* the most biblical of all the major streams of Christianity. For a Protestant need not believe in dogmas that seem obviously untruthful (like the assumption of Mary) or adhere to practices that seem obviously nonapostolic (like the veneration of icons)—but a Protestant also need not anathematize as unchristian those who inhabit traditions that *do* adhere to such beliefs and practices (the depth of Protestant concern about them notwithstanding).

Protestantism in its contemporary expressions has many imperfections and weaknesses. One of them, particularly in my context in the United States, is the frequent (though not universal) historical shallowness, as well as the general lack of sacramental, liturgical, and aesthetic richness. These are areas where Protestants have often drifted and must humbly listen and improve—including by learning from the non-Protestant traditions.

The great, shining glory of Protestantism—that which stands out above all else, perhaps—is its radical focus on the simplicity of the gospel. Protestantism is relentlessly and structurally focused on the all-sufficiency of the person and work of Christ himself. The non-Protestant traditions may share this value in principle. But we worry that they have inadvertently added requirements on to the gospel that Christ himself would not require. (Mariology, as we have surveyed in this book, is a clear example.) We also have concerns that the freedom and certainty of the gospel is at times obscured in these other traditions—for example, in the theology of indulgences, or the necessity of confession to a priest. While we can share the core gospel message with many of the traditions outside Protestantism, certain of their practices and beliefs have the unfortunate effect of both blurring it and adding on to it. Protestantism keeps the gospel central and clear. The net result is clarity and assurance.

My guess is that many reading this book lack that sense of assurance. Exploring these deep ecclesial questions often generates deep unsettledness and anxiety. Since my deepest aim in writing this book is not just to convince people of this or that particular doctrine but also to encourage them toward a settled gospel assurance, let me conclude by giving some pastoral advice to the person struggling with their ecclesial placement and considering making a change.

First, take your time. The issues that separate the different Christian traditions are complicated. There is no way to arrive at an adequate understanding of the major differences in a few weeks or months. It takes study, reflection, prayer, and a deeply existential investment in the search for truth—and there are no shortcuts for this process.

This does *not* mean you need to be an expert. Not everyone will get a PhD in theology or history, and let me alleviate that burden from you by saying that even if you did, it would not make everything easy. And, indeed, it is possible to take too long as well. However, I have observed people move too quickly much more often than too slowly. It is easy to get enamored with one view and make a decision too rapidly, and perhaps too emotionally. Many who do this, though not all, come to later regret it.

The amount of time that is best will vary for each person, of course. I am not trying to place a legalistic burden on anyone's conscience here. But I want to advocate for each person to arrive upon a peace and reasonably settled conviction before making such a major change. My grandfather used to say, "When you are not sure what to do, don't do anything." Again, this advice could be abused toward a perpetual indecision. But it is not compromise to wait until you feel *peace* about the decision you make. For such a significant decision, and one that will profoundly affect you and those closest to you, this is not only appropriate but also responsible and wise.

Second, read and engage the *best* of each tradition. It is easy, especially in the context of a change, to study the professional theologians of another tradition while relying on your anecdotal experiences in your own tradition. I see this happening all the time with those considering leaving Protestantism. They leap from their observations of their current church (and perhaps some dialogue with their pastor) to the best of the apologetics and arguments of the other traditions—in the process bypassing Bavinck, the Puritans, the scholastic Lutherans, the Anglican greats, and other significant Protestant representatives. This obviously skews the picture.

We must be careful not to assume that we understand the best arguments for a particular tradition just because we grew up in it. Consider this analogy: The fact that someone grew up in a democracy does not mean they understand the historical reasons why democracy came to be or the best arguments for why it is so valuable. So it is with churches.

Again, not everyone will be a theological expert, reading scores of books on every topic. That is fine. But at least make sure you are not focusing only on one tradition to the neglect of others. Let it be a fair fight. If you read Philip Schaff, read John Henry Newman as well. If you read Thomas Aquinas, read Gregory Palamas. If you read the church fathers, read the Puritans. Lopsided reading leads to a skewed result. I realize this is somewhat simple advice, but I often see it violated. In the context of the excitement or angst regarding a possible change, it is easy to get swept off our feet.

Third, avoid triumphalism. The issues that divide different Christian traditions are not simple. Intelligent, sincere people disagree about them. If you think you can defeat the other side in ten seconds, you probably haven't fully understood their position. Unfortunately, each tradition has various spokespeople and advocates who will portray the differences as though all the intelligent and good people are (obviously!) on their side. It is best not to listen too much to those voices, or at least to balance them out with other voices that more accurately reflect the truth. Thankfully, each tradition also has thoughtful advocates who will help you perceive where the differences lie and the best arguments for each side.

Finally, and most importantly, remember that the most important parts of the process are prayer and simple trust in God. While it is important to study each side, that is not usually where peace and certainty issue forth. Rather, peace usually comes in a more existential way—through a full-blooded commitment to seeking truth. How we decide which church to join is a decision that can and should be brought under Proverbs 3:5–6, like all important decisions in our lives: "Trust in the Lord with all your heart, and do not lean on your own understanding. In all your ways acknowledge him, and he will make straight your paths."

This is a comforting promise. Peace in your decision does not come from being smarter than the next person who decided differently. It comes from wholly casting yourself upon the Lord. This is an exceedingly simple note on which to end this book, but I believe it is entirely appropriate: *Trust God.* If you have sought the truth to the best of your ability and made the best decision you can before God, you can rest in a posture of simple faith. Do not be anxious. God has no desire to damn you and is not looking to deceive you. He loves you. As you trust in him, he will never abandon you—to all eternity.

Notes

Epigraph Page

1. John Calvin and Jacopo Sadoleto, *A Reformation Debate*, ed. John C. Olin (New York: Fordham University Press, 2009), 56.

Introduction: How I Accidentally Became a "Protestant Apologist"

1. This clip can be viewed at Relevant, "Francis Chan on Communion: "Everyone Saw It as the Literal Body and Blood of Christ," https://relevantmagazine.com/culture/francis-chan-on -communion-everyone-saw-it-as-the-literal-body-and-blood-of -christ, accessed August 5, 2022.

2. I am referring to the famous dispute between two monks: Ratramnus, who advocated for a spiritual interpretation of the Eucharist in which the elements represent Christ's body and blood figuratively, and Paschasius Radbertus, who advocated for more of a realist view in which the elements are identified with Christ's body and blood at the moment of consecration. At this time neither view was condemned (as Berengar of Tours's symbolical view would be two centuries later). For a helpful overview of this medieval development, see Brett Salkeld,

Transubstantiation: Theology, History, and Christian Unity (Grand Rapids: Baker Academic, 2019), 57–137.

3. See Peter Martyr Vermigli, *The Oxford Treatise and Disputation on the Eucharist*, trans. and ed. Joseph C. McLelland, The Peter Martyr Vermigli Library, vol. 7 (Moscow, ID: Davenant, 2018), 48–62; Thomas Cranmer, *A Defense of the True and Catholic Doctrine of the Sacrament of the Body and Blood of Our Saviour Christ* (Eugene, OR: Wipf & Stock, 2004), 45–63.

4. On the patristic roots of Vermigli's view, see George Hunsinger, *The Eucharist and Ecumenism: Let Us Keep the Feast* (Cambridge: Cambridge University Press, 2008), 39–46.

5. Harper Lee, *To Kill a Mockingbird* (New York: Grand Central, 1960), 39.

6. E.g., see my video, "The Essence-Energies Distinction: A Protestant Reflection," Truth Unites, May 30, 2022, YouTube video, 1:08:57, https://youtu.be/gvfPICJGcHo.

Chapter 1: Protestantism's Core Identity

1. Philip Schaff, *The Principle of Protestantism*, trans. John Nevin, ed. Bard Thompson and George H. Bricker, Lancaster Series on the Mercersburg Theology 1 (Philadelphia: United Church Press, 1964), 59, italics in the original.

2. Schaff, *The Principle of Protestantism*, 57.

3. Schaff, *The Principle of Protestantism*, 47.

4. Schaff, *The Principle of Protestantism*, 74.

5. Philip Schaff, "What is Church History? A Vindication of the Idea of Historical Development," in *Reformed and Catholic: Selected Historical and Theological Writings of Philip Schaff*, ed. Charles Yrigoyen and George M. Bricker (Pittsburgh: Pickwick, 1979), 139.

6. Schaff, *The Principle of Protestantism*, 215.

7. Schaff, *The Principle of Protestantism*, 225.

8. Schaff, *The Principle of Protestantism*, 112.

9. Schaff, *The Principle of Protestantism*, 160.

10. Schaff, *The Principle of Protestantism*, 129–55.

11. Schaff, *The Principle of Protestantism*, 169, italics in the original.

12. Nevin, "Introduction," in *The Principle of Protestantism*, 37.

13. Schaff, *The Principle of Protestantism*, 153.

14. Schaff, *The Principle of Protestantism*, 201.

15. Nevin, "Introduction," 42.

16. Schaff, *The Principle of Protestantism*, 76–77.

17. Schaff, *The Principle of Protestantism*, 83.

18. Schaff, *The Principle of Protestantism*, 84.

19. Schaff, *The Principle of Protestantism*, 85.

20. Schaff, *The Principle of Protestantism*, 85–86.

21. Schaff, *The Principle of Protestantism*, 98.

22. Schaff, *The Principle of Protestantism*, 101.

23. Schaff, *The Principle of Protestantism*, 99.

24. Jaroslav Pelikan, ed., *Luther's Works, vol. 26, Lectures on Galatians 1535: Chapters 1–4* (St. Louis: Concordia, 1963), 24.

25. *Luther's Works, vol. 26*, 24.

26. Conrad Bergendoff, ed., *Luther's Works, vol. 40, Church and Ministry II* (Philadelphia: Fortress, 1958), 231–32.

27. Bergendoff, ed., *Luther's Works, vol. 40*, 232.

28. Calvin and Jacopo, *A Reformation Debate*, 69.

29. John Calvin, *Institutes of the Christian Religion* 4.2.12, vol. 2, ed. John T. McNeill, trans. Ford Lewis Battles (Louisville: Westminster John Knox, 2006), 1052, italics in the original.

30. Calvin, *Institutes of the Christian Religion* 4.2.11–12, vol. 2, 1052–53.

31. Francis Turretin, *Institutes of Elenctic Theology* 14.1.3, vol. 3, ed. James T. Denniston, trans. George M. Giger (Phillipsburg, NJ: P&R, 1997), 121.

32. Turretin, *Institutes of Elenctic Theology* 14.1.3, 121.

33. Richard Hooker, *The Ecclesiastical Polity and Other Works of Richard Hooker*, ed. Benjamin Hanbury (London: Holdsworth and Ball, 1830), 201–02.

34. Calvin, *Institutes of the Christian Religion* 4.2.2, vol. 2, 1043.

35. Calvin, *Institutes of the Christian Religion* 4.2.2, vol. 2, 1043n5.

36. George Mastrantonis, *Augsburg and Constantinople: The Correspondence Between the Tübingen Theologians and Patriarch Jeremiah II of Constantinople on the Augsburg Confession* (Brookline, MA: Holy Cross, 1982), 27–28.

37. Mastrantonis, *Augsburg and Constantinople*, 29.

38. See the summary in "Protestant-Orthodox Relationship: The Moment That Defined It," Truth Unites, June 12, 2023, YouTube video, 17:41, https://www.youtube.com/watch?v=u95i1nSrWzA.

39. Mastrantonis, *Augsburg and Constantinople*, 30.

40. Mastrantonis, *Augsburg and Constantinople*, 210.

41. Mastrantonis, *Augsburg and Constantinople*, 210.

42. Mastrantonis, *Augsburg and Constantinople*, 305.

43. Mastrantonis, *Augsburg and Constantinople*, 306.

44. Mastrantonis, *Augsburg and Constantinople*, 313.

45. Mastrantonis, *Augsburg and Constantinople*, 314.

46. Mastrantonis, *Augsburg and Constantinople*, 149.

Chapter 2: "The One True Church"

1. For example, Augustine, *City of God* 1.35, in *Nicene and Post-Nicene Fathers*, first series, vol. 2, ed. Philip Schaff (1885; repr. Peabody: Hendrickson, 2012), 21; Augustine, *On Baptism, Against the Donatists* 3.19.26–28, in *Nicene and Post-Nicene Fathers*, first series, vol. 4, 444–46; Augustine, *On Rebuke and Grace* 20–22, in *Nicene and Post-Nicene Fathers*, first series, vol. 5, 479–80.

2. For an overview of Justin, Irenaeus, Clement of Alexandra, and Origen on this point, see Francis A. Sullivan, *Salvation Outside the Church? Tracing the History of the Catholic Response* (Mahwah, NJ: Paulist, 1992), 14–17.

3. Cyprian, "Epistle 72," in *Ante-Nicene Fathers*, vol. 5, ed. Alexander Roberts (1885; repr. Peabody: Hendrickson, 2012), 379–86.

4. For a classic articulation of several of these themes, see Alexei Stepanovich Khomiakov, *The Church is One* (1863; reprint, London: Fellowship of St. Alban and St. Sergius, 1968).

5. Schema-monk Metrophanes, *Blessed Paisius Velichkovsky: The Life and Ascetic Labors of Our Father, Elder Paisius, Archimandrite of the Holy Moldavian Monasteries of Niamets and Sekoul* (Platina, CA: Saint Herman of Alaska Brotherhood, 1976), 201.

6. Metrophanes, *Blessed Paisius Velichkovsky*, 201.

7. Metrophanes, *Blessed Paisius Velichkovsky*, 202.

8. *The Confession of Dositheus* in *The Holy Standards: The Creeds, Confessions of Faith, and Catechisms of the Eastern Orthodox Church*, ed. Joshua Schooping (Olyphany, PA: St. Theophan the Recluse, 2020), 25–86. For reference to Protestants as heretics, see, e.g., Decrees 2 and 3.

9. *The Confession of Dositheus*, "Decree 10," in *The Holy Standards*, 42.

10. *The Confession of Dositheus*, "Decree 10," in *The Holy Standards*, 45.

11. "Encyclical of the Eastern Patriarchs, 5.xv, http://orthodoxinfo.com/ecumenism/encyc_1848.aspx, accessed September 20, 2022.

12. "The Patriarchal Encyclical of 1895," XXIV, http://orthodoxinfo.com/ecumenism/encyc_1895.aspx, accessed May 30, 2023.

13. "Longer Catechism of St. Philaret of Moscow," in *The Holy Standards*, 191. Again, bear in mind that historically, the Eastern Orthodox Church has referred to itself as "Catholic."

14. Another example would be the series of anathemas against Roman Catholics and all Western Christians, employing the standard ark of Noah imagery, in the "Sigillion of 1583"—though I refrain from including it here because it has a disputed textual history.

15. Timothy Ware, *The Orthodox Church: An Introduction to Eastern Christianity, 3rd ed.* (New York: Penguin, 2015), 240.

16. *The Catechism of the Catholic Church* 2nd ed. (New York: Doubleday, 2000), 847; hereafter cited as *CCC* with paragraph number).

17. See *CCC* 839–841.

18. Pope Boniface VIII, "Unam Sanctam, https://www.newadvent.org/library/docs_bo08us.htm, accessed May 31, 2023. The Unam Sanctam was also significant for laying out the medieval theory of the two swords (the spiritual and the temporal), which was used to justify terrible violence.

19. Sullivan, *Salvation Outside the Church?*, 103.

20. As cited in Christopher E. Reyes, *In His Name* (Bloomington, IN: AuthorHouse, 2010), 45.

21. As cited in Reyes, *In His Name*, 45, italics mine.

22. As cited in Reyes, *In His Name*, 45.

23. "The Confession of Dositheus," Decree 17, in *The Holy Standards*, 65. Recall that "Catholic" here does not mean "Roman Catholic."

Chapter 3: Catalysts for Reformation

1. The Council of Trent, Session 25, Third Decree, http://www.thecounciloftrent.com/ch25.htm, accessed May 31, 2023.

2. "Pope Leo X," in *The Catholic Encyclopedia*, https://www.newadvent.org/cathen/09162a.htm, accessed May 31, 2023. A ducat was a form of monetary currency.

3. See Scott H. Hendrix, *Martin Luther: Visionary Reformer* (New Haven: Yale University Press), 57.

4. For an overview of some of these efforts, see Helen Parish, *Clerical Celibacy in the West: C.1100–1700* (London: Routledge, 2010), 123–24.

5. Justo Gonzalez, *The Story of Christianity: The Reformation to the Present Day*, vol. 2 (San Francisco: HarperSanFrancisco, 1985), 6.

6. Martin Chemnitz, *Examination of the Council of Trent*, trans. Fred Kramer, vol. 4 (St. Louis: Concordia, 1986), 228–33.

7. Chemnitz, *Examination*, vol. 4, 230.

8. Chemnitz, *Examination*, vol. 4, 232.

9. See especially Nikolaus Paulus, *Indulgences as a Social Factor in the Middle Ages*, trans. J. Elliot Ross (1922; reprint; Honolulu:

University Press of the Pacific, 2001). For a classic Protestant account, see Henry Charles Lea, *A History of Auricular Confession and Indulgences in the Latin Church*, vol. 3 (Philadelphia: Lea Brothers & Co, 1896). For an overview of more recent scholarship on the historical development of indulgences, see Ethan Leong Yee, "Lest the Keys Be Scorned: The Implications of Indulgences for the Church Hierarchy and Thirteenth-Century Canonists' Resistance to the Treasury of Merit," *Traditio* 76 (2021): 248–49.

10. E.g., The Synod of Ancyra, canon 22, https://www.newadvent .org/fathers/3802.htm, accessed May 31, 2023.

11. For an older but lucid discussion of this historical development, see John F. Sullivan, *The Externals of the Catholic Church: Her Government, Ceremonies, Festivals, Sacramentals, and Devotions* (New York: P.J. Kenedy & Sons, 1917), 297–99.

12. Paulus, *Indulgences as a Social Factor*, 14.

13. Chemnitz, *Examination*, vol. 4, 208.

14. Enrico dal Covolo, "The Historical Origin of Indulgences," italics in the original, https://www.catholicculture.org/culture /library/view.cfm?recnum=1054#1, accessed May 31, 2023.

15. Thomas Schirrmacher, *Indulgences: A History of Theology and Reality of Indulgences and Purgatory: A Protestant Evaluation*, 2nd *ed.* (Bonn: Culture and Science, 2012), 33.

16. Yee, "Lest the Keys Be Scorned," 252–53, observes that there is no evidence for the common claim that Hugh of St. Cher was the first to formulate the theory.

17. Lea, *A History of Auricular Confession and Indulgences in the Latin Church*, 35–38, outlines the influence of the introduction of the treasury of merit on papal power.

18. For an overview, see *The Catholic Encyclopedia*, "Holy Year of Jubilee," https://www.newadvent.org/cathen/08531c.htm, accessed May 31, 2023.

19. Schirrmacher, *Indulgences*, 69.

20. Schirrmacher, *Indulgences*, 27–31, 39–40.

21. As cited in Schirrmacher, *Indulgences*, 28.

22. For example, Mark Gregory Pegg, *A Most Holy War: The Albigensian Crusade and the Battle for Christendom* (Oxford: Oxford University Press, 2008), 188–90, defends this categorization for the Albigensian Crusade, an early thirteenth-century crusade initiated by Pope Innocent III.

23. *Luther's Works, vol. 40*, 232.

24. Thomas A. Fudge, *The Trial of Jan Hus: Medieval Heresy and Criminal Procedure* (Oxford: Oxford University Press, 2013), xxi.

25. See Fudge, *The Trial of Jan Hus*, 29–30. At the same time, Fudge acknowledges "disgraceful disorder, disruption, and dishonor" during the public hearings of the trial, which in his view were not only "shameful" but contrary to canon law (343).

26. Fudge, *The Trial of Jan Hus*, 347.

27. Fudge, *The Trial of Jan Hus*, xix, notes as representative of this school of thought the claim of David R. Holeton, "The Celebration of Jan Hus in the Life of the Churches," *Studia Liturgica*, 35.1 (2005): 58: "it can be demonstrated that the trial at Constance did not follow the legal norms of the time." Hus was also denied legal representation. The Czech medieval canon law specialist Jiří Kejř produced the only full-scale study of the Hus trial (*Husův process* [Prague: Vyšehrad, 2000]). Of course, legality is not the same as morality: as František Šmahel notes, Stalin's trials were *legal* as well (see František Šmahel, "Introduction," in *A Companion to Jan Hus*, ed. František Šmahel and Ota Pavlíček [Leiden: Brill, 2015], 5).

28. Fudge, *The Trial of Jan Hus*, 347–48.

29. John Paul II, "Address of the Holy Father to an International Symposium on John Hus," December 17, 1999, https://www.vatican.va/content/john-paul-ii/en/speeches/1999/december/documents/hf_jp-ii_spe_17121999_jan-hus.html.

30. Fudge, *The Trial of Jan Hus*, 17.

31. Fudge, *The Trial of Jan Hus*, 13.

32. Fudge, *The Trial of Jan Hus*, 13.

33. David S. Schaff, *John Huss: His Life, Teachings and Death, After Five Hundred Years* (New York: Charles Scribner's, 1915), 254.

34. Fudge, *The Trial of Jan Hus*, 13–14.

35. Fudge, *The Trial of Jan Hus*, 14.

36. For a classic study on why persecution increased dramatically in the medieval church, see R. I. Moore, *The Formation of a Persecuting Society: Authority and Deviance in Western Europe 950–1250, 2nd ed.* (Oxford: Blackwell, 2007); for an introduction to the Inquisition, see Cullen Murphy, *God's Jury: The Inquisition and the Making of the Modern World* (New York: Houghton Mifflin Harcourt, 2012).

37. Pope Boniface VIII, *"Unam Sanctam,"* https://www.newadvent.org/library/docs_bo08us.htm, italics mine, accessed May 31, 2023.

38. As cited in *Reading the Middle Ages: Sources from Europe, Byzantium, and the Islamic World*, ed. Barbara H. Rosenwein, 3rd ed. (Toronto: University of Toronto Press, 2018), 367.

39. Innocent IV, *Ad Extirpanda*, Law 1, see http://www.documentacatholicaomnia.eu/01p/1252-05-15,_SS_Innocentius_IV,_Bulla_%27Ad_Extirpanda%27,_EN.pdf, accessed May 31, 2023.

40. On this point, see Schaff, *John Huss*, 249.

41. See Oscar Kuhns and Robert Dickie, *Jan Hus: Reformation in Bohemia* (Stornoway, Scotland: Reformation Press, 2017), 79–80.

42. Schaff, *John Huss*, 213–27, provides a helpful overview of these 39 articles.

43. Schaff, *John Huss*, 113–14.

44. For an account of Jerome's life and thought, who is an important thinker in his own right and not merely an echo of Hus, see Thomas A. Fudge, *Jerome of Prague and the Foundations of the Hussite Movement* (Oxford: Oxford University Press, 2016).

45. For a fascinating historical account of the early history of the Hussite movement, see *Origins of the Hussite Uprising: The Chronicle of Laurence of Brezona (1414–1421)*, trans. Thomas A.

Fudge (Routledge Medieval Translations; New York: Routledge, 2020). For a contemporary introduction, see *The Crusade against Heretics in Bohemia, 1418–1437: Sources and Documents for the Hussite Crusades*, ed. Thomas A. Fudge (Crusade Texts in Translation; New York: Routledge, 2016).

46. Euan Cameron, *The Reformation of the Heretics: The Waldenses of the Alps, 1480–1580* (Oxford: Oxford University Press, 1984), 72.

47. Cameron, *The Reformation of the Heretics*, 76–79.

48. Cameron, *The Reformation of the Heretics*, 30–32.

49. Lea, *A History of Auricular Confession and Indulgences in the Latin Church*, 377.

50. Lea, *A History of Auricular Confession and Indulgences in the Latin Church*, 373–74. Flagellants are those who whip themselves as a form of penance.

51. Lea, *A History of Auricular Confession and Indulgences in the Latin Church*, 379.

52. Lea, *A History of Auricular Confession and Indulgences in the Latin Church*, 377–78.

Chapter 4: The Recovery of *Sola Fide*

1. Kurt Aland, ed., *Martin Luther's 95 Theses* (St. Louis: Concordia, 2004), 55.

2. As cited and narrated in Lyndal Roper, *Martin Luther: Renegade and Prophet* (London: Random House, 2016), 4.

3. Denis R. Janz, ed., *A Reformation Reader: Primary Texts with Introductions* (Minneapolis: Fortress, 1999), 82.

4. Janz, *A Reformation Reader*, 82.

5. Ashley Null, "Sola Gratia," in *Reformation Anglicanism: A Vision for Today's Global Communion* (The Reformation Anglicanism Essential Library, vol. 1; Wheaton, IL: Crossway, 2017), 106. Thanks to Sean Duncan for pointing me to this passage.

6. For a helpful overview, see Timothy George, *Theology of the Reformers* (Nashville: Broadman and Holman, 1988), 62–73.

7. For a helpful overview of Catholic-Protestant dialogue

throughout the latter half of the twentieth century, see Anthony N. S. Lane, *Justification by Faith in Catholic-Protestant Dialogue: An Evangelical Assessment* (New York: T&T Clark, 2002).

8. *CCC* 1989.

9. Michael Horton, *Justification*, vol. 1 of *New Studies in Dogmatics* (Grand Rapids: Zondervan, 2018), 25.

10. As cited in Lane, *Justification by Faith in Catholic-Protestant Dialogue*, 181.

11. Hans Küng, *Justification: The Doctrine of Karl Barth and a Catholic Reflection* (Louisville: Westminster John Knox, 2004), 221.

12. These are spelled out, for example, in The Council of Trent, Session 6, Chapter 7, http://www.thecounciloftrent.com/ch25.htm, accessed May 31, 2023.

13. This point is well made by Henri Blocher, "The Lutheran-Catholic Declaration on Justification," in *Justification in Perspective: Historical Developments and Contemporary Perspectives*, ed. Bruce L. McCormack (Grand Rapids: Baker Academic, 2006), 211–12.

14. J. I. Packer, "Crosscurrents among Evangelicals," in *Evangelicals & Catholics Together: Toward a Common Mission*, ed. Charles Colson and Richard J. Neuhaus (Dallas: Word, 1995), 147–174. See also, "Why I Signed It," *Christianity Today*, December 12, 1994: 34–37.

15. Calvin, *Institutes*, 3:11:20.

16. Alister E. McGrath, *Iustitia Dei: A History of the Christian Doctrine of Justification, 3rd ed.* (Cambridge: Cambridge University Press, 2005), 210–18.

17. For discussion and examples, see Lane, *Justification by Faith in Catholic-Protestant Dialogue*, 138–39.

18. John Chrysostom, Homilies on Second Corinthians 11.5, in *Nicene and Post-Nicene Fathers*, first series, vol. 12, 334.

19. John Chrysostom, Homilies on Romans 7, in *Nicene and Post-Nicene Fathers*, first series, vol. 11, 378.

20. John Chrysostom, Homilies on Romans 7, in *Nicene and Post-Nicene Fathers*, first series, vol. 11, 380.

21. John Chrysostom, Homilies on Romans 8, in *Nicene and Post-Nicene Fathers*, first series, vol. 11, 380.

22. See especially Horton, *Justification*, vol. 1, 39–91.

23. Jaroslav Pelikan, *The Riddle of Roman Catholicism* (Nashville: Abingdon Press, 1959), 49, 51–52.

24. As cited in Lane, *Justification by Faith in Catholic-Protestant Dialogue*, 94.

Chapter 5: The Case for *Sola Scriptura*

1. "The Confession of Dositheus," Decree 2, in *The Holy Standards*, 28.

2. *CCC* 107.

3. Anthony N. S. Lane, "*Sola Scriptura*? Making Sense of a Post-Reformation Slogan," in *A Pathway into the Holy Scripture*, ed. P.E. Satterthwaite and D.F. Wright (Grand Rapids: Eerdmans, 1994), 324.

4. So Oliver D. Crisp, *God Incarnate: Explorations in Christology* (New York: T&T Clark, 2009), 17. See his fuller construal of these categories and terms on 9–17.

5. "The Thirty-Nine Articles of Religion," Article 20, in *Creeds, Confessions, and Catechisms: A Reader's Edition*, ed. Chad Van Dixhoorn (Wheaton, IL: Crossway, 2022), 123.

6. Turretin, *Institutes of Elenctic Theology* 2.20.2, vol. 1, 154.

7. On the distinction between the sufficiency of Scripture and *sola Scriptura*, as well as where they overlap, see Lane, "*Sola Scriptura*? Making Sense of a Post-Reformation Slogan," 318–27.

8. The Thirty-Nine Articles, http://anglicansonline.org/basics/thirty-nine_articles.html, accessed March 27, 2023.

9. For a good summary of Luther's position, see George, *Theology of the Reformers*, 80–81.

10. *The Westminster Confession of Faith* 1.6 (Glasgow: Free Presbyterian, 1966), 22.

11. Prolegomena are items discussed first in the task of theology; often they concern matters of method that are helpful to address before the content of Christian doctrine is engaged, just as getting the right prescription of glasses is necessary before you can inspect the painting.

12. John R. W. Stott, *The Message of 2 Timothy: Guard the Gospel* (Downers Grove, IL: InterVarsity, 1973), 101–02.

13. Benjamin B. Warfield, *The Inspiration and Authority of the Bible* (Phillipsburg, NJ: Presbyterian & Reformed, 1948), 137.

14. For why this phrase is best taken as referring to the Old Testament Scriptures, see Douglas J. Moo, *The Epistle to the Romans*, New International Commentary on the New Testament (Grand Rapids: Eerdmans, 1996), 182–83.

15. *CCC* 81.

16. *CCC* 80–82.

17. *CCC* 2035.

18. *CCC* 66. On this point, see Keith A. Mathison, *The Shape of Sola Scriptura* (Moscow, ID: Canon, 2001), 165–66.

19. E.g., see Georges Florovsky, *Bible, Church, Tradition: An Eastern Orthodox View* (Wellington, New Zealand: Crux Press, 2022). Different Eastern Orthodox theologians construe the precise relationship between Scripture and tradition differently. For a brief overview, see Michael Horton, *The Christian Faith: A Systematic Theology for Pilgrims on the Way* (Grand Rapids: Zondervan, 2011), 186–87.

20. E.g., Trent Horn, *The Case for Catholicism: Answers to Classic and Contemporary Protestant Objections* (San Francisco: Ignatius, 2017), 40–44.

21. D. A. Carson, *Matthew*, in *The Expositor's Bible Commentary*, vol. 8, ed. Frank E. Gaebelein (Grand Rapids: Zondervan, 1984), 348.

22. As cited in Mathison, *The Shape of Sola Scriptura*, 173.

23. John R. W. Stott, *The Message of Acts: The Spirit, the Church, & the World* (The Bible Speaks Today; Downers Grove, IL: InterVarsity, 1990), 274.

24. See the discussion and quotations in William Goode, *The Divine Rule of Faith and Practice* (London: J. Hatchard and Son, 1842), 323–23.

25. *The Church History of Eusebius* 5.24, in *Nicene and Post-Nicene Fathers*, second series, vol. 1, 242–44.

26. *Against Heresies* 2.22.5, in *Ante-Nicene Fathers*, vol. 1, 391–92.

27. See the discussion and quotations in Goode, *The Divine Rule of Faith and Practice*, 330–43.

28. On this point, see Goode, *The Divine Rule of Faith and Practice*, 344–45.

29. Edward Feser and Joseph M. Bessette, *By Man Shall His Blood Be Shed: A Catholic Defense of Capital Punishment* (San Francisco: Ignatius, 2017), 11–12.

30. *CCC* 2267.

Chapter 6: Objections to *Sola Scriptura*

1. E.g., Decrees of the First Vatican Council, Session 3, Chapter 2, https://www.papalencyclicals.net/councils/ecum20.htm, accessed May 31, 2023.

2. For helpful examples, see Richard A. Muller, *Post-Reformation Reformed Dogmatics, vol. 2: Holy Scripture: The Cognitive Foundation of Theology* (Grand Rapids: Baker, 1993), 358–88.

3. As cited in Horton, *The Christian Faith*, 193.

4. As cited in Kenneth J. Collins and Jerry L. Walls, *Roman but Not Catholic: What Remains at Stake 500 Years After the Reformation* (Grand Rapids: Baker Academic, 2017), 21.

5. As cited in Philip Edgcumbe Hughes, *Theology of the English Reformers* (Grand Rapids: Eerdmans, 1965), 36.

6. Muller, *Post-Reformation Reformed Dogmatics, Vol. 2*, 361.

7. Muller, *Post-Reformation Reformed Dogmatics, Vol. 2*, 358–63. McGrath, *The Intellectual Origins of the European Reformation* (Grand Rapids: Baker, 1995), 140–51, also draws attention to points of continuity between the Protestant position on this

point and a tradition of thought throughout the fourteenth and fifteenth centuries.

8. Collins and Walls, *Roman but Not Catholic*, 21.

9. For an overview of the canonization of the New Testament, see John D. Meade and Peter J. Gurry, *Scribes and Scriptures: The Amazing Story of How We Got the Bible* (Wheaton, IL: Crossway, 2022), 147–65.

10. Michael J. Kruger, *The Question of Canon: Challenging the Status Quo in the New Testament Debate* (Downers Grove, IL: IVP Academic, 2013), 119–54.

11. On this point, see Peter Balla, "Evidence for an Early Christian Canon (Second and Third Century)," in *The Canon Debate*, eds. Lee Martin McDonald and James A. Sanders (Peabody, MA: Hendrickson, 2002), 372–85.

12. For helpful discussion, see Meade and Gurry, *Scribes and Scriptures*, 111–20.

13. For discussion, see Steve Mason, "Josephus and His Twenty-Two Canon," in *The Canon Debate*, 110–27. The question of which Old Testament canon is the correct one is out of the scope of this chapter (I have addressed that elsewhere); our concern is to show that the recognition of Old Testament Scripture as such did not depend on an exercise of infallibility by the people of God. For a classic defense of the Protestant Old Testament canon, see William Whitaker, trans. William Fitzgerald, *A Disputation on Holy Scripture Against the Papists, Especially Bellarmine and Stapleton* (Cambridge: Cambridge University Press, 1849), 25–109.

14. For example, Josiah Trenham, *Rock and Sand: An Orthodox Appraisal of the Protestant Reformers and Their Teachings, 3rd ed.* (Columbia, MO: Newrome, 2018), 163.

15. Chemnitz, *Examination of the Council of Trent*, vol. 1, 219–307.

16. Chemnitz, *Examination of the Council of Trent*, vol. 1, 272.

17. Heiko A. Oberman, *Forerunners of the Reformation: The Shape*

of Late Medieval Thought, trans. Paul L. Nyhus (London: Lutterworth, 1967), 55. See also Heiko A. Oberman *Harvest of Medieval Theology: Gabriel Biel and Late Medieval Nominalism* (Grand Rapids: Baker Academic, 2000).

18. For an overview of the medieval development, see Alister McGrath, *Intellectual Origins of European Reformation*, 141–48, and Mathison, *The Shape of Sola Scriptura*, 19–81.

19. J. N. D. Kelly, *Early Christian Doctrines, rev. ed.* (New York: HarperOne, 1978), 47.

20. St. Basil the Great, *On the Holy Spirit* 7.16, trans. David Anderson (Crestwood, NY: St Vladimir's, 1980), 34.

21. Mathison, *The Shape of Sola Scriptura*, 15.

22. E.g., see Kevin J. Vanhoozer, endorsement of Collins and Wallins, *Roman but Not Catholic*; for an explication of this concern, Horton, *The Christian Faith*, 187–98.

23. Whitaker, *A Disputation on Holy Scripture*, 670–704.

24. Augustine, *On Baptism, Against the Donatists* 2.3.4, in *Nicene and Post-Nicene Fathers*, first series, vol. 4, 427.

25. See https://www.newadvent.org/cathen/12164c.htm.

26. Augustine, "Answer to Maximus the Arian," in *The Works of Saint Augustine: A Translation for the 21st Century, vol. 1*, ed. John E. Rotelle, trans. Ronald E. Teske (Hyde Park, NY: New City Press, 1990), 282.

27. E.g., such a rendering is nowhere documented in Charlton T. Lewis and Charles Short, *A Latin Dictionary* (Oxford: Oxford University Press, 1879), 640–41.

28. E.g., Augustine, *On Baptism, Against the Donatists* 2.4.5, in *Nicene and Post-Nicene Fathers*, first series, vol. 4, 427, in the next sentence, speaks of how Cyprian was "most willing to *correct* his own opinion" (my italics). There are several other instances of doctrinal "correction" in the immediate context; all involve a genuine error.

29. For one example, see *On Baptism, Against the Donatists* 5.23.31, in *Nicene and Post-Nicene Fathers*, first series, vol. 4, 475.

30. Augustine, *On Baptism, Against the Donatists* 2.4.5, in *Nicene and Post-Nicene Fathers*, first series, vol. 4, 427.

31. Cf. Lewis and Short, *A Latin Dictionary*, 1719.

32. Robert B. Eno, "Doctrinal Authority in Saint Augustine," *Augustinian Studies* 12 (1981): 137, 138. See also his summary on 133.

Chapter 7: The Papacy

1. Decrees of the First Vatican Council, Session 4, Chapter 1, https://www.papalencyclicals.net/councils/ecum20.htm, accessed April 2, 2023.

2. Decrees of the First Vatican Council, Session 4, Chapter 2, https://www.papalencyclicals.net/councils/ecum20.htm, accessed April 2, 2023.

3. Decrees of the First Vatican Council, Session 4, Chapter 4, https://www.papalencyclicals.net/councils/ecum20.htm, accessed April 2, 2023.

4. Decrees of the First Vatican Council, Session 4, Chapter 3, https://www.papalencyclicals.net/councils/ecum20.htm, accessed April 2, 2023.

5. Cyprian, *The Unity of the Church 4*, in *Ante-Nicene Fathers*, vol. 5, 422, italics mine.

6. As cited in Ed Siecienski, *The Papacy and the Orthodox: Sources and History of a Debate* (Oxford: Oxford University Press, 2017), 128, who provides other examples of this Cyprianic view throughout the patristic era as well.

7. John Chrysostom, Homily 33, in *Nicene and Post-Nicene Fathers*, first series, vol. 11, 207.

8. Augustine, Sermon 149.5–6, as cited in Siecienski, *The Papacy and the Orthodox*, 129.

9. Siecienski, *The Papacy and the Orthodox*, 116.

10. Augustine, *Retractions* 20.1, in *The Fathers of the Church: A New Translation*, trans. M. Inez Bogan (Washington DC: Catholic University of America Press, 1968), 90.

11. David Bradshaw, "Giving Honor to Whom Honor is Due: A Reply to Michael Root," in *The Gospel of John: Theological-Ecumenical Readings* (Eugene, OR: Wipf and Stock, 2017), 243.

12. Cited in W. J. Sparrow Simpson, *Roman Catholic Opposition to Papal Infallibility* (London: John Murray, 1909), 320.

13. Cited in Simpson, *Roman Catholic Opposition to Papal Infallibility*, 324.

14. John W. O'Malley, *Vatican I: The Council and the Making of the Ultramontane Church* (Cambridge, MA: Belknap, 2018), 197.

15. For various Eastern Orthodox perspectives on the papacy, see *The Primacy of Peter: Essays in Ecclesiology and the Early Church*, ed. John Meyendorff (Crestwood, NY: St Vladimir's Seminary Press, 1992).

16. "The Epistle of Ignatius to the Romans," in *Ante-Nicene Fathers*, vol. 1, 73. See also Ignatius's language about the Ephesian and Smyrnean churches.

17. Cyprian, *The Unity of the Church 4*, in *Ante-Nicene Fathers*, vol. 5, 422.

18. Cyprian, Letter 71 3.1, in *The Letters of St. Cyprian of Carthage*, vol. 4, trans. G. W. Clarke (New York: Newman Press, 1984), 50. The word "seniority" is the Latin word *primatus* and is often translated as "primacy" or "supremacy."

19. Brian Tierney, *Origins of Papal Infallibility, 1150–1350* (Leiden: Brill, 2022), 281.

20. *Lumen Gentium* 22, https://www.vatican.va/archive/hist _councils/ii_vatican_council/documents/vat-ii_const_19641121 _lumen-gentium_en.html, accessed April 3, 2023.

21. For a classic Protestant explication of this point, and replies to responses, see the older study of Edward Denny, *Papalism: A Treatise on the Claims of the Papacy as Set Forth in the Encyclical Satis Cognitum* (London: Rivingtons, 1912), 131–39.

22. *Lumen Gentium* 22, https://www.vatican.va/archive/hist _councils/ii_vatican_council/documents/vat-ii_const_19641121 _lumen-gentium_en.html, accessed June 1, 2023.

23. This is known as the "Three Chapter Controversy." The three figures involved were Theodore of Mopsuestia, Theodoret of Cyrus, and Ibas of Edessa. I have discussed the whole episode at greater length in my videos.
24. Richard Price, *The Acts of the Council of Constantinople of 553 With Related Texts on the Three Chapters Controversy* (Liverpool: Liverpool University Press, 2009), 56.
25. Price, *The Acts of the Council of Constantinople of 553 With Related Texts on the Three Chapters Controversy*, 56.
26. Price, *The Acts of the Council of Constantinople of 553 With Related Texts on the Three Chapters Controversy*, vol. 2, 101.
27. Klaus Schatz, *Papal Primacy. From Its Origins to the Present* (Collegeville: Liturgical Press, 1996), 53.
28. Price, *The Acts of the Council of Constantinople of 553 With Related Texts on the Three Chapters Controversy*, 57.

Chapter 8: Apostolic Succession

1. John Henry Newman, "Tract 1: Thoughts on the Ministerial Commission, Respectfully Addressed to the Clergy" in *Religious Controversies of the Nineteenth Century: Selected Documents*, ed. A.O.J. Cockshut (Lincoln, NE: University of Nebraska Press, 1966), 65.
2. Newman, "Tract 1: Thoughts on the Ministerial Commission, Respectfully Addressed to the Clergy," 65, italics in the original.
3. For an overview, E. Rozanne Elder, "Anglican-Orthodox Relations: A Long-Term Overview," in *One Lord, One Faith, One Baptism: Studies in Christian Ecclesiality and Ecumenism in Honor of J. Robert Wright*, eds. Marsha L. Dutton and Patrick Terrell Gray (Grand Rapids: Eerdmans, 2006), 262–83.
4. Stanley Archer, "Hooker on Apostolic Succession: The Two Voices," *The Sixteenth Century Journal* 24.1 (1993): 67.
5. Newman, "Tract 1: Thoughts on the Ministerial Commission, Respectfully Addressed to the Clergy," 65.
6. J. B. Lightfoot, *Saint Paul's Epistle to the Philippians, 3rd ed.* (London: Macmillan, 1873), 93.

7. Francis Sullivan, *From Apostles to Bishops: The Development of the Episcopacy in the Early Church* (Mahwah, NJ: Newman, 2001), viii.

8. Raymond Brown, *Priest and Bishop: Biblical Reflections* (Eugene, OR: Wipf and Stock, 1999), 72, 73.

9. *Catholic Encyclopedia*, "Bishop," https://www.newadvent.org/cathen/02581b.htm, accessed March 31, 2023.

10. Alistair C. Stewart, *The Original Bishops: Office and Order in the First Christian Communities* (Grand Rapids: Baker Academic, 2014).

11. Didache 15, https://www.newadvent.org/fathers/0714.htm, accessed March 31, 2023.

12. *The First Epistle of Clement* 42, in *Ante-Nicene Fathers*, vol. 1, 16.

13. *The First Epistle of Clement* 42, in *Ante-Nicene Fathers*, vol. 1, 16.

14. *The First Epistle of Clement* 44, in *Ante-Nicene Fathers*, vol. 1, 17. It is also significant that for Clement, presbyter-bishops who hold this office after the apostles died are appointed "with the consent of the whole church."

15. *The First Epistle of Clement* 47, 57, in *Ante-Nicene Fathers*, vol. 1, 18, 20.

16. Eamon Duffy, *Saints and Sinners: A History of the Popes, 3rd ed.* (New Haven, CT: Yale University Press, 2006), 10.

17. *The Pastor of Hermas*, Vision 2.4, 3.9, in *Ante-Nicene Fathers*, vol. 2, 14, 16.

18. The Epistle of Polycarp to the Philippians 5–6, in *Ante-Nicene Fathers*, vol. 1, 34. Polycarp opens the letter referencing "the presbyters with him," which can be interpreted in multiple ways but provides mild further support for a two-office view.

19. The Epistle of Ignatius to the Magnesians 6, in *Ante-Nicene Fathers*, vol. 1, 61.

20. Herman Bavinck, *Reformed Dogmatics, vol. 4, Holy Spirit, Church, and New Creation*, ed. John Bolt, trans. John Vriend (Grand Rapids: Baker Academic, 2008), 349.

21. Irenaeus, *Against Heresies* 4:26:2, in *Ante-Nicene Fathers*, vol. 1, 407.

22. Tertullian, *The Prescription Against Heretics* 32, in *Ante-Nicene Fathers*, vol. 3, 258.

23. Tertullian, *The Prescription Against Heretics* 32, in *Ante-Nicene Fathers*, vol. 3, 258.

24. Irenaeus, *Against Heresies* 3.3.3, in *Ante-Nicene Fathers*, vol. 1, 416.

25. Arthur C. Headlam, *The Doctrine of the Church and Christian Reunion: Being the Bampton Lectures for the Year 1920* (London: John Murray, 1920), 128.

26. Michael Ramsey, *The Gospel and the Catholic Church* (Cambridge, MA: Cowley, 1990), 82–85; Ramsey himself thinks the nature of the church makes the debate irrelevant.

27. *The Apostolic Tradition of Hippolytus*, trans. Burton Scott Easton (Cambridge: Cambridge University Press, 1934), 33.

28. *Constitutions of the Holy Apostles* 8.2.4, in *Ante-Nicene Fathers*, vol. 7, 481.

29. *Constitutions of the Holy Apostles* 8.2.4, in *Ante-Nicene Fathers*, vol. 7, 482.

30. Jerome, Letter 146, https://www.newadvent.org/fathers /3001146.htm, accessed March 31, 2023.

31. Jerome, Letter 146, https://www.newadvent.org/fathers /3001146.htm, accessed March 31, 2023.

32. *St. Jerome's Commentaries on Galatians, Titus, and Philemon*, trans. Thomas P. Scheck (Notre Dame, IN: University of Notre Dame Press, 2010), 289.

33. *St. Jerome's Commentaries on Galatians, Titus, and Philemon*, 289–90.

34. *St. Jerome's Commentaries on Galatians, Titus, and Philemon*, 290.

Chapter 9: Protestantism as Retrieval

1. John Henry Newman, *An Essay on the Development of Christian Doctrine*, 7th ed. (London: Longmans, Green, & Co., 1890), 8.

2. William Chillingworth, *The Religion of Protestants: A Safe Way of Salvation* (London: George Bell & Sons, 1888), 463.

3. Newman, *An Essay on the Development of Christian Doctrine*, 6. Just later he writes of historical Christianity, "I shall admit that there are in fact certain apparent variations in its teaching, which have to be explained" (7).
4. Newman, *An Essay on the Development of Christian Doctrine*, 7.
5. Newman, *An Essay on the Development of Christian Doctrine*, 9.
6. Newman, *An Essay on the Development of Christian Doctrine*, 6.
7. Newman wrote this passage in 1845, just prior to his reception into the Catholic Church. For an overview of the controversy within Catholic circles following the publication of Newman's theory of doctrinal development, see Kenneth J. Stewart, *In Search of Ancient Roots: The Christian Past and the Evangelical Identity Crisis* (Downers Grove, IL: IVP Academic, 2017), 187–206.
8. Newman, *An Essay on the Development of Christian Doctrine*, 11–12.
9. Kelly, *Early Christian Doctrines*.
10. Calvin, "Prefatory Address to King Francis," in *Institutes of the Christian Religion*, vol. 1, 18.
11. Calvin, "Prefatory Address to King Francis," 19–22.
12. Calvin, "Prefatory Address to King Francis," 19.
13. John Calvin, *Tracts Related to the Reformation*, trans. Henry Beveridge (Edinburgh: Calvin Translation Society, 1844), 37.
14. Calvin, *Tracts Related to the Reformation*, 37.
15. Calvin, *Tracts Related to the Reformation*, 38.
16. Calvin, *Tracts Related to the Reformation*, 39.
17. *The Augsburg Confession*, vol. 1, trans. Henry E. Jacobs (Philadelphia: G.W. Frederick, 1882), 67.
18. *The Augsburg Confession*, 57.
19. *The Augsburg Confession*, 61.
20. E.g., John Jewel, *An Apology of the Church of England*, ed. Robin Harris and Andre Gazal (Leesburg, VA: Davenant, 2020), 4–18.
21. Jewel, *An Apology of the Church of England*, 14.
22. Jewel, *An Apology of the Church of England*, 30–32.

23. Jewel, *An Apology of the Church of England*, 31.

24. Jewel, *An Apology of the Church of England*, 32–33.

25. Jewel, *An Apology of the Church of England*, 33.

26. Jewel, *An Apology of the Church of England*, 29–30.

27. Gelasius was a late fifth-century pope who commanded that communion be received in both kinds—that is, in both bread and wine—and who is often held to have opposed transubstantiation as well. For example, see the discussion in Philip Schaff, *History of the Christian Church, vol. 3: Nicene and Post-Nicene Christianity A.D. 311–600*, https://www.ccel.org/ccel/schaff/hcc3.iii.x.xxii.html#fnf_iii.x.xxii-p44.1.

28. See the discussion in *The Encyclopedia of Christianity*, ed. John Mbiti, Jan Lochman, et. al. (Leiden: Eerdmans/Brill, 2005), 96.

29. Calvin, "Prefatory Address to King Francis," 24.

30. Calvin, "Prefatory Address to King Francis," 25. Instead, Calvin maintained that the true church is recognized by pure preaching of God's Word and the lawful administration of the sacraments.

31. For more on this point, see my *Theological Retrieval for Evangelicals: Why We Need Our Past to Have a Future* (Wheaton, IL: Crossway, 2019), 23–44.

32. Turretin, *Institutes of Elenctic Theology* 18.13.19, vol. 3 (Phillipsburg, NJ: P&R, 1997), 105.

33. Turretin, *Institutes of Elenctic Theology* 18.15.9, vol. 3, 142.

34. Turretin, *Institutes of Elenctic Theology* 18.13.18–19, vol. 3, 105.

35. One could, perhaps, argue that contemporary Protestant weaknesses are logically necessary to Protestant positions. But that case would need to be made. And it is a difficult case to make, since both historically and today, many Protestant churches *do* have a high view of the sacraments, a catholic ethos, and so forth. Thus, the word "necessary" would be difficult to establish.

36. As cited in Chemnitz, *Examination of the Council of Trent*, vol. 3, 237.

37. The International Theological Commission, "The Hope of

Salvation for Infants Who Die Without Being Baptized," 21–25, https://www.vatican.va/roman_curia/congregations/cfaith/cti_documents/rc_con_cfaith_doc_20070419_un-baptised-infants_en.html, accessed August 8, 2022.

38. "The Confession of Dositheus," Decree 16: Of Holy Baptism, in *The Holy Standards: The Creeds, Confessions of Faith, and Catechisms of The Eastern Orthodox Church*, ed. Joshua Schooping, (Olyphant, PA: St. Theophan the Recluse Press, 2020), 56.

39. See my talk: "Gavin Ortlund | Worth Standing Up For: Hearing a 4th-Century Witness for Justice and the Gospel," OikonomiaNetwork November 29, 2021, YouTube video, 14:36, https://www.youtube.com/watch?v=YuuE_bA7G5U.

40. Thomas Aquinas, *Summa Theologica* I, Q. 92, Art. 1, trans. Fathers of the English Dominican Province (Notre Dame, IN: Christian Classics, 1948), 466.

41. Augustine, *The Literal Meaning of Genesis* 9.5.9, in *On Genesis*, ed. John Rotelle, trans. Edmund Hill (Hyde Park NY: New City, 2002), 380.

42. Jewel, *An Apology of the Church of England*, 65–66.

43. The same word is used in Luke 23:23 to describe the crowd's successful demands to Pilate: "but they were urgent, demanding with loud cries that he should be crucified. And their voices *prevailed*."

44. See D. A. Carson, *Matthew*, in *The Expositor's Bible Commentary*, vol. 8, ed. Frank E. Gaebelein (Grand Rapids: Zondervan, 1984), 370.

45. For an overview of the role of the emperor in the church, see Jeffrey Richards, *The Popes and the Papacy in the Early Middle Ages, 476–752* (New York: Routledge, 1979), 9–28.

46. C. S. Lewis, Letter to Lyman Stebbins, May 8, 1945, in C. S. Lewis, *The Collected Letters of C. S. Lewis*, vol. 2, *Books, Broadcasts, and the War, 1931–1949*, ed. Walter Hooper (New York: HarperSanFrancisco, 2004), 646–47.

Chapter 10: Case Study: Mary's Assumption

1. https://www.motherofallpeoples.com/the-petition, accessed August 9, 2022. The first two Marian dogmas are her divine motherhood and perpetual virginity.

2. *Munificentissimus Deus* 45, https://www.vatican.va/content/pius -xii/en/apost_constitutions/documents/hf_p-xii_apc_19501101 _munificentissimus-deus.html, accessed August 9, 2022.

3. *Munificentissimus Deus* 47, https://www.vatican.va/content/ pius-xii/en/apost_constitutions/documents/hf_p-xii_ apc_19501101_munificentissimus-deus.html, accessed August 9, 2022. A similar warning is attached to the definition of the Immaculate Conception of Mary in Pius IX's 1854 apostolic constitution *Ineffabilis Deus*: "If anyone shall dare—which God forbid!—to think otherwise than as has been defined by us, let him know and understand that he is condemned by his own judgment; that he has suffered shipwreck in the faith; that he has separated from the unity of the Church." *Ineffabilis Deus*, https://www.newadvent.org/library/docs_pi09id.htm, accessed August 9, 2022.

4. Eamon Duffy, *Saints and Sinners: A History of the Popes* (New Haven: Yale University Press, 2001), 353.

5. Eamon Duffy, *What Catholics Believe about Mary* (London: Catholic Truth Society, 1989), 17.

6. Stephen J. Shoemaker, *Ancient Traditions of the Virgin Mary's Dormition and Assumption*, Oxford Early Christian Studies (Oxford: Oxford University Press, 2006), 26.

7. Shoemaker, *Ancient Traditions of the Virgin Mary's Dormition and Assumption*, 282.

8. Shoemaker, *Ancient Traditions of the Virgin Mary's Dormition and Assumption*, 38–46, 146–68, 232–56. See also his more recent work, *Mary in Early Christian Faith and Devotion* (New Haven: Yale University Press, 2016), 24, 103.

9. Brian E. Daley, "'At the Hour of our Death': Mary's Dormition and Christian Dying in Late Patristic and Early Byzantine Literature," *Dumbarton Oaks Papers* 55 (2001): 72.

10. Daley, "At the Hour of our Death," 81.

11. Ludvig Ott, *Fundamentals of Catholic Dogma*, ed. James Bastible, trans. Patrick Lynch (Fort Collins, CO: Roman Catholic Books, 1954), 209–210. He is speaking of *Transitus Beatae Mariae*, an apocryphal text accepted by Gregory of Tours.

12. Walter J. Burghardt, "Mary in Western Patristic Thought," in *Mariology*, vol. 1, ed. Juniper Carol (Post Falls, ID: Mediatrix, 2018), 453.

13. See Shoemaker, *Ancient Traditions of the Virgin Mary's Dormition and Assumption*, 289.

14. Daley, "At the Hour of our Death," 72.

15. Brian Daley, "Introduction," in *On the Dormition of Mary: Early Patristic Homilies*, Popular Patristics 18 (Crestwood, NY: St. Vladimir's Seminary Press, 1998), 39fn16, where he notes that this is the earlier date; others (like Simon Mimouni) have argued for a sixth-century date.

16. Matthew Levering, *Mary's Bodily Assumption* (Notre Dame, IN: Notre Dame Press, 2015), 154.

17. Levering, *Mary's Bodily Assumption*, 153–54.

18. Levering, *Mary's Bodily Assumption*, 151.

19. *The Panarion of Epiphanius of Salamis, Books II and III. De Fide*, trans. Frank Williams, rev. ed. (Leiden: Brill, 2013), 635.

20. Burghardt, "The Testimony of the Patristic Age Concerning Mary's Death," 62.

21. *The Panarion of Epiphanius of Salamis*, 635.

22. *The Panarion of Epiphanius of Salamis*, 624–25.

23. The dogma simply asserts that "the Immaculate Mother of God, the ever Virgin Mary, having completed the course of her earthly life, was assumed body and soul into heavenly glory." *Munificentissimus Deus* 44, https://www.vatican.va/content /pius-xii/en/apost_constitutions/documents/hf_p-xii_apc

_19501101_munificentissimus-deus.html, accessed May 24, 2023.

24. Tim Staples, *Beyond Your Mother: A Biblical and Historical Defense of the Marian Doctrines* (El Cajon, CA: Catholic Answers, 2014), 225.

25. Andrew S. Jacobs, *Epiphanius of Cyprus: A Cultural Biography of Late Antiquity,* Christianity in Late Antiquity, vol. 2 (Oakland: University of California Press, 2016), 21.

26. Walter Burghardt, "The Assumption of Mary," in *Encyclopedia of Early Christianity*, ed. Everett Ferguson (New York: Garland, 1999), 134.

27. *The Panarion of Epiphanius of Salamis,* 641.

28. As cited in Luigi Gambero, *Mary and the Fathers of the Church: The Blessed Virgin Mary in Patristic Thought,* trans. Thomas Buffer (San Francisco: Ignatius, 1999), 375.

29. In support of the conclusion that Isidore thought Mary died, see Gambero, *Mary and the Fathers of the Church*, 375.

30. The authenticity of the passage is sometimes disputed; see Burghardt, "The Testimony of the Patristic Age Concerning Mary's Death," 59.

31. Burghardt, "The Testimony of the Patristic Age Concerning Mary's Death," 69.

32. As cited in Burghardt, "The Testimony of the Patristic Age Concerning Mary's Death," 65, italics added.

33. Burghardt, "The Testimony of the Patristic Age Concerning Mary's Death," 65.

34. Burghardt, "The Testimony of the Patristic Age Concerning Mary's Death," 92.

35. Burghardt, "The Testimony of the Patristic Age Concerning Mary's Death," 94. I am grateful to Jason Engwer for drawing my attention to these examples.

36. For example, Augustine, *Tractates on the Gospel According to St. John*, Tractate 8.9, in *Nicene and Post-Nicene Fathers*, first series, vol. 7, 61.

37. Augustine, *Expositions on the Book of Psalms*, XXXV, 14, in *Nicene and Post-Nicene Fathers*, first series, vol. 8, ed. Philip Schaff (Grand Rapids: Wm. B. Eerdmans Publ. Co, 1983), 83.

38. Kelly, *Early Christian Doctrines*, 479.

39. Augustine, *The Literal Meaning of Genesis* 10.18.32, in *On Genesis*, 417. The translator, Edmund Hill, adds an explanatory note stipulating that "the doctrine of the Immaculate Conception of Mary has not even begun to be formulated in Augustine's time."

40. Shoemaker, *Ancient Traditions of the Virgin Mary's Dormition and Assumption*, 11.

41. Tertullian, *On The Resurrection Of The Flesh* 58, in *Ante-Nicene Fathers*, vol. 3, 591. I am grateful to Jason Engwer for directing me to many of the following passages.

42. Tertullian, *A Treatise on the Soul* 50, in *Ante-Nicene Fathers*, vol. 3, 227. Here he stipulates that though Enoch and Elijah were preserved from death, they will suffer future martyrdom, as the witnesses in Revelation 11:3.

43. E.g., he discusses the nature of heaven and Elijah's assumption there in *Against Marcion* 5.12, in *Ante-Nicene Fathers*, vol. 3, 457.

44. Irenaeus, *Against Heresies* 5:5, in *Ante-Nicene Fathers*, vol. 1., 530–31.

45. Methodius, *From The Discourse On The Resurrection* 3:2:14, in *Ante-Nicene Fathers*, vol. 6, 376.

46. Origen, *Commentary On The Epistle To The Romans*, trans. Thomas Scheck (Washington, DC: The Catholic University of America Press, 2001), 5:4:3, 340.

47. *Constitutions of the Holy Apostles* 5.1.7, in *Ante-Nicene Fathers*, vol. 7, 440.

48. John Chrysostom, *Homilies on John*, 75, in *Nicene and Post-Nicene Fathers*, vol. 14, 278.

49. John Chrysostom, *Homilies on Hebrews* 22, in *Nicene and Post-Nicene Fathers*, vol. 14, 467.

50. Cyril of Jerusalem, *Catechetical Lectures* 3:6, in *Nicene and Post-Nicene Fathers*, second series, vol. 7, 15.

51. Cyril of Jerusalem, *Catechetical Lectures* 14:25, in *Nicene and Post-Nicene Fathers*, second series, vol. 7, 101. Enoch and Elijah are repeatedly appealed to in 14:25 also. In the Bel and the Dragon narrative, incorporated as the fourteenth chapter of Daniel, the prophet Habakkuk is miraculously translated by an angel to Babylon to feed Daniel when he is in the lions' den.

52. Jerome, *To Pammachius Against John of Jerusalem*, 29; https:// www.newadvent.org/fathers/3004.htm, accessed August 9, 2022.

53. Ambrose, On the Death Of Satyrus 2:94, in *Nicene and Post-Nicene Fathers*, second series, vol. 10, 189.

54. Augustine, *Reply to Faustus The Manichaean* 26:1, in *Nicene and Post-Nicene Fathers*, vol. 4, 320.

55. Augustine, *On the Grace Of Christ, And On Original Sin* 2:27, in *Nicene and Post-Nicene Fathers*, vol. 5, 246. Caelestius was one of Pelagius's followers.

56. Eusebius, *Church History* 6:42:3, in *Nicene and Post-Nicene Fathers*, second series, vol. 1, 285.

57. Shoemaker, *Ancient Traditions of the Virgin Mary's Dormition and Assumption*, 54.

58. In what follows, I simply sketch some representative examples. To work through these texts, see esp. Shoemaker, *Ancient Traditions of the Virgin Mary's Dormition and Assumption*, 78–141.

59. Shoemaker, *Ancient Traditions of the Virgin Mary's Dormition and Assumption*, 64. See the discussion in Daley, "At the Hour of our Death," 80; and also in Daley, "Introduction," in *On the Dormition of Mary*, 8–9.

60. Shoemaker, *Ancient Traditions of the Virgin Mary's Dormition and Assumption*, 29. See the discussion in Daley, "At the Hour of our Death," 80; and also in Daley, "Introduction," in *On the Dormition of Mary*, 8–9.

61. Shoemaker, *Ancient Traditions of the Virgin Mary's Dormition and Assumption*, 31.

62. As cited in Burghardt, "The Testimony of the Patristic Age Concerning Mary's Death," 71.

63. Shoemaker, *Ancient Traditions of the Virgin Mary's Dormition and Assumption*, 282.

64. See Shoemaker's lengthier summary of what is often called the "palm of the tree of life" traditions, *Ancient Traditions of the Virgin Mary's Dormition and Assumption*, 37–38.

65. Shoemaker, *Ancient Traditions of the Virgin Mary's Dormition and Assumption*, 59. Daley, "At the Hour of our Death," 82–83, discusses one of the narratives with the 206-day interval between Mary's death and assumption, delivered in a sermon by the sixth-century anti-Chalcedonian patriarch of Alexandria Theodosius around 566/567.

66. Shoemaker, *Ancient Traditions of the Virgin Mary's Dormition and Assumption*, 67.

67. An immediate assumption is more common among what Shoemaker calls the "Bethlehem traditions," e.g., the Six Books. See Shoemaker, *Ancient Traditions of the Virgin Mary's Dormition and Assumption*, 52.

68. See the discussion in Daley, "At the Hour of our Death," 81.

69. Shoemaker, *Ancient Traditions of the Virgin Mary's Dormition and Assumption*, 283.

70. The Ethiopic *Liber Requiei* 52, in Shoemaker, *Ancient Traditions of the Virgin Mary's Dormition and Assumption*, 320. Here and below, where the Ethiopic and Georgian text deviate, I follow the Ethiopic unless otherwise noted.

71. The Ethiopic *Liber Requiei* 25, in Shoemaker, *Ancient Traditions of the Virgin Mary's Dormition and Assumption*, 303; though there are manuscript differences at this point.

72. The Ethiopic *Liber Requiei* 5, in Shoemaker, *Ancient Traditions of the Virgin Mary's Dormition and Assumption*, 292.

73. The Ethiopic *Liber Requiei* 6, in Shoemaker, *Ancient Traditions of the Virgin Mary's Dormition and Assumption*, 293.

74. The Ethiopic *Liber Requiei* 17, in Shoemaker, *Ancient Traditions of the Virgin Mary's Dormition and Assumption*, 300 (cf. his discussion on 244).

Notes

75. The Ethiopic *Liber Requiei* 41, in Shoemaker, *Ancient Traditions of the Virgin Mary's Dormition and Assumption*, 314–315.

76. The Ethiopic *Liber Requiei* 41–89, in Shoemaker, *Ancient Traditions of the Virgin Mary's Dormition and Assumption*, 315–40.

77. The Ethiopic *Liber Requiei* 90–104, in Shoemaker, *Ancient Traditions of the Virgin Mary's Dormition and Assumption*, 341–47.

78. R. P. C. Hanson, *The Bible as a Norm of Faith* (Durham: University of Durham, 1963), 14.

79. Shoemaker argues that the *Six Books Dormition Apocryphon* may extend back into the fourth century (*Mary in Early Christian Faith and Devotion*, 25, 133–34).

80. Michael O'Carroll, *Theotokos: A Theological Encyclopedia of the Blessed Virgin Mary* (Wilmington, DE: Glazier, 1982), 57.

81. O'Carroll, *Theotokos*, 278. I am grateful to Jason Engwer for directing me to O'Carroll's work.

82. O'Carroll, *Theotokos*, 57.

83. This letter, *Cogitis Me*, was evidently written by Radbertus himself. It can be read online: https://epistolae.ctl.columbia.edu/letter/299.html. For discussion of its influence, see O'Carroll, *Theotokos*, 300.

84. O'Carroll, *Theotokos*, 7.

85. O'Carroll, *Theotokos*, 191.

86. O'Carroll, *Theotokos*, 283–84.

87. O'Carroll, *Theotokos*, 7.

88. Burghardt, "The Assumption of Mary," in *Encyclopedia of Early Christianity*, 135.

89. Daley, "Introduction," in *On the Dormition of Mary*, 27.

90. There are too many passages like this to cite, but G. K. Beale, *The Book of Revelation: A Commentary on the Greek Text* (Grand Rapids: Eerdmans, 1999), 625–31, gives a fuller list, noting in particular the usage of sun and moon imagery in some cases, such as Song of Solomon 6:10 and Isaiah 60:19–20. See also Robert H. Mounce, *The Book of Revelation, rev. ed.* (Grand

Rapids: Eerdmans, 1997), 232: "The OT frequently pictured Israel as a woman in travail."

91. Shoemaker, *Ancient Traditions of the Virgin Mary's Dormition and Assumption*, 13.

92. St. Andrew of Crete, Homily II, in *On the Dormition of Mary*, 126.

93. E.g., so Brant Pitre, *Jesus and the Jewish Roots of Mary: Unveiling the Mother of the Messiah* (New York: Image, 2018), 54–70.

94. Newman, *An Essay on the Development of Christian Doctrine*, 7.

Chapter 11: Case Study: Icon Veneration

1. Richard Price, *The Acts of the Second Council of Nicaea (787)*, Translated Texts for Historians, vol. 68 (Liverpool: Liverpool University Press, 2020), 577.

2. As cited in Price, *The Acts of the Second Council of Nicaea (787)*, 89.

3. As cited in Price, *The Acts of the Second Council of Nicaea (787)*, 90.

4. As cited in Price, *The Acts of the Second Council of Nicaea (787)*, 585.

5. As cited in Price, *The Acts of the Second Council of Nicaea (787)*, 588–89.

6. As cited in Price, *The Acts of the Second Council of Nicaea (787)*, 589.

7. E.g., see *CCC* 2131–2132.

8. Cindy Egly, "Eastern Orthodox Christians and Iconography," *Antiochian Orthodox Christian Archdiocese*, http://ww1.antiochian. org/icons-eastern-orthodoxy, accessed May 26, 2023.

9. Léonide Ouspensky and Vladimir Lossky, *The Meaning of Icons*, trans. G. E. H. Palmer and E. Kadloubovsky (Crestwood, NY: St. Vladimir's Seminary Press, 1982), 30.

10. Ouspensky and Lossky, *The Meaning of Icons*, 34–35.

11. Ouspensky and Lossky, *The Meaning of Icons*, 36.

12. Ouspensky and Lossky, *The Meaning of Icons*, 39.

13. Price, *The Acts of the Second Council of Nicaea (787)*, 3.

14. Price, *The Acts of the Second Council of Nicaea (787)*, 43.

15. Mike Humphreys, "Contexts, Controversies, and Developing Perspectives," in *A Companion to Byzantine Iconoclasm*, ed. Mike

Humphreys, Companions to the Christian Tradition 99 (Leiden: Brill, 2021), 54.

16. Ernst Kitzinger, *Byzantine Art in the Making: Main Lines of Stylistic Development in Mediterranean Art, 3rd-7th Century* (Cambridge, MA: Harvard University Press, 1977), 105.

17. Peter Brown, "A Dark-Age Crisis: Aspects of the Iconoclastic Controversy," *EHR* 88 (1973): 10.

18. E.g., Averil Cameron, "Images of Authority: Elites and Icons in Late Sixth-Century Byzantium," *Past & Present* 84 (1979), 3–35.

19. Leslie Brubaker and John Haldon, *Byzantium in the Iconoclast Era, c. 680–850: A History* (Cambridge: Cambridge University Press, 2011), 62. Also significant in this stream of scholarship is the work of Marie-France Auzepy and Paul Speck.

20. Paul Corby Finney, *The Invisible God: The Earliest Christians on Art* (Oxford: Oxford University Press, 1994), 293.

21. Brubaker and Haldon, *Byzantium in the Iconoclast Era, c. 680–850*, 63.

22. As noted by Brubaker and Haldon, *Byzantium in the Iconoclast Era, c. 680–850*, 2, 787.

23. Humphreys, "Contexts, Controversies, and Developing Perspectives," in *A Companion to Byzantine Iconoclasm*, 47–48.

24. Cyril Mango, *The Art of the Byzantine Empire 312–1453: Sources and Documents* (Toronto: University of Toronto Press, 1986), 150.

25. Finney, *The Invisible God*, 5.

26. For documentation and summary, see Finney, *The Invisible God*, 131, 290–93.

27. Justin Martyr, *First Apology* 1.9, in *Ante-Nicene Fathers*, vol. 1, 165; Athenagoras, *A Plea for Christians* 15, in *Ante-Nicene Fathers*, vol. 2, 135.

28. Municius Felix, *Octavius* 10, in *Ante-Nicene Fathers*, vol. 4, 178; a footnote observes this final phrase can be rendered "no consecrated images."

29. Municius Felix, *Octavius* 32, in *Ante-Nicene Fathers*, vol. 4, 193.

30. Origen, *Contra Celsus* 7.41, in *Ante-Nicene Fathers*, vol. 4, 627.

31. Origen, *Contra Celsus* 7.64, in *Ante-Nicene Fathers*, vol. 4, 637.

32. Origen, *Contra Celsus* 8.17, in *Ante-Nicene Fathers*, vol. 4, 645.

33. E.g., Origen, *Contra Celsus* 8.17–20, in *Ante-Nicene Fathers*, vol. 4, 645–47.

34. Clement of Alexandria, *Stromata* 2.18, in *Ante-Nicene Fathers*, vol. 2, 365.

35. Clement of Alexandria, *Stromata* 5.5, in *Ante-Nicene Fathers*, vol. 2, 451.

36. Clement of Alexandria, *Stromata* 7.5, in *Ante-Nicene Fathers*, vol. 2, 530.

37. Lactantius, Divine Institutes 2.19, in *Ante-Nicene Fathers*, vol. 7, 68.

38. Tertullian, *On Idolatry* 2, in *Ante-Nicene Fathers*, vol. 3, 62.

39. Tertullian, *On Idolatry* 4, in *Ante-Nicene Fathers*, vol. 3, 63.

40. Arnobius, *Against the Heathen* 6.9, https://www.newadvent.org/fathers/06316.htm, italics in the original, accessed December 28, 2022.

41. Arnobius, *Against the Heathen* 6.9.

42. For discussion of this translation and the relevance of the canon, see John B. Carpenter, "Answering Eastern Orthodox Apologists Regarding Icons," *Themelios* 43.3 (December 2018), https://www.thegospelcoalition.org/themelios/article/answering-eastern-orthodox-apologists-regarding-icons/.

43. Jensen, "Figural Images in Christian Thought and Practice Before ca. 500," in *A Companion to Byzantine Iconoclasm*, 135–6.

44. Another example comes in Irenaeus, *Against Heresies* 1.25.6, in *Ante-Nicene Fathers*, vol. 1, 351, where he references a particular Gnostic group that practices honoring images and claims to have an image of Christ made by Pilate; he describes their "modes of honouring these images" as being "after the manner of the Gentiles."

45. As cited in Jensen, "Figural Images in Christian Thought and Practice Before ca. 500," in *A Companion to Byzantine Iconoclasm*, 112.

46. Robin Jensen, "Aniconism in the First Centuries of Christianity," *Religion* 47.3 (2017): 419.

47. As cited in Mango, *The Art of the Byzantine Empire 312–1453*, 17. The date of this letter is uncertain. Its authenticity is sometimes questioned, but has been authoritatively defended by Stephen Gero, "The True Image of Christ: Eusebius' Letter to Constantia Reconsidered," *Journal of Theological Studies* 32.2 (1981): 460–470. His conclusion is that "inauthenticity has no single powerful argument in its favour, and a host of reasons, specific and general, against it" (470). See also Price, *The Acts of the Second Council of Nicaea (787)*, 663–64, who derives a similar conclusion.

48. As cited in Mango, *The Art of the Byzantine Empire 312–1453*, 18.

49. Eusebius, *Church History* 7.18, in *Nicene and Post-Nicene Fathers*, second series, vol. 1, 304.

50. Epiphanius, Letter 51.9, https://www.newadvent.org/fathers /3001051.htm, accessed December 29, 2022.

51. Epiphanius, Letter 51.9.

52. For one example, see Ambrosius Giakalis, *Images of the Divine: The Theology of Icons at the Seventh Ecumenical Council* (Leiden: Brill, 2005), 26. Brubaker and Haldon, *Byzantium in the Iconoclast Era, c. 680–850*, 47, note the "prevailing view" that this and other similar fragments are genuine, but themselves question this conclusion.

53. Augustine, Sermon on Psalm 115, in *Nicene and Post-Nicene Fathers*, vol. 8, 553.

54. Augustine, Sermon on Psalm 115, in *Nicene and Post-Nicene Fathers*, vol. 8, 553, italics mine.

55. See the discussion in Mango, *The Art of the Byzantine Empire*, 43–44.

56. Gregory, Book 9, Letter 105, in *Nicene and Post-Nicene Fathers*, second series, vol. 13, 23.

57. Gregory, Book 11, Letter 13, in *Nicene and Post-Nicene Fathers*, second series, vol. 13, 53–54.

58. Jensen, "Aniconism in the First Centuries of Christianity," 421.

59. As the exception to their 680 date for the emergence of the veneration of icons, Brubaker and Haldon, *Byzantium in the Iconoclast Era, c. 680–850*, 35–36, discuss the famous *acheiropoieta* (images "not made by human hand") that functioned as both relics and icons, and emerged in the latter half of the sixth century.

60. Brubaker and Haldon, *Byzantium in the Iconoclast Era, c. 680–850*, 50–51.

61. Price, *The Acts of the Second Council of Nicaea (787)*, 15n69.

62. George Florovsky, "Origen, Eusebius, and the Iconoclastic Controversy," *Church History* 19.2 (June 1950): 77.

63. For a helpful overview, see Humphreys, "Contexts, Controversies, and Developing Perspectives," in *A Companion to Byzantine Iconoclasm*, 31–42.

64. Constantine VI became emperor in 780 at age nine, but Irene exercised control over him, functioning until 790 as regent, later as co-ruler, and finally as empress once she deposed Constantine VI.

65. Humphreys, "Contexts, Controversies, and Developing Perspectives," in *A Companion to Byzantine Iconoclasm*, 78.

66. Price, *The Acts of the Second Council of Nicaea (787)*, 27. Price also notes rampant simony at Nicaea II (34, 54).

67. For discussion, see Andrew Louth, *Greek East and Latin West: The Church AD 681–1071*, The Church in History, vol. 3 (Crestwood, NY: St. Vladimir's Seminary Press), 54–60.

68. Giakalis, *Images of the Divine*, 16, who is himself sympathetic to Nicaea II, admits that the supposed oriental legates "were not sent personally by the patriarchs."

69. Price, *The Acts of the Second Council of Nicaea (787)*, 204.

70. For a helpful overview of the Carolingian view, see Thomas F. X. Noble, *Images, Iconoclasm, and the Carolingians* (Philadelphia: University of Pennsylvania Press, 2009).

71. As cited in Noble, *Images, Iconoclasm, and the Carolingians*, 193.

72. Noble, *Images, Iconoclasm, and the Carolingians*, 367.

73. Noble, *Images, Iconoclasm, and the Carolingians*, 204, notes that

Theodulf rejected these and other dubious sources appealed to by the bishops of Nicaea II.

74. For examples, see Noble, *Images, Iconoclasm, and the Carolingians*, 19.

75. Price, *The Acts of the Second Council of Nicaea (787)*, 164. The passages are cited as Psalm 26:8, 44:14, and 4:7.

76. Chemnitz, *Examination of the Council of Trent*, vol. 4, 114.

77. For discussion, see Jaroslav Pelikan, *The Spirit of Eastern Christendom (600–1700)*, The Christian Tradition, vol. 2 (Chicago: University of Chicago Press, 1974), 103.

78. Price, *The Acts of the Second Council of Nicaea (787)*, 40–41.

79. Humphreys, "Contexts, Controversies, and Developing Perspectives," in *A Companion to Byzantine Iconoclasm*, 65.

80. Humphreys, "Contexts, Controversies, and Developing Perspectives," in *A Companion to Byzantine Iconoclasm*, 65.

81. Price, *The Acts of the Second Council of Nicaea (787)*, 76.

82. John Henry Newman, *An Essay on the Development of Christian Doctrine*, 199.

83. Price, *The Acts of the Second Council of Nicaea (787)*, 576–77.

84. Price, *The Acts of the Second Council of Nicaea (787)*, 565; see footnote 58 for the reference to bowing and prostration.

85. Price, *The Acts of the Second Council of Nicaea (787)*, 566.

86. Price, *The Acts of the Second Council of Nicaea (787)*, 577.

87. Humphreys, "Contexts, Controversies, and Developing Perspectives," in *A Companion to Byzantine Iconoclasm*, 45.

88. As cited in Chemnitz, *Examination of the Council of Trent*, vol. 4, 131.

89. This way of arguing goes back to John of Damascus; in the contemporary literature, see Giakalis, *Images of the Divine*; so also John Meyendorff, *Byzantine Theology: Historical Trends & Doctrinal Themes* (New York: Fordham, 1992), 42–53.